Europe from Be

# Europe from Below

## An East–West Dialogue

———◆———

Edited by

## MARY KALDOR

**VERSO**

London · New York

First published by Verso 1991
Collection © Verso 1991
Translation © individual translators
All rights reserved

**Verso**
UK: 6 Meard Street, London W1V 3HR
USA: 29 West 35th Street, New York, NY 10001-2291

Verso is the imprint of New Left Books

**British Library Cataloguing in Publication Data**
Europe from below : an East–West dialogue.
   1. Western bloc countries. Foreign relations with Eastern
   I. Kaldor, Mary
   327.091713

   ISBN 0-86091-305-8
   ISBN 0-86091-522-0 (pbk)

**US Library of Congress Cataloging-in-Publication Data**
Europe from below : an East–West dialogue / edited by Mary Kaldor.
      p.     cm.
   ISBN 0-86091-305-8 (hardback) : ISBN 0-86091-522-0 (paperback) ;
    1. Europe–Politics and government–1989–   I. Kaldor, Mary.
   D2009.E87    1991
   320.94–dc20

Typeset in Times by Leaper & Gard Ltd, Bristol
Printed in Finland by Werner Söderström Oy

*In memory of Milan Šimečka, who did so much
to increase understanding among those in
opposition in both East and West*

# Contents

# Acknowledgements

This book was a joint effort together with Verso. Robin Blackburn encouraged me to edit the book, read the essays, and made many important suggestions. Lucy Morton and Jason Freeman took over much of the burden of editing the book. I am grateful to all of them.

Thanks are due to the contributors for giving permission for their pieces to be reproduced here. Those which have been published in English elsewhere are as follows: E.P. Thompson's 'Ends and Histories' has been published in different forms in *The Nation* and *New Statesman and Society*. Mary Kaldor's 'After the Cold War' was first published in *New Left Review*. J.K. Galbraith's 'Revolt in Our Time' appeared in an earlier form in the *Observer*. Anthony Barnett's 'Eastern Promise' was first published in *New Statesman and Society*; Timothy Garton Ash's 'Tell Me Your Europe' and Anthony Barnett's 'Reply' in the *Independent*; Neal Ascherson's 'Birds of an East European Feather' and 'Two Winners for Each Loser' in the *Independent on Sunday*. Robin Blackburn's 'The European Community and the Challenge of the New Europe' was first published in *New Statesman and Society*. Adam Michnik's 'The Two Faces of Europe' was first published in the *New York Review of Books*.

The royalties on the book will go to European Dialogue, the UK branch of the Helsinki Citizens' Assembly, 11 Goodwin Street, London N4.

# Introduction

Ten years ago, a group of us launched the European Nuclear Disarmament (END) Appeal for a nuclear-free Europe. The Appeal attracted thousands of signatures from all over Europe and beyond, and was one of the mobilizing documents of the new peace movement which sprang up in Western Europe in the early 1980s.

The Appeal called for nuclear disarmament through unilateral, bilateral and multilateral means, but it was also an appeal to end the Cold War. It accorded responsibility for the Cold War to both the United States and the Soviet Union, and insisted on the link between disarmament and democracy.

As well as campaigning against cruise and Pershing missiles during the 1980s, END placed increasing emphasis on what we called 'detente from below' – constructing links between peace, green and human rights groups in East and West; initiating a dialogue between citizens and not just between governments. This dialogue turned out to be an intensive learning process. We in the Western peace movement began to internalize the struggle for democracy in Eastern Europe, not only for its own sake, but also as a way of ending the arms race. Our friends in Charter 77 talked about political disarmament as opposed to technical disarmament, by which they meant the need to tackle the sources of the Cold War, not just the symptoms. For their part, our Eastern counterparts began to recognize that tackling the symptoms was also important; that the removal of Soviet troops from East-Central Europe would be best achieved within the framework of a pan-European disarmament process. The Prague Appeal addressed to the 1985 END Convention by Charter 77 expressed this point of view.

Ten years on, in the aftermath of the 1989 revolutions, many of the goals set out in the Appeal have been achieved. The East–West division of Europe is over. The Berlin Wall has been breached. Eastern Europe is in the throes of a far-reaching process of democratization. Germany is unifying. Substantial arms reductions are taking place, as a result both of multilateral talks and of unilateral or bilateral decisions. Soviet forces are being removed from Czechoslovakia and Hungary. Short-range nuclear weapons are probably going to be removed from Germany.

All the same, many old problems remain and many new problems are emerging. First of all, the process of democratization is still fragile. Nowhere is this more true than in the Soviet Union, which seems to be poised between disintegration and forcible reintegration; between the pressures for national and local self-determination in the individual republics, and the pressure from the military and from Russian conservatives for restoration of centralized control. In East-Central Europe, nationalist exclusivist tendencies threaten the delicate political balance so far achieved, especially in the Balkan countries. But it is not only in the East that democracy is a concern. The failure to stop the Euromissiles through the parliamentary process, despite the fact that majority opinion was opposed to deployment in all five deployment countries, indicated the degree to which formally democratic institutions are unable to respond to popular pressures and made clear the extent to which multinational institutions like NATO undercut domestic democratic processes. There is an urgent need to reinvigorate democracy in the West, especially at local levels and in international institutions like the European Community.

Second, Eastern Europe – and indeed most of the world – faces severe economic difficulties and a potentially catastrophic environmental crisis. So far, the debate has centred on how to introduce markets in Eastern Europe, and aid from the West is largely conditional on such an introduction. Unless a substantial and continuing programme of economic and ecological assistance is initiated, the old political division of Europe is likely to be replaced by a new economic division between a prosperous West and a poor, ecologically dying East.

Third, the opening up of East European societies has revealed an explosive combination of cultural suppression and socioeconomic underprivilege which is voiced in new nationalist and ethnic sentiment. The cultural diversity of Europe, in both East and West, does provide a possible basis for enriching experience and developing democracy and self-determination. But it also represents a terrifying potential for hatred, rivalry, exclusion and division. Already, the tragic situations in Kosovo, Nagorno-Karabakh and Transylvania illustrate the dangers. Multiculturalism is no less important in the West, where small nations like Wales or Friesland have demonstrated the possibilities for cultural nationalism, while exclusivist rivalries, in Northern Ireland or against racial minorities, threaten peace and democracy.

Finally, there is still a lot to do to sustain the process of disarmament and to establish for Europe a new security system which can cope with the myriad of new and old conflicts (nationalist, economic, ecological, and so on) in a peaceful, non-violent, democratic way. Up to now, the Western countries have been much slower to reduce armed forces and defence spending than the Soviet Union and East-Central Europe. Some of the authors in this book, writing in the spring of 1990, suggest that Arab dictators, constructed out of the oil-hunger of the West, could replace the Soviet threat as a reason for armament. Even before the Gulf crisis, the American, British and French governments explained the continued need for nuclear weapons and intervention capabilities in terms of the threat from countries like Iraq and Libya. Today, this argument is propelling forward demands for an integrated West European defence entity. Is the old East–West conflict to be replaced by a new North–South confrontation? Or even perhaps a confrontation between a rich consumerist West and emergent fundamentalisms of various kinds in both the East and the South? Can we construct a security system that is an institution for resolving conflicts, not keeping them alive through the threat of war? Can we integrate Europe without integrating European armed forces?

In order to face these problems, there is more than ever a need to intensify the process of detente from below, to exchange experiences and ideas. These are not problems that can be left to governments: they have to be debated publicly throughout Europe. There are, today, a number of new initiatives which could provide a catalyst for citizens to play an active role. The END Convention process continues. Solidarity in Poland has taken the initiative in organizing conventions on human rights. The first Helsinki Citizens' Assembly for Peace and Democracy, which arose directly out of the Prague Appeal of 1985, was held in Prague in October 1990.

This book is intended as a contribution to the new dialogue. The essays reflect a range of political opinion. Some authors describe themselves as left; others consider that the left/right division has little meaning in Europe today. What the essays share is a different perspective on the process of ending the Cold War from the one that usually appears in the press – the perspective of those engaged in detente from below rather than detente from above. It is from this perspective that the book puts forward some of the new issues and new ways of thinking that will have to be developed in the 1990s.

*Mary Kaldor*
*October 1990*

# PART I

# Goodbye to the Cold War

# 1

# Ends and Histories*

## E.P. Thompson

The lumpenintelligentsia of Washington think-tanks are still rabbiting on about 'the end of history',[1] but it would be more to the point if we looked at the history of END. For END, with its 'beyond the Cold War' programme, is perhaps the only group whose agenda clearly prefigured the transformations taking place in Europe now and which, hence, helps us to evaluate their significance.

END has stood for two things. First, the European Nuclear Disarmament Appeal, launched by a group of sponsors and by the Russell Peace Foundation in April 1980. This became a charter of the non-aligned Western peace movements, and the basis for annual Conventions in different European cities which still continue and are the gathering-ground of all the diverse political and social forces involved (Christian, feminist, green, Social-Democratic, Eurocommunist, and so on).

Second, END has stood for the British END Committee, and our specific strategies, as articulated above all in END Journal, edited for the past few years by Mary Kaldor with the support of an able collective.

*This essay went through several stages. It commenced as a Raoul Wallenberg lecture at Rutgers University, New Brunswick, in October 1989. It was revised after the Czechoslovak, GDR and Romanian 'revolutions', and passages were published in *The Nation* (USA) on 29 January 1990 and *New Statesman*, 12 and 26 January 1990. Acknowledgements and thanks to those journals. It has been further revised for this volume (in May 1990). I should explain that the personal tone of reminiscence over the history of the Cold War was induced in part by the fact that I was in hospital in intensive care during November 1989. As I wrote in an earlier version: 'during the Czechoslovak crisis I was on a ventilating machine, and the day the great crowds occupied Wenceslas Square was also the day that my condition took a turn for the better: Prague's lungs and my lungs seemed to recover their uses on the same day – "Dubček, Havel, Svoboda!"'

This remarkable journal, influential not only in Western Europe and United States peace circles but also read avidly 'on the other side', will come to be seen as the most innovative, well-informed and prescient journal of international affairs in Western Europe in the eighties. It is greatly discouraging that the *Journal* had to suspend publication, through lack of finances, just at the moment when events have vindicated its whole record.

The END Appeal, which was signed by thousands of influential people in the West but only a handful on 'the other side', was precipitated by the NATO 'Euromissile' decision of December 1979 to install cruise and Pershing II missiles. But it opposed these from the first within a 'beyond the Cold War' perspective. As we declared: 'We must commence to act as if a united, neutral and pacific Europe already exists. We must learn to be loyal, not to "East" or "West", but to each other, and we must disregard the prohibitions and limitations of any national state.' This – together with our refusal to attribute guilt for the Cold War exclusively to one side or the other – was calculated to infuriate the habit-formed Cold Warriors of both sides. 1980–83 were interesting years. On the one hand, END supporters were playing leading parts in the Western peace movement, CND and so on. On the other hand, we were caught in the crossfire of the rival ideological camps.

If I take examples from my own case, this is only because I know it best. The liberal establishment in the United States has always confined its expertise to the minutiae of arms control, and has been complacently insensitive to the politics of the Cold War. In the *New York Review of Books* George Ball found my views (which he did not review or cite) 'disgraceful'. Theodore Draper was equally dismissive and again avoided any discussion of our agenda. Leon Weiseltier arraigned me in the *New Republic* (again without mentioning END's strategy, which for years was unmentionable by American liberals or conservatives) and General Bernard Rogers denounced me before the House of Representatives Committee on Armed Services.

But from the other side the aggression was even more ferocious. I and other members of the non-aligned (and END) peace movement – notably Mient Jan Faber, a leader of the Dutch Inter-Church Peace Council (IKV) and Mary Kaldor – were regularly denounced by the World Peace Council and the Soviet Peace Committee as agents of the CIA infiltrated into the European peace movement. Georgi Arbatov of the US–Canada Institute informed Dutch peace workers that he knew from special sources that END was 'a CIA affair'. *Rudé Právo* (Prague) alleged: 'Thompson is a notorious anti-Communist working on behalf of the CIA to influence the peace movement according to Washington's ideas.' G. Lokshin, Secretary of the Soviet Peace committee, wrote:

In NATO's arsenal of methods of subversion directed against the anti-war movement, an ever-greater place is being given to ideological warfare. This is carried out partly with the help of various front organizations and groups that insinuate themselves into the anti-war movement . . . E.P. Thompson, historian and sociologist, widely publicized of late, a former professor at Oxford University [not guilty] is the noisiest mouthpiece of these anti-Soviet conceptions. (*International Life*, June 1984)

And Mr Lokshin went on to explain that Mient Jan Faber and I were trying to draw the anti-war movement into a 'crusade against the socialist fraternity, while cynically hiding themselves behind stolen banners of peace'. The jackal-affiliates of the World Peace Council took up the lines assigned to them, Mark Solomon of the US Peace Council dutifully writing *Death Waltz to Armageddon: E.P. Thompson and the Peace Movement* ('Thompson regularly ignites the combustible materials that inflame the Cold War') – a booklet which, in these days of glasnost, even the author must know it was silly to have written.[2]

Why should this old history concern us now? There are three reasons. First, despite the incessant media projection of the peace movement as captively pro-Soviet, the END alliance was clearly, from 1980 onwards, an independent and non-aligned political agent. The END Appeal had insisted upon this from the outset:

We must resist any attempt by the statesmen of East or West to manipulate this movement to their advantage. We offer no advantage to either NATO or the Warsaw alliance. Our objective must be to free Europe from confrontation, to enforce detente between the United States and the Soviet Union, and, ultimately, to dissolve both great power alliances.

(Thus the Appeal in 1980, but with each year, at successive Conventions, this agenda was stated more explicitly.)

Second, a significant struggle was enacted between 1981 and 1984 for the hegemony of the Western peace movement, between non-aligned (END) and pro-Soviet (World Peace Council) forces. Yuri Zhukov, President of the Soviet Peace Committee, was the main aggressor, as ugly and unpeaceful a political operator as it has ever been my misfortune to sit around a table with. (He was sacked a year or two ago, but some of his deputies, like Lokshin, serve on.) On 2 December 1982 Zhukov went on to the full offensive, circulating peace movements and inidividuals throughout the West with a long letter denouncing END's plans to hold the Convention in Berlin the following summer: END was unmasked as a group whose true objective was 'to split the anti-war movement and infiltrate Cold War elements into it'. True peace

fighters had to understand that *all* the guilt in the Cold War lay on
NATO's side: the peace-loving Soviet Union was (for the previous forty
years) wholly innocent. In a calm and reasoned reply the British END
Committee argued for an ideological 'healing process' – 'Barbed wire
divides not only the territories of the two blocs, there is also barbed wire
in people's minds and hearts.' And we pointed out (more opportunisti-
cally) that:

> If all those whom you regard as 'anti-Soviet elements' were to be purged from
> the Western peace movement, then that movement would be reduced in
> numbers from hundreds of thousands to mere hundreds. It would be reduced
> to a handful of small pro-Soviet committees, without influence or inde-
> pendence.

A serious political and ideological conflict took place, from which END –
and the non-aligned movements – emerged victorious: as the vast
spectrum of opinions represented at successive annual END Conventions
– Brussels, Berlin, Perugia, Amsterdam, Paris, Coventry, Lund, Vitoria
(Basque Country), Helsinki – testifies. END Appeal strategies were
endorsed by majority peace movements in Finland, Scandinavia,
Holland, Belgium, West Germany, Britain, Spain, Italy, Greece, Austria
and Switzerland, leaving only the PCF-dominated movement of France,
and also Portugal, as major WPC exceptions. In the United States, the
multitude of movements was more distanced from the politics of the
Cold War, but they were not WPC-captives. We had stopped being just a
bunch of intellectuals talking about a possible 'third way'. We were a
real confederation of political forces, and we *were* the third way.

Increasingly, the movements within the END loose 'confederation'
came to adopt an explicitly peace *and* human rights agenda. This placed
us in the very eye of the ideological storm: Cold War dogma insisted
that one must be for 'human rights' or for 'peace', but one could not be
for both. The non-aligned peace movements broke that dogma, showing
solidarity with independent peace groups on the other side (like the
Moscow Trust Group), co-operating with Hungarian Dialogue,
discussing the issues in public with members of Czechoslovakia's
Charter 77. At the annual END Conventions influential 'independents',
like Zdena Tomin, Zhores Medvedev and George Konrad, took part.
A few independents managed to get across from the East. There were
fraught negotiations with official Eastern peace committees, and Yuri
Zhukov and his cronies were apoplectic.

People are sometimes surprised when they learn about these raging
ideological battles which so much preoccupied a few of us. Why were
they not kept informed? Well, we were also taking leading parts in our

own national peace movements, more concerned with restraining Reagan and Thatcher than with the petty skulduggery of Zhukov. Unless one was a close reader of the peace movement press, one saw no mention of these matters. The liberal establishment in the USA didn't want to know about the politics of the Cold War, and it was easier to write off the European peace movement as pro-Soviet and 'disgraceful'. This makes its sudden discovery of the issues at the centre of our work for years all the more bathetic.

And the British media Establishment is in general the most complacent, ill-informed, bigoted, provincial and sub-intelligent in West Europe. It behaves as if tedious commentators have the right to define what are the 'real' political issues – that is, those that are convenient for party-politicians – and to ignore what is really going on. (The important END Convention in Coventry in 1987 went almost unreported in Britain, apart from the Left weeklies and a report in the *Guardian*.)

But the British Establishment's repression and marginalization of the END agenda was more conscious than that. One illustration was the Dimbleby Lecture affair in 1981. When, to my surprise, I was invited by BBC General Features in spring 1981 to submit a proposal for the lecture, I chose the theme 'Beyond the Cold War'. According to a trustworthy account (Michael Leapman, *The Last Days of the Beeb*) my synopsis was approved by Features and by the BBC managing director, Alasdair Milne. I was phoned and invited to get on with the script. Then in the summer the director-general, Sir Ian Trethowan, learned of the invitation and promptly forbade it. He noted that I was a prominent supporter of CND and of unilateral nuclear disarmament for Britain. Although my talk did not address this issue, he knew that Mrs Thatcher and her ministers would be furious. Leapman comments: 'By banning Thompson before the government had time to make a fuss ... Trethowan had diverted a potential new assault on the Beeb by Thatcher and her supporters.'

If one looks at what Mrs Thatcher and her security services have done to the BBC and our major media subsequently, one need not linger over such trivia as the Dimbleby Lecture affair. My point is simply to indicate one instance of the way in which the agenda of the non-aligned peace movement was marginalized or suppressed. Thereafter (I am told) I was banned from the BBC. The media decided that there was only one peace issue – 'unilateralism' as they chose to define it. Any other issue which CND or END was taking up (the politics of the Cold War) was unmentionable (and still is).

My banned Dimbleby Lecture, 'Beyond the Cold War' (1981) was, essentially, an argument prefiguring the situation of Europe today. It had a pessimistic and an optimistic set of propositions. The pessimistic

propositions started from the proposal that the Cold War had long
outlived the historical conditions of its formation: it was no longer (in
Europe) a conflict of interests, but an inertial condition – it was 'about
itself'. But this was not a comforting conclusion, since the inertia was
embodied in ideological, bureaucratic and military-industrial forms and
was *self-reproducing*. The dynamic of this reproduction was driven by
the reciprocal influence, the antagonistic contradiction, of the rival
military blocs, which continually summoned forth each other's militarist
resources and ideological malice. As I put it in the even more pessimistic
essay, 'Exterminism: the Last Stage in Civilization?': 'It is a non-
dialectical contradiction, a state of absolute antagonism, in which both
powers grow by confrontation, and which can only be resolved by
mutual extermination.'

'Exterminism' belongs to early 1980, before the mass peace movement got going, and it was pessimistic. I was rebuked by Raymond
Williams for using a determinist metaphor to describe exterminism as a
mode of production, and I accepted his criticism on that point. It has
also been suggested recently that 'Exterminism' was overstated and that
it has been disproved by events. That is true in some part, although I
argued at the time that 'the economies and ideologies of either side
could buckle' under the acceleration of Cold War II. And I also
envisaged an international movement of resistance as a counter to
exterminist logic. But I am still unwilling to abandon the fearsome
concept altogether. The material basis for exterminism has been little
reduced, even if the ideological structures of the Cold War are tottering.
And my 1980 definition indicated that the institutional basis of exterminism is 'the weapons-system, and the entire economic, scientific,
political and ideological support-system ... the social system which
researches it, "chooses" it, produces it, polices it, justifies it, and
maintains it in being'.[3]

This is still lying there, in central compartments of both economies,
waiting for the opportunity to resume its logic. The 'modernization' of
weaponry continues. The Soviet Union has made significant unilateral
reductions in weaponry, but it remains one of the world's two great
ranchers of nuclear weapons. And in November 1989 the Stockholm
Peace Research Institute published sobering figures, which showed that
the USSR has stretched well ahead of the USA in the arms trade. Her
exports of arms last year amounted to $63.8bn, the USA following with
$50.3bn. These huge figures are an index to the vast surplus capacity of
the USA and USSR's respective military-industrial complexes. Not many
Soviet or American arms firms, it seems, had by 1988 gone over to
making breakfast food. The thrust to exterminism has certainly been
checked, but the potential remains.

On the optimistic side, in *Beyond the Cold War* I noted that the very high ideological content of Cold War II might provide the peace movement with opportunities to contest it. And I envisaged a possible alternative, in an East–West confluence of popular movements for peace and human rights:

> What I have proposed is improbable. But, if it commenced, it might gather pace with astonishing rapidity. There would not be decades of detente, as the glaciers slowly melt. There would be very rapid and unpredictable changes; nations would become unglued from their alliances; there would be sharp conflicts within nations; there would be successive risks. We could roll up the map of the Cold War, and travel without maps for a while.

As the causes of peace and freedom came together, so 'the trans-continental discourse of political culture can be resumed'.[4] Or, as I wrote in 'Exterminism Reviewed' (1982), the confluence will 'shatter or transform or transcend the ritualized and long-inert categories of "Communism" and of "Social Democracy". . . . It is not that the Second International will make it up and enter a marriage with the Third. New forces and new forms will replace them both.' In 1981 and 1982 these ideas were regarded as too impossibly utopian to merit any discussion. Now that their time has arrived, media conductors assure us that no one could possibly have anticipated today's events.

At about that time (1982) I also put forward a more concrete agenda. I proposed that we work for a settlement of the Cold War by the year 2000, with the mutual withdrawal of US and Soviet military bases and forces from European territories. The date was at first thought to be implausible, but the demand was slowly adopted by non-aligned European peace movements. The dissolution of NATO and of the Warsaw Pact came to be seen not just as an ever-distant 'New Jerusalem' but as a practicable political agenda with intermediary steps, including the 'Finlandization' of parts of Eastern Europe, the detachment of nations from the alliances, the growth of grey areas.

## The Cold War Today

Let us now lift our eyes from the past to our own time, and regard the Cold War as we find it in 1990.

In the last months we have witnessed astonishing events, coming pell-mell one after another, rising to a surrealistic crescendo in the final two months of 1989. The first signals were ideological, with the overthrow of fifty-year-old taboos, with the publication of non-authors and the rehabilitation of non-persons. Thence in the Soviet Union the curbing of the

KGB and the forward surge of glasnost. Then the astonishing televised
theatre of the Soviet Parliament; the defeat and humiliation of Party
officials in elections; the waves of strikes, especially that of the miners;
the outburst of nationalisms. The rapid loosening of controls in East and
Central Europe – the virtual dissolution of the Hungarian CP (I never
thought to see the sacrosanct Leninist dogma, the 'leading role' of the
CP, withdrawn by the Party itself). Power-sharing in Poland; the spec-
tacle of thousands upon thousands of East Germans crossing to the
West through Hungary or Czechoslovakia; then the peaceful 'revolution'
in the GDR and the opening of the Wall. Even the cautious Bulgarians
joining democracy's chorus; the exciting days which transformed
Czechoslovakia; and, as a final climax to the year, which compressed all
the lessons of 'Stalinism' into one fearsome week of bloodshed, the
partly nineteenth-century and partly TV-inspired revolution in Romania,
the Christmas Day execution of the Ceauşescus.

How (it must seem) could it be possible for any system to be more
discredited than Communism, or any set of ideas be exposed as more
bankrupt than Marxism–Leninism? The question is enforced by the total
loss of self-confidence in the ruling Communist circles in Eastern
Europe and (very widely) in the Soviet Union.

No wonder Western Cold Warriors are sounding off their triumphal
notes. It would be strange if they did not. Francis Fukuyama, in 'The
End of History?', celebrates the 'unabashed victory of economic and
political liberalism', whose consequence will be 'the universalization of
Western liberal democracy as the final form of human government'.
Professor Allan Bloom is even more ecstatic:

> This glorious victory ... is the noblest achievement of democracy, a miracle of
> steadfastness on the part of an alliance of popular governments ... over a
> fifty-year period.... This victory is the victory of justice, of freedom over
> tyranny, the rallying of all good and reasonable men and women. It is the
> *ideas* of freedom and equality that have animated the West and have won ...

I must thank Professor Bloom for voicing with such naivety the thoughts
of so many others, and for giving me a text to interrogate. This text says:
'*We* have won the Cold War', and this victory is due to the ideas and
steadfastness of 'the West'.

But it does not seem to be 'the West' but the Soviet, Polish,
Hungarian, East German, Czech, Bulgarian and Romanian peoples who
have started to settle their own accounts. The ideas of the 'free West'
have never, I think, been greatly at risk in the West from Communist
tyranny – indeed, that tyranny has often been a foil to set Western freedoms off to greater advantage. Certainly, notions of human rights have

been strongly endorsed in some Western codes and institutions, albeit imperfectly practised. But the peoples on 'the other side' are not being dispensed these rights by some Western charity, they are obtaining them by their own efforts.

Indeed, one might call in question the whole triumphalist script on several grounds:

1. So far from the NATO posture hastening these changes, it can be argued that Cold War aggression delayed all these events. Nothing is more obvious than the fact that the changes were long overdue, and that we are seeing the release of pent-up pressures. Brezhnev and his clique derived their only legitimacy precisely from the Western 'threat' and from the need to 'defend' against a heavily armed nuclear adversary. No human rights were ever introduced by the threat of nukes.

2. One is also perplexed by the smug notion that over there they are adopting 'our values'. I only wish I knew what 'our values' are. In fact the 'free West' has had somewhat negligible influence – apart from the negative one of delay – upon these changes. In terms of challenge to 'Stalinism' and Communist orthodoxy, one major stream has always been that of Communist self-reform: from Khrushchez, from Rajk, Nagy and Maleter, from Dubček to Gorbachev. Another has certainly been human rights 'dissidents', but anyone familiar with Charter 77 or with the Hungarian opposition in the past few years will know what a wide and diverse spectrum of ideas and values are involved: there is no simple transfer to the ideas of the 'free West'.

3. In the winter of 1989–90 much of the Western media was obsessed with the ludicrous notion that the whole of Eastern and Central Europe was intent upon hurling itself helter-skelter into a 'market economy', the institution of capitalism in a Thatcherite or Milton Friedmanite form. Certainly the absurdities and absolute failures of the Communist command economies made many heads turn in that direction, and these were often the heads that spoke English and could talk with Roger Scruton, Timothy Garton Ash and the endless flow of American, British and German funders, advisers, political and academic voyeurs, business agents, and others flooding through Prague, East Berlin, Warsaw and Budapest.

But already (in mid 1990) one can observe more thoughtful and complex responses, as well as a perceptibly widening gap between a new political class of intellectuals (for example Solidarność's 'nomenklatura') and the proletarian founding members (for example Lech Wałęsa's old constituents) who are falling out of the national discourse. Polish prices

and unemployment are increasingly painful, and the other nations of
Central Europe are watching. People are beginning to ponder more seriously problems of public services and of health care. German reunification can no longer be viewed as an unmixed blessing.

This is to say only that these are times of great political plasticity, of
impetuous and rapid swings in moods and fashions. Despite all the
trumpeting of 'democracy', events in the East have been guided by a
very small Westernphile intellectual class, and working people more
generally have not yet been involved, nor learnt how to use their democratic muscle. (And this learning process will certainly not be encouraged
by Western business and political advisers.)

It will probably be three or four years before the full implications of
the events of autumn 1989 have worked their way through and given
rise to new demands, new programmes, new institutions. I cannot share
the view that the political parties of the new post-Communist societies
will be simple copies of parties in the 'free West', whether reigning or in
opposition. One may expect new projects and new ideas to emerge.

4. In any case, what is absurd is the notion that the only available alternatives are Fukayama's Western liberal democracy, with its free-market
imperatives, and 'Stalinism' or Communist centralized statism. This
century has seen Leninism and Stalinism subjected to dozens of other
critiques. There have been critiques which shared Communist premisses
– those of Luxemburg, Victor Serge, Kollontai, and thence to Bukharin,
Trotsky, and so on. There has been the major social-democratic critique
and alternative, in all its variety. Now there is the 'green' environ-
mentalist critique, alternative models of workers' control and smaller-
scale autonomous and co-operative units. And much more. So we must
watch and listen before predicting the outcome – and the outcome may
well be different in different nations. New forms and improvisations may
be discovered, drawing upon social-democratic, co-operative and
private initiatives. One can also envisage a bleaker outcome, in which
Middle Europe becomes a dumping-ground and a cheap labour
resource for West German and Japanese capitalists, and variants of
'vodka-kola' thrive.

In all this we are repeatedly told that everything that is now
happening is extraordinary, unprecedented, quite unpredictable. Yet the
very substantial confederation of political forces gathered around END
strategy not only predicted some of it, but has been actively working for
it over the last decade. From 1980 onwards we put the causes of peace
and freedom together. We repeatedly crossed East–West frontiers,
entered into dialogue with official and unofficial voices, and prised open
the doors through which the events of 1989 came. To our surprise, after

1985 our own words started to come back to us – from Moscow. It was Gorbachev now who took our lines, who spoke of ridding Europe of nuclear weapons 'from the Atlantic to the Urals', who proposed a practical agenda for the dissolution of both blocs and advocated the withdrawal of Soviet and US troops within their own borders by the year 2000.

The habit-formed executives of the Cold War have been feeling increasingly threatened. It is not only Lawrence Eagleburger who is made uneasy by the relaxation of the Cold War compulsions which were 'characterized by a remarkably stable set of relations between the great powers'.[5] One of the advantages of that system (in the eyes of its executives) was that it did not only hold the 'enemy' in an assured place; it also held client states and potentially insurgent peoples in their places. It was always an *internal* police system and a means of *internal* ideological control, as much as an external one. The events 'on the other side' have utterly destroyed the credibility of Cold War military scenarios. As Hans-Dietrich Genscher asked: 'Do we really want to acquire new nuclear rockets that can reach the Poland of Lech Wałęsa . . . or the Hungary of humaneness and democratization?'

All this has fulfilled, and overfulfilled, a good half of END's agenda, but not the whole of it. We had always proposed a mutual and reciprocal process of disengagement and withdrawal. We are still waiting for the other shoe to drop. This 'other shoe' is not just Western economic aid, even some 'Marshall Plan'. It is certainly an expectation of something more than Western applause, human rights rhetoric, and French food parcels to Romania.

It is Mrs Thatcher's humour to pretend that Mr Gorbachev is her man in Moscow. She sees events over there mainly as photo-opportunities. It is now safer for her to go on walkabout in Moscow or Budapest than in Leeds or Liverpool. But she has not moved one inch in response to the Soviet Union's unilateral cuts in weaponry; instead she is multiplying Britain's offensive power with the ill-fated Trident (as the Labour Party also promises to do) while refusing to place British nukes on any bargaining table. She is the leading advocate in NATO for the development of air-launched cruise missiles (TASM), and she is offering British airfields for the launch. Despite gushing professions of approval for perestroika, her effective stance is like that of a victor in war, imposing terms on the defeated.

And this is exactly the tone of the United States administration. How else may one interpret the extraordinary demand that a united Germany should take its place in NATO, with perhaps a concession permitting the Soviet Union to station some troops on former East German territory for a year or two more? The historical injustice of this proposal must astound anyone with living memories of World War II. The Soviet Union fought the heaviest battles of that war and suffered the heaviest losses, both military and civilian, of any combatant. Any Soviet leadership which accepted such a one-sided resolution would not long survive in the face of public memory.

Yet this is precisely what insensitive unreconstructed Cold Warriors in Washington are demanding. As the *New York Times* reports (12 April 1990): 'The underlying attitude in the Administration toward Moscow on this issue was described by one official as: "We won, you lost. Your allies are asking you to leave, ours are asking us to stay, so we are not equals." '

Moods are swinging fast on the other side. Leaving aside scenarios of a backlash – and of a Bonapartism imposed by a frustrated military, all of which depends more upon internal Soviet problems than upon the actions of the West – we may soon encounter a different level of response, in reviving Soviet self-respect and national pride. The Soviet people are not going to be humiliated for ever as the defeated in a war which they have done much more to bring to an end than has the West. They will not be pushed around for ever, as if they had thrown up their arms in unconditional surrender.

These immensely dangerous policies and postures of NATO and of the United States, which guarantee to extend conflict into the next century, have been inadequately contested by Western peace forces. The only possible answer to that arrogant American attitude is to make it clear that the time for a United States presence in West Europe is drawing rapidly to an end, and that whatever the experts and the paid commentators say, a majority of West Europeans are *not* 'asking American forces to stay'.

Most certainly there has been plenty of evidence in the past year that the Soviet governing elite is utterly demoralized, to the point of a collapse of national self-respect. This collapse is merited and necessary, and is the inevitable nemesis of Stalinism. But I see no reason for the Western peace movement to endorse the surrender of all positions to aggressive Western policies.

Whatever private messages Soviet diplomats may have been sending to Washington, the public message of the European peace movement, East and West, must be clear. A united Germany must be wholly denuclearized and severely limited in its conventional arms. (Germany's enhanced strength as an economic competitor, in consequence of arms limitations, will act as a pressure upon other nations – France and Britain – to disarm also.) Since Germany is to be a member of NATO, the peace movement has to ensure that NATO increasingly becomes an irrelevance in shaping the future of Europe. To achieve this, Germany has to take part in an active agenda designed to dissolve the bloc system and to create, in the spirit of the Helsinki agreement, the institutions of common security.

It is of the greatest importance that Western peace forces make their influence felt on this question urgently. If they fail to do so, they may become involuntary accomplices in United States strategies of 'roll-back' (after the model proposed by John Foster Dulles in the 1950s), a euphemism for the roll-forward of Western militarism and aggressive capitalism. To see the militarist forces of the Soviet Union checked and reduced is a great victory for the forces of peace. But as yet we have seen no corresponding victory over the militarist forces and ideologies in the West, and these – with their long historical formation and their secure institutional bases – may well prove the most difficult of all to bring under control.

Above all, the Western peace movement, and allied forces, must seize this opportunity, not only to heal the two blocs and promote the widest discourse between them but also to enforce some major concessions from the West to match those made by the East. Let me give examples. The Brezhnev doctrine has been explicitly renounced. But there has as yet been no sign whatsoever of the renunciation of the Truman Doctrine (1947) by which the USA asserted a 'right' not only to intervene in Greece and Turkey but also to intervene when *any* nation was threatened by Communist 'subversion'. Nor has there been any repudiation of the Eisenhower Doctrine (1957) which extended the US sphere of direct intervention to the Middle East (further extended by Carter to the Persian Gulf). The Truman Doctrine was nothing less than the direct passing-on of ugly British imperialist and royalist strategies to the United States during Attlee's bankrupt second post-war Labour administration. These doctrines license the perpetual presence in the Mediterranean and Persian Gulf of the US 7th Fleet. If Gorbachev can take his nuclear submarines out of Baltic waters, which lap against Soviet shores, it is surely time some elements of the US navy were pulled out of the Mediterranean? (The question may provide its own answer: the Cold War with the Soviet Union is not the true occasion for the deployment of the fleet, but the pretext – the plausible excuse for a wider exercise in imperialist control facing towards the Near East and North Africa, an excuse made less plausible every day.)

The Soviet withdrawal from Afghanistan (and self-criticism of its military adventure there) has been matched by no such self-criticism by the USA of its fomenting of civil war and intervening in elections in Nicaragua. Gorbachev now speaks of his willingness to withdraw Soviet troops and bases from Central and Eastern Europe as part of a reciprocal agreement with NATO, but there are no serious steps to respond by removing United States bases from Italy, Turkey, Greece, Spain, Britain, Belgium, West Germany, or Norway.

One could go on down a lengthening agenda, in which the Cold War is ending, but with one-sided concessions. If the Soviet leadership is, for the time being, satisfied with this, the peace movement in the West cannot be. There is work enough for us to do.

## The End of History?

How on earth can these prestigious persons in Washington rabbit on about an 'end to history'? As I look forward into the twenty-first century I sometimes agonize about the times in which my grandchildren and their children will live. It is not so much the rise in population as the rise in universal material *expectations* of the globe's huge population which will be straining its resources to the very limits. North–South antagonisms will certainly sharpen, and religious and nationalist fundamentalisms will become more intransigent. The struggle to bring consumer greed within moderate control; to find a level of low growth and satisfaction, which is not at the expense of the disadvantaged and poor; to defend the environment and to prevent ecological disasters; to share more equitably the world's resources and to ensure their renewal – all this is agenda enough for the continuation of 'history'.

It is an agenda which will not find all its answers in an unconstrained 'market economy'. On the contrary, we are going to need the fullest repertoire of forms – co-operative, individual enterprise, social-democratic, the centralized planning of some resources, autonomous units – as well as new forms and ways not yet invented, based upon families, communities and neighbourhoods, with new forms of self-government and simplified lifestyles. In all this, 'socialism' has not been discredited, although command-economy Communism has; socialism is part of the inheritance we shall need, although we must draw upon it critically and selectively. The most viable future may well be a kind of socialism, albeit a green and individuated kind with strong anti-state resistances.

If indeed the Cold War is now ending (and I think that with our help it may be) then my generation – my exact age-cohort – have now seen the whole episode through from start to finish, and sometimes Dorothy and I and our close political friends have been bit-part actors in it. I would date its first onset not to 1946 but to 1944. In 1944 I was a soldier in Italy: at the end of the year my regiment stood by for service against the Greek ELAS. That was when the present peace movement started for me. In 1946–56 we took a very active part in the largely World Peace Council-directed programme for peace – the Stockholm

Appeal, campaigns against German rearmament, against British imperial exploits in Malaya, Cyprus, Kenya, Guiana, the French war in Algeria; above all the movement against the Korean War. Even these sometimes manipulated and co-opted movements did raise the level of anti-nuclear consciousness, and inhibited General MacArthur and other warriors from using nuclear weapons.

In 1956 we took a leading part in the autocritique which swept the world Communist movement, forming an opposition journal within the British Communist Party, which resulted in our departure from the Party after the suppression of the Hungarian insurrection. From that time forward we developed in little journals, and then with the first British New Left – in association with friends in West Europe and C. Wright Mills in the USA – a new strategy of 'active neutrality' and a third way of peace and human rights. We converted the mass British peace movement (CND) to some of these positions and then, after 1980, converted it again. We reached out, after 1956, to voices in Gomulka's Poland (Adam Wazyk, Leszek Kolakowski) and in the thawing USSR. In 1968 we suffered the agony of witnessing the worst Brezhnevite repression outside the Soviet Union's borders – the repression of the Prague Spring. Since 1980 we have steadily advanced and developed in every way our former strategies, which have come to command a vast spectrum of non-aligned opinion.

It is profoundly moving to see the forms of the old Cold War dissolving before one's eyes. The Cold War has not been a heroic episode, an occasion for triumphs, but the most futile, wasteful, humanly destructive no-through-road in history. It has led to inconceivable investment in weapons with inconceivable destructive powers, which have threatened – and continue to threaten – the very survival of the human species (and of other species perhaps more worthy of survival). It has nourished and reproduced reciprocal paranoias; enlarged authoritarian powers and the license of overmighty security services; deadened imagination with a language of worst-case analysis and a definition of half the human race as an enemy Other. Its refraction into internal ideological and political life, on both sides, has been malign. I need not document the offences against human rights on the other side. On this side we have had absurd spy games, McCarthyism and Red-baiting, the purging of trade unions and academies, the inhibition or closure of many intellectual areas.

I could even regard those forty-five years of waste and ideological terror with distaste and a sense of personal grievance. How much of our lives went into restraining that Coldness from becoming Hot! There have been compensations in working with successive peace movements – high-spirited, voluntary, generous movements – the best people I

know. But I am astounded that Mr Fukuyama can find the end of the
Cold War 'a very sad time'. In his retrospect, 'the worldwide ideological
struggle called forth daring, courage, imagination and idealism', whereas
in the future politics will be reduced to mundane regulation of consumer
needs: 'I can feel in myself, and see in others around me, a powerful
nostalgia for the time when history existed.'

But I am not as astounded as all that. For four decades the Cold War
has been some people's professional employment – it was their job to
keep it going by every possible means. There are naturally little eddies of
panic now in the State Department and around Whitehall, a natural fear
of redundancy. What is astounding is that these people should now
come forward and claim that they are the victors, that they brought the
Cold War to an end. These are the people who have systematically
screwed up relations between East and West on every occasion;
published in their journals lampoons and direct lies about independent
intellectuals; used undisclosed agents and secret service money to
penetrate and confuse trade unions, democratic organizations, journals
and publishing houses; denied on every occasion that Communism or
'totalitarianism' could ever be capable of self-reform; and whose
activities contributed significantly to delaying and inhibiting that
process. If these people are now finding themselves bereft of some
functions and a little bored, that is a comfort to the rest of us.

If these were not the agents that influenced the end of the Cold War,
who were? Historians will argue this for decades. One major factor, of
course, has been the crippling burden of the arms race upon the
superpower economies, especially the Soviet economy. Another has
been the overflow of the long-pent-up waters of Soviet and East
European renewal. But another factor has been the influence of the
Western peace movement. This has been influential in two ways. First,
its massive education of consciousness, especially on nuclear weapons,
has been a shield against chaos. It has modified the language and even
the strategies of politicians and militarists, and redefined the political art
of the possible.

There is a second, less visible influence, which is more difficult to
demonstrate. I have argued that Cold War II, while underscored by
military-industrial complexes, was held together within an ideological
structure. If this was so, then the non-aligned (END-ish) Western peace
movement played a critical part in the 'ideological moment' when that
controlling ideological field-of-force was broken open.

It is of real significance that even at the height of the Euromissile
crisis, the major Western peace movements maintained their autonomy
and did not become captive pro-Soviet auxiliaries. At some point
between 1982 and 1985, matters came to a crisis. In our contacts with

'officials' on the other side we could feel a palpable sense of uncertainty and reorientation. We became aware of more flexible responses, from Moscow think-tanks and younger researchers.[6] The Soviet ideologists were becoming aware that millions had been demonstrating for peace in European and American cities who were not World Peace Council auxiliaries; who made demands upon the USSR as well as upon NATO; who had a growing traffic with 'dissidents' yet could not possibly be written off as 'anti-Soviet'; who were ardently resisting the weapons programmes of their own governments; who showed goodwill not to the ruling CPSU(B) but to the Soviet people; who had a strategy 'beyond the Cold War' which, while never reported on the BBC, Radio Free Europe or the Voice of America, did trickle through to the other side.

I have one point of agreement with Mr Fukuyama, and that is in his emphasis on the power of ideas. At certain moments history turns on a hinge of new ideas. I think that there was such an ideological moment in 1982–85, in which peace and human rights movements together broke the Cold War field-of-force and gave history a new hinge. In any case, the non-aligned peace movements made a large contribution to the end of the Cold War and is one of the only traditions to emerge from it with any honour.

We also prefigured again and again the events of 1989. The little tracks which we made in the East–West exchanges of the 1980s led directly to today. Roy Medvedev, the sole Soviet resident who signed the initial END Appeal, is now an influential member of the Soviet Parliament. Many of our Hungarian friends of different tendencies, whom we visited and argued with in the early 1980s, are now very active in Hungarian political life. Jiři Dienstbier, the new Czech Foreign Minister, was a contributor to the last Penguin Special (*Prospectus for a Habitable Planet*) which I co-edited, and we had long prepared the way for common understanding by visits and published debate with Charter 77 and individual members. Dialogue with Poles was sometimes more difficult but many exchanges have taken place, and Jaček Kuron (now Polish Minister of Labour) came to the END Convention in Lund in 1988.

One case may be taken for all. In 1981 British END's Churches and German groups made contacts with the first independent peace in-itiatives in the GDR – led by Robert Havemann and Pastor Rainer Eppelmann. END activists paid visits, as did Dutch and West German peace workers. Some were denied visas, others were thrown out. Later, visitors from British CND received similar treatment. A member of END committee, Barbara Einhorn, was held in a GDR prison for several days. Exchanges were also made with a small women's peace movement in East Berlin, of which Bärbel Bohley and Ulrike Poppe were leading

members. Rainer Eppelmann is now (May 1990) Defence and Disarmament Minister in the GDR government, while Bohley and Poppe
were founders and are leading members of New Forum and New
Democracy respectively. In September 1989 Bohley reported that New
Forum had 1,500 members. In November New Forum claimed 100,000.

When the time is ready, ideas can flow like the rivers of China in
flood. I think that 'we' helped to throw down the banks and let those
pent-up waters through. Those waters are not just those of the rejection
of all forms of socialism. They are also those of renewal; of those (like
Christa Wolf) who decided to stay and to remake their own societies. So
when I speak of a healing process I do not mean that this process should
start today or tomorrow. I mean that it has long been the hidden and
unreported script; for a decade the forces of peace and freedom, or a
'green' libertarian socialism, have been recognizing each other. The
events of late 1989 were a part of that healing. It is already far
advanced.

Of course, the long process of finding our friends, of mutual
recognitions and rejections, of forming new alliances and establishing
new projects, will not be the work of five or six months. New Forum and
New Democracy did not emerge as victors in the GDR elections, nor did
the Free Democrats in Hungary; rather, victory went to some of those
ardent democrats who had spent the previous twenty years sitting in
armchairs in front of the television, doing nothing whatsoever for liberty
or peace or 'dissent'. The pioneers of the democratic revolution – those
who, for years, had faced bans and police harassment – were over-
whelmed by the tides of revulsion against anything reminiscent of statist
socialism, and by the tides of Western money and media hype.

We learn, for neither the first nor the last time, that it is a terribly long
and thankless task to try to influence the course of history by little
movements 'from below'. Yet such minority positions, through most of
recorded human history, have been the only honourable places to be;
nor do they always fail in the long run. Today there is nothing to prevent
these minorities, East and West, from growing in strength and
discovering common strategies. The citizens' search for a common
project, bringing together widening constituencies in a direct discourse
unmediated by Cold War agencies or media, is the urgent task of our
time.

## Notes

1. References are to Francis Fukuyama, 'The End of History?', *National Interest*, no.
16, Summer 1969; and to subsequent discussion in later issues and sundry half-baked

comments in the United States and European press.

2. These attacks from both sides are documented and discussed in my *Double Exposure* (Merlin Press, London 1985), which is also included in the American edition of my *Heavy Dancers* (Pantheon, New York 1985).

3. 'Exterminism: the Last Stage in Civilization?' first appeared in *New Left Review*, May–June 1980; reprinted in *The Heavy Dancers*. An extensive discussion of the issues by several hands (including Raymond Williams and Roy and Zhores Medvedev) was published in the collection *Exterminism and Cold War* (Verso, 1982), together with my reply, 'Europe, the Weak Link in the Cold War'. For criticisms of the notion, see Bromley and Rosenberg, 'After Exterminism', *New Left Review*, no. 168, and Martin Shaw, 'Exterminism and Historical Pacifism', in Harvey J. Kaye and Keith McClelland, eds, *E.P. Thompson: Critical Perspectives* (Oxford, 1990).

4. *Beyond the Cold War* was first published as a pamphlet (Merlin Press, 1982), then reprinted in the collection *Zero Option* (Merlin, 1982); in the USA as *Beyond the Cold War*, (Pantheon, 1982).

5. See Alan Riding, 'Redoing Europe', *New York Times*, 15 April 1990: ' "Historical change is happening in a way it was not meant to happen," said an American defense expert as NATO headquarters in Brussels. "Instead of a slow, drawn-out process, it has happened precipitously. It's natural for people to want a return to order and predictability." '

6. See Tair Tairov's account of changes in Soviet response in this volume, pp. 43–8.

# 2

# After the Cold War[1]

## *Mary Kaldor*

East Europeans always emphasize the power of words. This has been the essence of much of Havel's political writings. The way we describe the world, the words we use, shape how we see the world and how we decide to act. Words and history – a collection of words used to describe the past – have demonstrated their power in East-Central Europe over the last few months.

The Cold War has always been a discourse, a conflict of words, 'capitalism' versus 'socialism'. Both Left and Right used the same words. They disagreed about which word was good and which was bad. Even though the Western Left was, for the most part, sharply critical of Stalinism, it still characterized the Cold War as a conflict between capitalism and socialism. It described the West as 'capitalist' and the East as 'socialist', and explained the conflict in terms of the expansionary nature of capital and the unwillingness of capitalism to tolerate any alternative.

Now the political systems in Central Europe have collapsed and the Soviet system is under severe challenge. The Right is claiming the revolutions of 1989 as its victory. What is happening, according to mainstream commentators, is the decisive defeat of socialism and the triumph of liberal (actually neo-liberal) values and policies. Fukuyama, the new favourite author of the neo-liberal Right, talks about the 'end of history' and the final victory of the 'universal homogeneous state', defined as 'liberal democracy in the political sphere combined with easy access to VCRs and stereos in the economic'.[2]

It is very important, in this climate of euphoric opinion, to think again about the words and their meanings, and to redefine recent history. What is it that has collapsed? Socialism? Yes, if what we mean by socialism is nationalization, central planning, bureaucracy, paternalism, the belief in the ability of government experts to solve social and economic problems. Socialism, in this sense, has collapsed in *both* East and West. More gradually in the West, under pressure both from the neo-liberal Right and the post-1968 generation of social movements. Explosively in the East, once these systems were no longer propped up in fact by the Soviet Union.

And what has won? Liberal values have certainly won, but has capitalism won? In what sense can the West be described as 'capitalist'? In all Western countries, including the United States, government spending is more than 50 per cent of Gross Domestic Product. Has the neo-liberal approach of Thatcher and Reagan won? Or have Japan, West Germany and other successful West European economies won? These economies are capitalist in the sense that they are market-orientated and dominated by large private corporations. But compared with the United States or Britain, much greater emphasis is placed on education, social services, public investment, local planning, worker participation, and so on.

And what does it mean to say the West has won? Does it mean that the West is stronger economically or militarily? Does it mean that Western strategies contributed to the downfall of socialism? Or does it mean that East European countries will adopt a Western political and economic model? And if so, which model? The East Europeans want Western liberal values, but do they want Americanization or Swedish social democracy? And what will they get? 'Third Worldization' or 'Mexicanization', as some are suggesting? Or perhaps an entirely new indigenous model of economic and social organization?

The answers to these questions are not yet determined. Indeed, what is taking place, in the aftermath of 1989, is a political struggle for the future of Europe. Whether 1989 was a victory for the neo-liberal Right or a victory for the new-style social movements that came to prominence in the 1980s; whether East-Central Europe is to be annexed, economically, socially and culturally, by the West, or whether we can expect a new evolution of systems in both East and West – all this depends on politics, on our own contributions to the debates and campaigns of the 1990s. In what follows, I shall explore these questions in relation to the East, the West and, finally, the East–West relationship.

Gorbachev was the trigger for the revolutions of 1989. He signalled his unwillingness to underwrite the old regimes. His spokesman Gerassimov talked about the Sinatra Doctrine: 'I did it my way.' And evidence is accumulating that in October 1989, he intervened to prevent a German Tiananmen Square (I am told that hospitals were, at that time, being mobilized to expect some 100,000 casualties). It was after this that the fear pervading East Germany and Czechoslovakia began to evaporate. 'I feel more happy than frightened but a bit frightened as well,' a young Czech peace activist told me during the second week of November.

Once the fear had gone, the regimes toppled one by one like a house of cards. Their collapse revealed the emptiness of the prevailing systems, the fact that change was long overdue.


## A War Economy

What was the system that characterized the so-called People's Democracies of East-Central Europe? It was a weird and brutal kind of socialism that was imposed in the late 1940s on the countries occupied by the Red Army during World War II. The system was the outcome of a peculiar mixture of Russian history, socialist ideas, and the specific experience of war.

Oscar Lange described the Stalinist system as a war economy.[3] By this he meant that it 'resembled the wartime organization of capitalist countries in its concentration of all resources to avoid leakages to anything that was considered non-essential – that is, not connected to the prosecution of the war'. Lange was of the view that the 'methods of the war economy' were 'necessary in a revolutionary period of transition', but he did not think these methods were intrinsically socialist. For example, compulsory deliveries of food were introduced 'by the occupation Army of Kaiser Wilhelm the Second whom I do not think anybody regards as a champion of socialism'.

The analogy of the war economy can be taken further, in the sense that the system was geared for war and really functioned efficiently only in wartime. The prosecution of war, or Cold War, was the primary goal of the Stalinist system from 1928 onwards. Even today, military spending, according to official estimates which are thought to be low, amounts to 12–15 per cent of Net Material Product. Industrialization was determined by the need to prepare for war. Moreover, the wartime atmosphere, the notion of an ever-present external threat, provided a basis for social cohesion and discipline and a legitimation for oppression.

The newly created Soviet Union was, of course, internationally beleaguered and threatened militarily from abroad. Yet in explaining the emergence of a war economy in the late 1920s and the 1930s, it is difficult to disentangle the role of outside pressures from the Russian heritage. Tsarism was, after all, shaped by the need to protect Russia from waves of invasion. Paranoia, insecurity, war psychosis had nurtured the rulers of Russia, the state apparatus, and even the Russian revolutionaries for generations.

In fact, despite the pre-war efforts, the Red Army was unprepared for the German invasion in 1941. Soviet weapons proved inferior to German weapons and the Soviet arms industry was destroyed in the first few weeks of the war. The system, however, displayed an extraordinary capacity for recovery. The arms industries were moved to the East and the design of weapons was adapted to the experience of battle. In the end, Soviet war production was comparable to American war production, and although lendlease was important, this was primarily an indigenous effort. Thus the experience of war appeared to confirm the pre-war predilections of the systems.

The imposition of Stalinism on East-Central Europe was probably inevitable once the Soviet Union had occupied these territories in the early 1940s. From an early date, Communists were put in charge of the police and the armies. Brutality and fear are self-reproducing. The argument of such diverse writers as Hannah Arendt and Fernando Claudín that Stalinism could not tolerate alternatives for fear of revealing the truth about past crimes is rather convincing. The Communists were held together, says Šimečka, by 'above all, an awareness of sharing the "original sin"'.[4]

All the same, Western behaviour helped. Although, technically, it was the Russians who refused to allow the East-Central European countries to accept Marshall Aid, it is now clear that the Americans (and the British) imposed conditions that they hoped the Russians would refuse.[5] The East European countries were much poorer than the West European countries and had suffered proportionally more war damage. In the absence of Western aid, the methods of the war economy were the most obvious to deal with the horrendous problem of reconstruction. The establishment of the Cominform and Zhdanov's Two Camp Doctrine took place after the decision not to provide Marshall Aid to East-Central Europe. Subsequently, the formation of NATO, the introduction of nuclear weapons into Western Europe, and the rearmament of West Germany substantiated the Western threat hypothesis and reinforced the psychosis of war.

During the years 1948–52, the Stalinist system was imposed on East-Central Europe down to the last detail, in the name of the struggle for socialism against capitalism. Plans for autarkic self-sufficient industrial development were drawn up (often replacing national plans), with considerable emphasis on steel and heavy industry and, after Korea, the production of armaments. Agriculture was forcibly collectivized. Autonomous private life, such as cafés or non-political clubs, was strictly curtailed. Soviet army regulations were imposed on East European armed forces and Soviet army officers were put in positions of command. 'Home' Communists were purged and Soviet control was tightened over local Parties, the security forces, and the nomenklatura system. Personality cults were introduced in all East European countries in which local leaders basked in Stalin's reflected light.

## Eastern Europe after Stalin

The history of Soviet-type systems after 1952 is a history of attempts to escape the Stalinist inheritance. It is a history in which the ruling parties sought to remain in power while correcting some of the worst abuses of the system – the paranoid atmosphere which engulfed the rulers as well as the ruled, and the intractable economic problems which they faced once the immediacy of war had been removed. All these countries were subject to perennial shortages because of the inherent tendency in planned economies to exceed planned expenditure. (This is similar to the cost-overrun problem in Western defence industries. Investment plans are always underestimated, either deliberately in order to 'hook on' to the plan, or because of unforeseen difficulties, or merely because there are no penalties for excess cost, as in a market economy.[6]) In the absence of war and of democracy, the goals of the plan are no longer determined by the requirements of battle but by bureaucratic pressures based on Stalinist structures. Today, the Soviet budget deficit is estimated to be 20 per cent of Net Material Product. The corollary to shortage is waste and inefficiency and an inherent tendency to squeeze consumption and agriculture in order to fulfil investment plans. Hence the typical cycle of investment drives followed by austerity.

Since 1953 there have been periodic attempts at reform, generally involving the introduction of a market element into the planning system. These reforms – which included the replacement of administrative directives by financial indicators, greater autonomy for enterprises, tolerance towards small-scale private enterprise, liberalization of agriculture (decollectivization, abolition of compulsory deliveries, acceptance of private plots, and so on), liberalization of foreign trade and greater emphasis on consumption – went furthest in Hungary. But in all cases, the momentum was halted by bureaucratic resistance in the absence of political reform. Without a central shift in the goals of the plan, which was impossible without political change, the reforms could do little other than marginally increase the efficiency with which the plans were fulfilled. And any serious attempt at political reform was liable to be crushed – as became evident in Hungary in 1956 and in Czechoslovakia in 1968. In some senses, 1968 was the crucial turning point: when the Brezhnev regime turned its back on reform, and remaining hopes for the democratization of socialism were dashed. It was after 1968 that opposition shifted from revisionism to outright dissidence.

The detente of the 1970s can be interpreted as an attempt to substitute imports for reform, to raise standards of living through the mechanism of what Brezhnev called the 'foreign reserve' while maintaining tight political control. By solving short-term bottlenecks, meeting immediate consumer demands (as in Poland) and importing Western technology, it was hoped that shortage could be overcome. However, imports created a chain of supplementary demands (for parts, appropriate raw materials, and so on), and in the absence of reform it was extremely difficult to assimilate Western technology. Moreover, the post-1973 recession in Western Europe, competition with Southern Europe as well as the newly industrializing countries of the Far East (which were competing for the same low-cost manufactured goods patch of the market) and the new protectionism made it impossible to generate sufficient exports to pay for increased imports. In the late 1970s and early 1980s, all the East European countries were forced to cut back on trade with the West and to introduce austerity policies. All, in varying degrees, were heavily indebted, although the problem was less serious in East Germany and Czechoslovakia. Romania managed to repay the debt through a particularly virulent return to nationalist totalitarianism.

So it was that by the mid 1980s, all avenues of change short of democracy had been exhausted. The remaining shreds of legitimacy, the remaining claims for socialism, disappeared with the cuts in welfare and consumption that were introduced in the years of austerity. Despite Reagan's efforts to help these regimes with his nuclear-war-fighting strategies and his aggressive rhetoric, the last remnants of belief in a Western threat vanished along with increased trade and travel. One had only to observe the joy on both sides of Berlin when the Wall was opened up to realize that *no one*, any more, believed in a conflict between East and West.

## The Atlanticist Compromise

If Stalinism came to fruition in World War II, the system that came to predominate in the Atlantic region was also profoundly shaped by the Anglo–American experience of that war. Atlanticism can be viewed as more than a geographical alliance. It constituted a specific phase of capitalist history, a specific statist variant of capitalism. It can be described as a kind of compromise between Fordism and Fabianism.

World War II solved the problems of the Depression, which had been caused by a disjuncture between production and consumption, between economics and politics. The huge expansion of productivity in the United States which was the consequence of the growth of Fordist methods of production was not matched by a corresponding increase in demand. This was both because of the domestic distribution of income within the United States and because international institutions still reflected the dominance of Britain. But then the big increase in military spending and the provision of lendlease mopped up unemployment in the United States. It also encouraged the spread of mass-production techniques and new inventions like the computer and radar which were to have profound implications after the war. For the duration of World War II, US income increased by 65 per cent. At the end of the war, the USA accounted for 40–45 per cent of world output, and enjoyed a huge trade surplus.

The Cold War reproduced the World War II experience. NATO provided a mechanism for a continuous transfer of resources from the USA to Europe, to sustain demand in the USA and to underpin the global financial system. It was a way of coping with the dollar shortage. NATO also encouraged the creation of a common infrastructure and a common set of technological priorities which facilitated the spread of Fordist methods of production.

This is not to suggest that what happened was mechanistic, that the Cold War began for economic reasons. (It is true, however, that Bevin, for example, seems to have regarded the Soviet threat as a way of persuading the Americans to make a permanent economic commitment to Europe.) There were other ways in which pre-war economic problems could have been solved – through welfare spending, for example, or through an international clearing union, as proposed by Keynes.

The reasons for the Cold War were political and had to do with both American and European domestic politics. The American political spectrum shifted to the right immediately after the war, while the European political spectrum shifted dramatically to the left. Socialist or left-leaning coalition governments in West Europe introduced varying mixtures of planning, nationalization and welfare policies. On the one hand, anti-Communism enabled a bipartisan consensus in the United States: it was a way of persuading the Republican Right to support a global role for the country. On the other hand, it was a way of persuading the United States to make a long-term economic commitment to Western Europe, despite differences of political outlook. Anti-Communism was a way of legitimizing Labour or socialist governments in Britain, France, Italy and the Netherlands, *vis-à-vis* the United States.

In practice, the Cold War divided the Left in Western Europe and allowed for the partial rehabilitation of the pre-war West European establishments. Radical policies were curbed: welfare gave way to warfare. During the 1950s, a new Atlanticist elite was formed with a common commitment to managed capitalism and to high levels of military spending.

J.K. Galbraith's book *The New Industrial State*, published in 1969, envisaged a new convergence between East and West around the planning system which characterizes both large corporations and the modern state. What he observed, it can be argued, were the institutions associated with Fordist patterns of production which were shaped by the shared legacy of World War II.

Unlike in the East, economic restructuring took place in the West during the 1970s and 1980s. Fordist patterns of industrial development have been increasingly replaced by more flexible, decentralized resource-saving methods of production, applicable to both manufacturing and services and based on the revolution in what are known as information technologies.[7] The pole of capitalist accumulation has shifted from the United States to Japan and, to a lesser extent, West Germany and the smaller West European countries.

Instead of facilitating the international economic system, the Cold War now represents a cause of economic problems. Continued high levels of military spending in the United States, as well as Britain and France, contribute to global economic imbalances and divert science and technology so that those countries which spend most on military research and development are the least competitive in international trade. The successful capitalist economies are those which have spent least on armaments and have responded to demands for spending on education and the environment, or introduced local community development programmes or worker participation schemes. Indeed, the economic problems of the 1970s can be explained by a new disjuncture between production and consumption and economics and politics – a disjuncture between the new pattern of industrial development centred on Japan and West Europe, and Fordist political institutions dominated by the United States.

## New Challenges

During the 1970s and 1980s, the Cold War compromise has come under challenge from both Right and Left. The neo-liberal Right challenged the Fabian elements of the compromise. It criticized the role of big government and welfare, or trade unions and inflation. It retained the emphasis on Cold War policies and the Soviet threat but advocated a return to the market, the abandonment of planning and state intervention, the eradication of 'socialism'. On the Left, the post-1968 new social movements put more emphasis on the Cold War element of the compromise. They were critical of the paternalistic and militaristic nature of state intervention, not of state intervention *per se.* They favoured democratization rather than liberalization and privatization.[8]

The new Cold War of the early 1980s was a victory for the neo-liberal Right. It helped to curb, at least temporarily, the influence of the post-1968 Left in Western Europe. It provided a reason for tolerating a growing US deficit and thus renewing, at least temporarily, American economic vigour. But is the end of the Cold War a victory for the neo-liberal Right? Does it not imply big reductions in military spending and a shift in political power to West Germany and Japan? And, in the absence of a Soviet threat, is it possible to explain away the neglect of welfare or the environment?

I have tried to suggest that the Cold War was not a conflict of systems. There were two distinct social systems: one was called 'socialism', the other was called 'capitalism'. They were specific variants of socialism and capitalism, but they became archetypal because all other variants were excluded. These two systems, which I call Atlanticism and post-Stalinism, were not in conflict but were *complementary*, tied together by the same historical experience. Each needed the other. Both required high levels of military spending and a permanent external threat. The existence of each provided a legitimation for the other.

Both systems, for different reasons, are in crisis. Atlanticism was the social and political expression of the Fordist era of capitalist development which is now exhausted. Crisis may be too strong a word for the West; both because of democratic pressures and because of the lessons learnt in the 1930s, it is perhaps more accurate to talk about the problems associated with the erosion of Atlanticism. Post-Stalinism has never functioned effectively in East-Central Europe; it has experienced a long-suppressed crisis which exploded dramatically as the lid was lifted from the mounting failures. In both East and West, the Cold War is ending for primarily internal reasons.

In so far as the West did play a role in the revolutions of 1989, it was not the neo-liberal Right but the new social movements – and especially the peace movements – which hastened the collapse of actually existing socialism. It was the fact that parts of the peace movement broke with the Left tradition of regarding the conflict as a conflict between capitalism and socialism in which the West was primarily responsible that undermined the words and language of the Cold War.

The neo-liberal Right legitimized its belief in deregulation and privatization in terms of a contrast with 'socialism' that existed in the West under Labour and Social Democrat governments and was identified with actually existing socialism in the East. Hence the coming to power of Reagan and Thatcher was associated with a renewal of Cold War rhetoric, increased emphasis on nuclear weapons, and higher levels of military spending. The New Cold War of the 1980s *legitimized* the renewed autarky of East European countries as a response to the debt crisis. It can be argued that the New Cold War helped to justify an interruption in the evolutionary process towards political reform that seemed to be occurring in the late 1970s.[9] It was, after all, in December 1981 that the crackdown in Poland took place in the midst of Warsaw Pact military manoeuvres on Poland's borders. E.P. Thompson wrote in 1981 that the future of Europe hangs on two hinges: whether we can halt cruise missiles in the West and whether Solidarity can succeed in the East.[10] In a double motion, these processes were stopped for a while. When the cruise missiles were finally deployed in 1983, there was a severe backlash against those who had opposed the Soviet missiles in East Germany and also in Hungary.

The effectiveness of the New Cold War was severely weakened by the emergence of a mass peace movement in Western Europe in the early 1980s. It is worth recalling that the movements were comparable in scale to the democracy movements in Eastern Europe in the late 1980s. Five million people demonstrated in the capitals of Western Europe in autumn 1981, and again in autumn 1983. What made this different from earlier peace movements was the explicit link between peace and human rights, the emphasis on the Cold War as a 'joint venture', which was expressed in the END Appeal of April 1980 and E.P. Thompson's essay on exterminism.[11] This helped to legitimize the peace movement in the West, to show that there was genuine concern about nuclear weapons and that this was not orchestrated by Moscow. But it also helped to provide space for the emergence of new social movements in the East. From 1983 onwards, parts of the Western peace movement like END, or the Dutch Inter-Church Peace Council (IKV) and the West German Greens, began to focus their activities on 'detente from below', on building links with peace, green and human rights groups in the East, and on pressing upon official peace committees and Warsaw Pact governments the argument that their initiatives for disarmament could not be taken seriously if they did not permit the right to campaign freely for peace.

## Solidarity and Democracy in Eastern Europe

In the 1980s, the individual isolated dissident gave way to social movements as a new form of opposition in East-Central Europe. By far the most important was Solidarity. It can be argued that the peace movement represented a new phenomenon in the West because of its insistence on democracy in both East and West; because it challenged the notion that Western governments were the guardians of freedom and the Soviet government stood for peace – it decisively changed the perception of the peace movement as a tool of the Kremlin! For its part, Solidarity similarly undermined Cold War ideology because it was a workers' movement in a society in which the rulers claimed to represent the working class, the struggle for socialism against capitalism. Subsequently, other movements, clubs and initiatives emerged in East-Central Europe. Peace movements were especially important – Swords into Ploughshares (a mass Church-based peace movement) in the GDR and the Hungarian Dialogue Group in the early 1980s, and substantial peace movements in Poland (Freedom and Peace), Czechoslovakia (the Independent Peace Association or NMS) and Slovenia in the late 1980s. The convergence of ideas that developed through the process of detente from below did profoundly influence 'New Thinking' in the Soviet Union, as can be observed from Gorbachev's speeches, and insistent pressure on Eastern governments did increase the political space within which the new movements could operate.

Where did the democracy movements of 1989 come from? They represented an outburst of popular feelings but these feelings were articulated and organized by those who had gained experience in the new peace, green and human rights movements of the 1980s. Both Václav Havel and Jiři Dienstbier had been engaged in an intensive dialogue with END and IKV during the 1980s. Dienstbier is a signatory of the END Appeal and a contributor to the END *Journal* – one of the people we would telephone regularly for tactical advice. Ulrike Poppe (Democracy Now) and Bärbel Bohley (New Forum) were part of East German women's groups who collaborated closely with the END Women's Committee. The END German–German group organized Bärbel's six-month stay in Britain in 1989 after she was expelled temporarily as a result of the officially organized demonstration to commemorate Rosa Luxemburg, in which demonstrators displayed posters carrying a quotation from Luxemburg: 'Freedom is the freedom to think differently.' In the short-lived East German government, the Minister for Disarmament and Defence, Foreign Minister and Finance Minister were all pacifists and END signatories. In recent years, much of END's energy has been devoted to supporting the rights of independent

Czech peace activists; now these same peace activists are playing a key role in Civic Forum. And in Hungary, the Young Democrats (FIDESZ), who participated in the Round Table talks with the government about Hungary's future and are now the third largest party in Hungary, were formed by a group of students who had initially got together to organize and engage in an East–West dialogue with groups like END and IKV. And the list could go on.

## Where Now?

But if it was not a victory for the West, in the sense that Western policies contributed to the collapse of socialism as it actually existed, is it a victory in the sense that East European countries will adopt a Western model?

The answer to that question depends as much on what happens in the West as on what happens in the East. In the West, the Left–Right division dominates politics and is supposed to reflect the East–West division. In the East, the Left–Right division is not really appropriate as a way of characterizing politics. The main political division in the East is between nationalist/authoritarian tendencies and democratic/cosmopolitan tendencies. In a sense, both Communists and nationalists are drawn from the same tradition. In the last years of Communist rule, socialist ideology in several countries was replaced by nationalist ideology. The authoritarian–democratic division also appeared to be reflected in the East–West division. To be pro-West is to be progressive; it is part of the outward-looking democratic tendency. If by Left/Right we mean a concern with social justice, then the full Left/Right political spectrum is visible in both authoritarian and democratic tendencies. On the whole, however, the most radical pro-market views are to be found amongst the more progressive democratic sections of political opinion – the Mazowiecki government in Poland, Civic Forum in Czechoslovakia, or the Free Democrats in Hungary. Being pro-market is seen as a radical negation of the Communist past, a (political) way of destroying the overheavy bureaucratic structures inherited from the Stalinist years. The victory of the nationalist/Christian Democratic Forum in Hungary, or the Communists in Bulgaria and Romania, can, I believe, partly be understood in terms of popular anxiety about the consequences of a radical break with the past. And these anxieties are not only economic. They have to do with fear of self-responsibility; to some degree, people have grown used to paternalism.

This generalization about East European politics does not, of course, apply to Germany, where Western-type parties rapidly took over the political landscape – even in Eastern Germany, however, the parties are different from their Western counterparts. It does apply to the Soviet Union, where this political division reflects the historic division between Slavophiles and Westernizers.

Paradoxically, the Western model will win in the long term in Eastern Europe only if the West itself changes. At present, public rhetoric in the West is dominated by the neo-liberal Right, which propounds the notion that it is only through unrestrained markets and so-called capitalist 'shock therapy' that East Europe will acquire the consumer goods which so attract their populations. Economic assistance has to be based on strictly commercial criteria. The exception, of course, is the former GDR, which will receive huge subsidies to facilitate unification. The capitalist shock therapy may succeed in undermining the old economic structures. But without substantial economic aid (grants or debt reduction) to build a new infrastructure, to solve environmental problems, and so on, I am doubtful whether sufficient entrepreneurial creativity will be released to generate economic growth. Markets are both destructive and creative. So far, the Polish shock therapy has reduced output by 40 per cent. Private enterprise has been squeezed by the fall in output, higher input prices and high interest rates. Foreign capital does not seem to be interested in investing in a country where the telephone does not work. In so far as there are Left pressures for Keynesian stimuli, social safety nets, and so forth, these are severely constrained by the conditions imposed by Western creditors.

It is worth noting that in the West the neo-liberal Right is very reluctant to reduce military spending – for reasons partly political and partly economic. In the absence of welfare, military spending is an important mechanism for regulation. It is argued that NATO must be maintained because it is the chief instrument of stability in Europe today, and the European Community must acquire a defence dimension in order to become a political entity and to integrate a united Germany. East-Central Europe will have some kind of associate status, but cannot fully join the European Community until it reaches a similar level of development. Hence the neo-liberal formula is a formula for excluding East-Central Europe. What one can envisage is a kind of Americanization of Western Europe, with high military spending, high levels of private consumption, a kind of unifying materialist culture, and a new economic division of Europe, with East-Central Europe reverting to nationalist, authoritarian government as the consequences of the neo-liberal approach are experienced.

A major weakness of the neo-liberal approach is the absence of an enemy to justify high levels of military spending and the absence of actually existing socialism to legitimize unrestrained markets. Who will

Western Europe arm against? One answer is the Soviet Union. Western intransigence could legitimize the reimposition of centralized control by the Red Army, thus re-creating a military division along the Western borders of the Soviet Union. Alternatively, the area that is now the Soviet Union could retreat – not necessarily to a pre-Gorbachevian system but to an undemocratic, unstable politics, riven with economic and ethnic problems. This is all the more likely if the West does not increase East–West co-operation. Another answer, which is already provided by Mrs Thatcher and other Western leaders, is proliferation, the spread of military technology to 'fundamentalists', drug traffickers, terrorists, and so on, in the Third World. It is possible to envisage a new Cold War between the 'modern' North and the 'fundamentalist' South. All the same, is Western military power the answer to the problems of proliferation and Third World violence?

And how will Western governments justify the neglect of social problems – the poor, the environment, public services, and so forth – in the absence of an authoritarian model to serve as a warning of what has to be avoided? Nostalgia for the welfare state, however paternalistic, is likely to grow.

An alternative direction for Europe, proposed by the new social movements, emphasizes their concerns about peace, the environment, gender, multiculturalism, and democracy. This would involve a more equal relationship between East and West Europe in which there was change in the West as well as the East. There would be big reductions in military spending, generous increases in expenditure on welfare and on the environment, and substantial increases in economic assistance on a continuing basis from surplus countries like West Germany and Japan to Eastern Europe and the Third World. Moreover, this assistance would be based not on commercial criteria but on social and ecological criteria determined through a democratic process involving both donors and recipients, achieved through the democratization of new and existing trans-European institutions. This approach is reflected in certain new initiatives in Europe today, like the Czech-sponsored Helsinki Citizens' Assembly held in Prague in October 1990.

At the time of writing, the first direction is winning the battle of words. The 1990s may well go down in history as the moment when Europe (and the world) took the wrong direction because of a commitment to capitalist orthodoxy. The dreaded word 'socialism' is no longer printable. The peace issue, however, could be the pivot which determines the future direction. The democratic tendencies in East-Central Europe may favour the Western Right in their economic policies, but they are much closer to the Western Left in their peace policies. Joint pressure to create an alternative security system for

Europe, based on the principles of non-violence, could result in a change of thinking on economic issues. Just as the Cold War provided a framework for a particular set of American- and Soviet-dominated socioeconomic approaches, so an alternative to the Cold War would require a different kind of economic underpinning. Except possibly in Hungary, there is no sign that the new governments of East-Central Europe wish to join NATO, and they all favour a pan-European security system that would supplant military blocs. Indeed, if we were to try to pinpoint the real contribution of the Western peace movement to the revolutions of 1989, one could say that it was the dialogue of the 1980s that led to a common conception of a Europe beyond the blocs, a new approach to peace in Europe.

In an essay addressed to the END Convention in Amsterdam in 1985, entitled 'The Anatomy of Reticence',[12] Václav Havel tried to explain to Western peace activists why the word 'peace' had been so discredited in Soviet-type societies and why, therefore, those who opposed the system were so reluctant to enter a dialogue with the Western peace movement. In a recent acceptance speech written for a German peace prize, Havel now says that 'one important word [peace] has been rescued from total debasement':

> In spite of that lengthy process of systematically divesting the word 'peace' of all meaning – worse than that, investing it instead with quite the opposite meaning to that given in the dictionary – a number of Don Quixotes in Charter 77 and several of their younger colleagues in the Independent Peace Association have managed to rehabilitate the word and restore its original meaning.... And it is not just a question of saving a word.... Something far more important is saved.[13]

So can the word 'socialism' be restored? Can a new European peace process result in a new socioeconomic model for both the East and West that we could call 'socialist'? I think it is difficult to use the term. 'Socialism' is discredited not just because of the inner contradictions of actually existing socialism but also because the Left failed to oppose actively what was happening in the Soviet Union and East-Central Europe. It was the peace movement which championed the cause of human rights. Social Democrat and Labour Parties promoted detente from above, good relations between ruling parties, which was important, but they argued wrongly that this was incompatible with detente from below. They argued that peace came before human rights. Likewise, much of the Left was reluctant to put its energies into democratic struggles in the East, in part because these countries were viewed as 'socialist', however distorted.

And there is something in the argument. Socialism is not such a straightforward word as peace. It does contain the notion of a strategy for social justice, a method of social organization that replaces capitalism. Because socialists failed to address the problem of state power, the portrayal of statist forms of economic organization as 'socialist' does have some truth. Yet the absence of an appropriate word with which to pursue the goals of material equality and economic democracy, the absence of a framework within which to discuss problems of ownership and control, uneven development and social policy, leaves a vacuum. These concerns will become increasingly important in the coming years, and we need to be able to conceptualize and articulate them. Moreover, if actually existing socialism has left a negative legacy, it is important to recall the proud and honourable socialist tradition in Europe – of workers' movements, ideas and education – which must not be discarded. Is social justice an adequate substitute for the term 'socialist'? Do we have to begin the painful and isolating task of redefining and resuscitating socialism? Or should we attempt to develop a new term that encompasses new concerns about democracy, the environment, gender and race, as well as traditional concerns? This is the debate we have to conduct with our new friends in the East.

## Notes

1. Part of the argument is taken from my book *The Imaginary War: Understanding the East–West Conflict*, Blackwell, 1990.

2. Extracted in *The Independent*, 20 and 21 September 1989.

3. In a lecture given in Belgrade in 1957, one year after Gomulka's accession to power. Lange was then head of the Planning Commission. See 'Role of Planning in a Socialist Economy', in Oskar Lange, ed., *Problems of Political Economy of Socialism*, New Delhi, 1962.

4. Milan Šimečka's 'From Class Obsessions to Dialogue: Detente and the Changing Political Culture of Eastern Europe', in Kaldor, Holden and Falk, eds, *The New Detente: Rethinking East–West Relations*, Verso, 1989.

5. See William C. Cromwell, 'The Marshall Plan, Britain and the Cold War', *Review of International Studies*, 8, 1982. See also George Kennan's account in *Memoirs*, vol. 1, Hutchinson, 1968.

6. For a theoretical exposition of this problem, see János Kornai, *The Economics of Shortage*, North-Holland, Amsterdam 1978; and Támás Bauer, 'Investment Cycles in Planned Economies', *Acta Oeconomica*, vol. 21, no. 3, 1978.

7. See Robin Murray, 'Life After Henry (Ford)', *Marxism Today*, October 1988; and 'Benetton Britain: The New Economic Order', *Marxism Today*, November 1985.

8. Hilary Wainwright, 'The State and Society: Reflections on a Western Experience', in *The New Detente*.

9. See Adam Michnik's article 'A New Evolutionism', written in 1978, in *Letters From Prison and Other Essays*, University of California Press, 1985.

10. *Beyond the Cold War*, Pantheon, 1982.

11. See *Exterminism and the Cold War*, Verso, 1982.

12. See *END Journal*, Issue 16/17, Summer 1985.

13. 'Words on Words', *New York Review of Books*, 18 January 1990.

# 3

# From New Thinking to a Civic Peace

*Tair Tairov*

Although, for many in the West, perestroika and changes in the foreign policy of the Soviet Union seem to be a kind of one-man operation or Gorbachev's personal innovation, broad circles of the public at large in the Soviet Union believe that internal developments had long ago set up a timetable for desperately needed reforms. It was evident that without urgent and dramatic changes, the militarily burdened economy and the geriatric totalitarianism would result in unpredictable internal and external crises. The situation was objectively ripe for reform.

However, the fact that the most radical changes were in foreign policy and unilateral reductions in armaments has to be explained in terms of the influence of Western peace movements, especially the principles and spirit elaborated in the END Appeal. I shared the frustration of the Soviet leadership, which almost in agony tried in the late 1970s and early 1980s to stop the arms race, but could not adopt an imaginative approach to the popular demands coming from disarmament campaigns and peace research institutions. It became increasingly clear that the Soviet economic situation and stagnating political structures could no longer allow the old Soviet leaders to maintain a status quo in the country.

Internal economic and social developments have created a situation in which only radical reforms can meet popular expectations. Nevertheless, Gorbachev's reforms still seem to be far from synchronizing with each other so as to cover all major fields and establish the viability of the Soviet system.

After he came to power, Gorbachev began by announcing his economic reforms. He spoke of possible changes within Party life, but waited five years – until 1990 – to start them. He introduced glasnost in the media (which is still progressing slowly), but never mentioned political reforms until 1988. It was four years before he realized that economic reforms could not be successful unless the political system became more flexible. Nor did he allow public debate on this matter before he himself started to make speeches about the coming political reforms.

Meanwhile, he did initiate very far-reaching steps in disarmament fields, in particular the signing of the INF Treaty. Unusual steps in foreign policy, openness and willingness to discuss possible compromises with foreign partners changed the old image of the Soviet Union, and produced a generally favourable atmosphere and climate of expectation abroad. The Soviet people were also very sensitive to foreign policy issues. But confirmation of the new thinking in foreign policy is not possible without changes in the political system. Only in 1989, with semi-democratic elections (where Party and state bureaucracy maintained their positions through corporate representation of public organizations in the Soviet Parliament) and dramatic and open dealing in the Parliament, has a wave of new thinking that really affects Soviet society become more visible.

Zigzags in economic and political reform did not affect perestroika in the field of foreign policy. Changes in this field preceded internal reforms. Questions concerning continuing intervention in Afghanistan and the mounting loss in human lives, growing military expenditure coupled with public outcry in the West against the deployment of SS-20s could not wait until the next Communist Party Congress. It was impossible to make radical changes inside the Soviet Union without large cuts in military spending. It was also apparent that internal changes could not take place without the creation of a favourable international climate. It was clear that sooner or later Western peace movements' demands for nuclear disarmament had inevitably to be met by the superpowers. And Gorbachev rightly decided to take the lead.

The Western peace movements played an instrumental role both in creating an international climate for the changes in Europe and in putting forward an arsenal of peace proposals which contributed to new thinking. But before new thinking could be implemented, what was needed was a change of personnel in the Kremlin and the emergence of a leader who possessed a sense of reason. Unfortunately, a leadership transition in Soviet society could not take place through democratic procedures but only as a result of the deaths of three Soviet leaders. This is why the changes started so late against a background of Cold War rhetoric.

The reaction of the previous Soviet leadership towards Western public opinion on the growing arms build-up in Europe was not simple. Not until 1979 did Moscow start to express growing concern about the coming NATO double-track decision on deployment of new US missiles in response to Soviet SS-20s. At the time, I was appointed Soviet representative to the World Peace Council and was asked to put all my energy into mobilizing WPC members to prevent NATO's decision. In fact I was told that the main purpose of my new job in Helsinki was to campaign against new US missiles. Despite the supposed influence of the Soviet Union at the WPC, I failed to convince almost all my colleagues in Helsinki to make the anti-missile campaign a priority issue. Instead I was strongly rebuffed by WPC secretaries, who argued that I was Eurocentric and was disregarding the needs of the Third World.

As it turned out, the campaign to stop the deployment of both Soviet and American missiles was completely independent of the WPC. Gorbachev, as a new Soviet leader, could not fail to know that the zero option proposed by President Reagan was a consequence of the mass demonstrations in Western Europe in autumn 1981. Moscow was always asking me to inform the Soviet leadership about the trends in the Western peace movements – what were the priority issues, and so on. Although the Soviet media – and especially articles by the Soviet peace committee leaders – described the END conventions as an anti-Soviet happening, the Soviet Party leaders took the END movement very seriously and the Central Committee was anxious to know as much as possible about it. Zhukov, Lokshin and others described END as a pro--NATO, anti-socialist movement, referring to its emphasis on human rights; the politicians wanted to exploit its disarmament platform for Moscow's foreign policy without paying a price for it. And the price was very simple – to agree to the elimination of *both* Soviet and American missiles and proceed with implementation of the Helsinki accords.

An upsurge of unprecedented movements against nuclear missiles demonstrated the tremendous energy and power of this new social force. The zero option was achieved by the people's demands and demonstrated the possibilities of mass non-violent protests in Europe. In fact I believe that mass demonstrations in the early 1980s were a prelude to the people's revolutions in Eastern Europe in 1989: people learned from each other. And it was the turn of the Eastern Europeans to grasp opportunities created by Gorbachev's new thinking and act non-violently against totalitarian regimes.

The INF Treaty and the 50 per cent reduction of strategic nuclear arms are undoubtedly achievements of the peace movements as well as of governments. During the last twenty to thirty years, peace research institutes, disarmament campaigns, civil rights activists and outstanding individuals in Europe have elaborated a long list of peace proposals. This market of common sense has been awaiting reasonable customers from both East and West. What Gorbachev did was to face the challenge of common sense presented in those peace proposals. Thus he himself has been shaped, as far as foreign policy is concerned, by peace and new social movements in Europe and inside the USSR as well; part of Gorbachev is the work of millions in the streets of Europe and the result of the tireless efforts of human rights activists.

However, new developments in the USSR, such as modernization, collapse of the Warsaw Treaty organization, withdrawal of Soviet troops from Hungary and Czechoslovakia in turn create new complications. On the one hand, all these events have helped the positive historic changes in Europe. Yet the whole process of new thinking is more and more conditional on what may happen to the USSR. Will it continue to exist as a unitary state, or will it develop into a number of confederated states? Worse, will it disintegrate into a number of warring states? The results of this process will influence further changes in USSR foreign policy and Western reaction to it. Meanwhile, what is becoming most important in the Soviet Union itself is its integrity and the continuation of the process of democratization.

I do not believe that a giant like the USSR, with its deeply rooted totalitarian culture, can in such a historically short time transform itself into a democratic and modern society. Before it does so, it is necessary for the emerging and fragile civil society in the Soviet Union to demonstrate what I call a *civic peace*. This peace should not be based on the use of Soviet tanks on Soviet or any other territory: rather, it should be based on political and socioeconomic equality of all Soviet citizens and ethnic communities. Civil peace in the Soviet Union is an urgent priority for the present Soviet leadership. But it cannot simply be achieved by the new thinkers in the leadership: it is necessary to act also at grass-roots levels. A civic peace based on international law and trust, not on military force and mistrust, has been long awaited by the Soviet people, and we in the USSR owe a great deal to Western peace movements for making detente from below the main issue in the 1980s and for raising many key issues of disarmament. This educated and helped perestroika, which has been able to use the fertile soil of European public opinion created by the peace movements. Had it not been for the process of European Nuclear Disarmament, we would not have been witnesses to the wonderful changes in Europe today.

The integrity of the Soviet Union is inseparable from the process of national identification of millions of people who have long been denied elementary rights on national grounds. The Soviet Union, despite perestroika, continues to be an enormous imperial structure. As such it cannot become part of the European home. What it needs is trans-formation into a form of flexible entity which allows its part to be independent in economic activities and – to a certain degree – in political activities. Despite political reforms, the imperial structure has not altered. Strong centralized bureaucratic machinery with chauvinistic prejudices continues to function, though with a new mantle of democratic vocabulary. It is an absolutely legitimate and morally grounded demand of the peoples of the republics that the right to full separation be granted and guaranteed by the constitution. The separation of republics will not mean that they are going to move to some other continent. They will continue to maintain their close co-operation with the rest of the USSR or with the Russian Federation, but on an equal basis.

The case of the Baltic republics is of particular significance. It is within the constitution that any republic, through its local Supreme Soviet, could declare its secession. Previously they could not have done so only because there were no free elections and local Supreme Soviets did not dare to challenge Moscow. There is no legal basis for Gorbachev to deny the Lithuanian Supreme Soviet's declaration of independence, especially since Lithuania was annexed territory and did not join the USSR in 1940 through a referendum.

If in foreign policy we have witnessed the best of Gorbachev's achievements, in national policy we are watching his worst. The blockade of Lithuania was neither more nor less than a grave violation of human rights and an act of aggression against a sovereign republic and independent state. Just as Gorbachev's foreign policy is a result of the demands and expectations of ordinary people and democratic pressure, more pressure for the self-determination of the Baltic republics would allow him to use this as an argument against his conservative wing – army, chauvinist pro-imperial apparatus, dogmatic Party comrades. With only one or two exceptions he has chosen very conservative people for his Presidential Council; people who are known for faithful service to Brezhnev and who, without doubt, are devoted to the semi-colonial, semi-imperial structures of the USSR. Gorbachev has demonstrated the ability to change – for instance by moving from his categorical refusal to abolish Article Six of the Constitution providing for monopoly rule by the Communist Party. In the case of the Baltic republics he is demonstrating classic old thinking.

Unless democratic forces in Europe and in the USSR swallow this bitter pill of totalitarianism in the Baltics, Gorbachev may be made to change his mind. The freedom and independence of these republics is a test-case of perestroika and democracy. If, as a result of the disintegration of the USSR, new constitutionally independent republics emerge, this should be considered not as a source of instability in Europe but as the natural consequence of perestroika – a consequence

we must welcome. However, whether Gorbachev and the Presidential
Council would welcome it remains a big question.

What we have today in the Soviet Union is a *State* peace – a policy
based on the power of the totalitarian structures: bureaucratic
machinery, repressive apparatus, police and security forces which
*enforce* a peaceful relationship between different ethnic groups and
nationalities. State peace answers the needs of the ruling bureaucratic
machine and counters democratic changes in Soviet society. The path to
democracy should create the conditions for a voluntary, non-violent
expression of the peaceful aspirations of all Soviet citizens. In short,
transition from totalitarian regimes to democracy should be combined
with the transition from state peace to civil peace.

# 4

# From Communism to Democracy

*George Konrad*

Where and when did it all start? In Budapest in 1956? In Prague in the spring of 1968? In Gdansk in the late summer of 1980? On those rare but ever more frequent occasions when those who dwelt in the Eastern empire told speakers sent by the Centre that this was not how it was at all? When friends here and there started to cyclostyle writings that no censor's eye had seen? When peasants and agricultural labourers, with unbelievable ingenuity, started to produce for the market on the tiny plot of land left to them after collectivization? When Western radio stations were no longer jammed? When average Eastern Europeans, travelling abroad, returned through the Iron Curtain and with a shock of recognition grasped the link between backwardness and the single-party system? When people started to long for freedom of expression and freedom of enterprise as they longed for colour television and video recorders? When governments started to think it more prudent merely to isolate dissidents, not to imprison them? When young printers first took the risks involved in printing opposition texts in secret? When intellectuals first honestly answered the questions put to them by Western journalists, and the answers came back over the airwaves to hundreds of thousands of listeners? When the Western media regularly fed back beyond the Iron Curtain what had been said and done there in the first place? When cost-effectiveness calculations replaced ideological priorities? When Members of the Academy first said no to Party headquarters, relying on the knowledge available to them?

When journalists and political scientists, with great effort and persistence, reintroduced 'pluralism' to the vocabulary of tolerated words? When the classics of the language that had earlier been disowned reappeared in the bookshops? When Hungarians living in a country where more concessions were made began to visit their kith and kin in Transylvania, which is now part of Romania, the Transcarpathian Ukraine that now belongs to the Soviet Union and the old Up-Country which is now Slovakia within the Czech and Slovak Federal Republic, where they lived under the greater rigour of dual oppression, both civic and national? When pop groups screamed to the world that servitude made them sick? When religious communities became thick on the ground?

When hundreds, even thousands, signed joint protests? When people dared to lay charges against the agents of authority who had assaulted them? When, on the anniversary of 15 March 1848 – that is, on Free Press Day – some hundreds, then thousands, of students assembled in a march, although the previous year's experience had taught them that rubber truncheons would be in evidence? When demonstrators discovered that being hit by a rubber truncheon was not the end of the world, and shouted 'Democracy! Democracy!' with multiplied strength? When family and friends dared to join the voices to demand a proper burial for the victims of the post-1956 retaliation whose bones rested in a remote cemetery corner, patrolled on occasion by the political police, in unmarked graves, overgrown by weeds?

When people unexpectedly compelled to pay income tax, and thus raised to the rank and status of taxpayers, realized that the state had sold the country from under their feet, accumulating a debt as high as the total value of the country's assets? When paternalism no longer meant a modest rate of acquisition but, on the contrary, accelerating impoverishment? When an epidemic started of opening your mouth wide, after lips had for so long been sealed tight by fright? Your true *Homo socialisticus* sees nothing, hears nothing, says nothing.

When newspapers turned rebellious and started to print what they heard, saw and thought? When people were infected by the fever that we should all be what we are? That there was no longer any need to pretend something stupid and false, no need to create an appearance of agreement with, or at least, toleration for, something they rejected? When the office-holders of the dictatorship themselves show resignation: it's no go, counter-pressure is growing, and even they find bourgeois democracy more attractive than hardline Communism? They too have taken a trip or two West; and extracts from the Western press, in translation, are there on their desk every morning.

When did it all start? At the end of the eighties, a year or two ago, when a growing number of peaceful citizens began to be irritated by their own dreary loyalty? When a growing minority suddenly realized that they would have to change the strategy that governed their lives? When a tide of euphoria cries out to be seized: it is now that the freedom and sovereignty of which we were robbed must be reclaimed.

Who were the most important actors? The composition of the company differed from country to country, but the intellectuals were the protagonists everywhere. Slow and fast revolutions elevated different groups of oppositional intellectuals. In Poland many million members of the working class lined up behind thirty intellectuals. In East Germany, Czechoslovakia and Romania insurrections and revolutions exploded, as it were, on a symbolic date. In East Berlin the breakthrough that brought down the Wall, and in Prague a demonstration repeated a few times, proved sufficient to prompt the regime to throw in the towel. In Bucharest that day was soon covered in blood; right from the start the smell of blood shed in Timişoara was in the air.

In Hungary the metamorphosis took a different course, step by step, in stages: many different dates could be mentioned. Neither bullets nor truncheons drew blood. Social pressure was enough to induce the Party state to go into voluntary liquidation. The established Party apparatchiks were pushed aside by the Reform Communists. The latter, having transformed themselves into would-be social democrats, reluctantly – but nevertheless – subjected themselves to the rules of the game of democracy and obtained the support of a tenth of those who cast their vote, but no more: fewer votes than there were Party members a year ago. Of former Party members and their families, only one in four gave them their vote in the first free elections. The system was melted down from within, its office-holders accepted that things just did not work that way. They no longer believed that the Leninist single-party system could be reformed, and they no longer entertained the illusion that they could discover some sort of third way between it and a multiparty system.

Neither sceptics nor pessimists can deny that Hungary is *en route* to democracy. You can found a party, start a newspaper, establish a publishing house; you can demonstrate if you wish, and assemble in public places in great numbers; and you can talk, talk as much as you like, as long as you can get someone to listen. New faces, names and concepts emerge – and submerge. It is easy to become fashionable – and to become unfashionable. If anything deserves publicity, it will most probably get it. The press has an insatiable appetite, and viewers expect the small screen to provide them with the truth, maybe even with wisdom. Are they getting any? They are somewhat disappointed: they get as much as there is. Stocks of wisdom are low. The country presents itself. There were no masterpieces in the desk drawers. It turned out that the country was not given democracy as a gift, and moreover, it was also short of democrats.

It is not easy to create a firmly founded democracy in a country that is in the midst of an economic crisis: fearing the rigours of the world market, afraid that its labour and property – indeed, its whole existence – will be devalued, that the switch to a market economy will result in a new kind of insecurity and servile incertitude. If the switch does not work out because of our own slowness and lack of concentration, our indebtedness and backwardness will grow. But even if we manage, many will have to pay for it, if only because they will not be able to continue their former lives. The pace will quicken, demands will rise, and competition will be tougher. The parties, one by one, reject the past that has lasted up to the present, but when it comes to the future as imagined by them, it's all words – mostly abstract words.

The less well-informed voter found it difficult to distinguish between speakers: they were all fine upstanding men, none promised anything concrete, and they said nasty things about each other. Two out of five entitled to do so did not turn up at the first round of the elections to cast their vote; by the second round it was already three out of five who did not exercise their right to choose their representative. The new government will be based on the majority of the minority that chose to vote. The majority rejected the previous system, but they are uncertain about the parties that opposed it. Many feel that little depended on them in the past, and that this will be so in the future as well. A few are upwardly mobile, some will go down in the world, the majority will stay in their place and, for a time at least, will be further impoverished. Those who know that they are at the bottom and will stay there watch the political stage with alienated sarcasm. Some argue: 'Well, Sir, no doubt it suits the actors to be on stage, but I am not all that certain that it benefits me that they're there.' The sullen people votes by not casting its vote.

The single-party state created the single-party people. The conditioning of the system created the personality. Those who learned to be afraid of those above and to bully those below will perhaps continue to practise such skills. Communism inherited authoritarian man from pre-war society and strengthened in him the priority of the principle of authority. The authoritarianism of the Right was succeeded by the authoritarianism of the Left. Few families went through the change to Communism without suffering damage, without having wounds inflicted on them. Passions have once again swung the pendulum to the Right, at least to Right of Centre. Will this new Right of Centre be a stranger to authoritarianism? Some fear and expect that it too will practise censorship, that it will occupy the high ground of the media, that it will narrow down the scope of freedom of thought by a new discriminatory rhetoric, by sticking pins into the images of new enemies. Some are anxious that the state desired by the Christian Nationalist Right of Centre is certainly not neutral but pretty ideological.

Liberal and social democrats are needed if liberal and social democracy is to take root, people whose ideas are in harmony with their behaviour and their environment. Such people are thin on the ground. Many take their own national identity to be the *fons et origo* of their thinking, and what they prize most. The strengthening of national feeling, and many different kinds of national renaissance, are the most powerful solvents acting on the glue that holds together the Soviet or Russian empire. Nationalism, not liberalism, is the most palpable alternative to Communism; it puts the national idea at the head of the pecking order, replacing the pseudo-internationalism of Communism. Nationalist fundamentalists have put in an appearance in every single Eastern European country. These are ideologies that judge everything, good or bad, by the standard of the presumed national interest. The practitioners of the nationalist rhetoric are the self-appointed custodians of this national interest. The ideological nationalist is intuitively aware of what, and who, can be described as national, who is un-Hungarian, un-Romanian or un-whatever, or perhaps cosmopolitan, or even a traitor to his or her country. Those who do not share their vocabulary and universe of discourse are suspect and taken to be deficient in their morals.

The Reform Communists and the dissidents had an important role in the dissolution of Communism; however, the odds are against them when it comes to making up the bulk of the post-free-election political elite. It is likely that neither liberals nor social democrats, let alone Reform Communists, will come to the top once the Communist power monopoly melts away, but instead the populist Christian Nationalists. It could be that, in accordance with the pendulum of parliamentary politics, the conservatives will be followed by liberals once again, but that is still a long way off.

Professional men and women of peasant or working-class parentage occupied the first circle of power in the years of Communism if they joined the Party, and the second if they did not but had professional skills and displayed loyalty. The latter were inclined to respect authority, but their preference was for national symbols, not for the dubious Red Star iconography. They wished to speak of a Thousand Years of History, not of the past forty years, that insalubrious episode. The first circle will be largely vacated now, offering places to the more successful members of the second. They will be joined by the sons and grandsons of the pre-war ruling and middle class who had been discriminated against precisely because of their parentage in the heyday of Communism. Suffering will become as much part of family history as rarer good luck; the heirs will inherit family mythologies that abound in insults and injuries suffered. Thanks to the national idea, a professional class of peasant origin will move up into the past of the gentry. It is part of the nature of good jobs that more or less talented people can be welded to them, allowing the meeting of role and personality more or less to acquire the dignity of necessity. The electoral success of the Christian Nationalists can be recognized as the meeting point of the professional class of peasant origin with that of gentry origin – that is, the reporting for duty of a feasible, new political elite. He who stood nearest the door enters the room first.

Nationalization or embourgeoisement? That, to my mind, is the major dilemma with which the societies of Central and Eastern Europe are faced. Nationalization favours the civil servants: justifies the growth in the number of public service jobs. Embourgeoisement requires reduced taxes instead – that is to say, a slimming-down of the bureaucracy. The worship of the state – whether the liturgy be socialist or nationalist, or both – preserves over-regulation and oppresses enterprise. In recent decades numerous statist regimes came into being in the Third World which used economic nationalism to maintain the backwardness of their countries. It proved necessary to overthrow the power of the Communist nomenklatura precisely in order to make it possible for the professional class that replaced it to open the gate to private enterprise. If there is no strong business- and property-owning middle class, if the bulk of the professional class depends on the state for its living, if there is no forceful private sphere, then democracy lacks firm foundation. If all that happens is that a Nationalist bureaucracy replaces the Communist bureaucracy, and one jargon replaces another, if the enemy merely acquires a new face, if the fundamentalist dualism of thought – we over here are the good; they over there are evil – is restored, if the new bureaucracy does not use positive discrimination to further the growth of an entrepreneurial bourgeoisie – of a private sphere that is independent of it – then our situation will change only inasmuch as others will cause the national debt to grow.

Hungarian post-Communist society is still dominated by the state. Ninety per cent of the economy is still in state hands, 90 per cent of the employed are still employed by the state. Private enterprise has not made a breakthrough yet, it is still a long way from domination, the line of state monopolies still holds. Enterprises expect instructions, regulations and subsidies from an above, from the government – now already a non-Communist government.

Subsidies have grown smaller, so debts and invoices cannot be paid. Everybody owes everybody. Many firms have liquidity problems; creditors, however, are patient. They do not want to drown each other, since that would probably mean that they would go under themselves. They hang on to each other instead, to stay on the surface.

You cannot call the Hungarian economy an operating market

economy – a good few years are needed before it will become that. No doubt it will have to become an operating market economy before the West European Common Market will open its gates to it. Sober forecasts predict that this will happen in the second half of the decade, more likely towards its end.

People are aware that the Soviet Union is slowly moving out. The West, however, is not moving in in its place. One of the major current troubles is that Hungary exports to the Soviet Union but the Soviet Union does not pay – indeed, raw material supplies, including oil and natural gas, are reduced. There are similar difficulties with other former Soviet bloc countries, though on a more modest scale. Enterprises, and whole industries, that have been geared to that market and are unable to find new Western customers at short notice have serious liquidity problems.

A paternalist society has lost its parent at home and abroad. It has no father but it has not yet grown up: a state of interregnum. The West cautiously speaks of support for a Central European integration, and sceptics question the utility of linking up all our crises. Western links do not grow to the same degree as Soviet links diminish, and this gives rise to insecurity in a post-paternalistic society. The post-paternalistic character manifests itself in the political class and authority as well: society has liberated itself from the old fathers; the new leaders, however, are not accepted as fathers – indeed, their very credentials for high office are doubted.

Yesterday's Communist Party ideology erected a barrier between skilled professionals and the exercise of power. Will the hands of the Christian Nationalist governmental coalition be tied by ideology when choosing the new administrative class? That is the question. No one escapes doubts concerning their ability to run the country since, in fact, none of them has any experience of office. Such doubts are in no way diminished by the knowledge that – to put it mildly – the country did not do all that well under the previous administration.

Many professional people feel that at times like these it is better to go elsewhere: to go West, to look for their individual happiness in places where their skills and knowledge can be turned to good account. The visiting professors and foreign workers are off, hoping to scrape together the price of half a house, and this naturally prompts the anxiety-ridden press and public opinion to speak of a brain drain.

The term 'intellectuals' as used in Eastern Europe had its ambiguities. Statistically it was defined as all those holding jobs requiring tertiary educational qualifications, the closest English equivalent being professional people. At the same time, ideologically, intellectuals thought of themselves as heirs to the intelligentsia while they aspired to be an educated middle class. The new political class is recruited from these people and so are a great many of the new businessmen, democratically called entrepreneurs even when they operate no more than a small workshop, or work from their own homes, and employ only two or three people, or just themselves. The new, younger and democratically elected Parliament includes many historians, economists, sociologists and literary figures. Much more mental capital is accumulated there than in the previous one. Better-educated, more articulate and more interesting men and women now occupy the political stage. The older ones are always open to accusations of earlier political servility, which gives more scope to the younger ones who had less of a chance to compromise themselves. It is certainly true that older personalities were more closely confined by faint-heartedness and resignation.

Intellectual authority is in demand; politics and the media are in great need of it. Clever people, therefore, have more irons in the fire; they are involved in a deal or two, but they hang on to their position in the academy. Names with a good ring to them are needed for all sorts of business deals. Those for whom the craft of intellectual was only an instrument of upward mobility now take their leave of the guild.

Strategies of life tend to spread more than before; some go one way, some another; abroad, or they switch parties, or professions. Unexpected mobility can be observed, people have less time for each other. The professional class dissolves, falls apart, and merges into a new middle class which is more extensive and structured. What are called professional people today – intellectuals in Hungarian – will remain an integral, perhaps central, factor, but businessmen, a property-owning bourgeoisie, will also acquire weight.

University teaching and research are badly paid. The only ones who stay are those who truly like it there. Those who are genuinely more interested in thought than in power or money will gladly continue as academics or intellectuals. Those who are more interested in action than in contemplation or observation find plenty to do these days in Hungary. Doers can't complain: the exchange rates for resignation are falling; those for experiment are going up and up.

The number of students is growing; classes have doubled in size. Many want to obtain qualifications, but few desire the life of the mind. Those who have not produced poems so far will not do so in future either, and given the choice between writing a novel and owning a BMW, they'd choose the latter. One thing is certain; the new novel will not pay for a BMW. The impoverishment of writers is on the way, unless the many new papers act as a parachute checking their free fall.

Under Communism everyone wanted to graduate and join the professions. Compulsory ideological drill compelled everyone to behave as a member of the intelligentsia, to fill his mind with the abstractions of social philosophy – at the very least in irritation, shown in the company of close friends, talking to oneself, complaining of the imbecilities one was told. One may have rejected the official answer, but the jargon in which the question was couched persisted in one's thinking. The official ideology of the state, or kicking against its pricks, acted as a bond, and provided a common explanation for one's strategy and the way one lived. Communism was truly a one-dimensional society.

The university, both as a mechanism of selection and as a training institution, allowed the appropriate young people to climb the upper rungs; it was up to them which hierarchy they chose. There were two pretty well closed hierarchies: that of political power and that of the respective professions – one could call them two nomenklaturas. You could say that you had really made it if you were in both, if you enjoyed the respect of both. And then there were the invisible people in the eyes of the state, the dissidents, whom the law-abiding members of their own profession – their own college – looked on with a sympathy tempered by irritation. There was plenty of jostling for power at the court of János Kádár during his long reign, but by and large the pecking order was pretty stable.

But look, now the strategies diverge. The paternalistic intimacy is coming to an end, that socialist *Biedermeier* in which the anti-princes of the spirit confronted King Kádár and his whole court. Yesterday state culture was still a whole world, and the *bien pensants* – that is, normal people – had their place in it. At least they did not extricate themselves from it, they did not feel that censorship was an intellectual barrier. They were part of it and, as a response to external rigour, they created the nooks and crannies of a kind intimacy. Now everyone leaves that intimate society, everyone in his own way.

Those up to their necks in Party business are irritated by irony. It makes sense that politicians should prefer the company of politicians, and that businessmen should focus their social life on the chance to do business. The old professional class is falling apart, the fledgeling politicians are taking flight, and so are the media managers, all those who need literature or science or scholarship for something different from its proper purpose, which is the luxury of understanding.

Many think they have to consider their own salvation, and now – they cannot wait for the redemption of the country. The country manages as well as it can; they certainly stand on firm ground. They're all right, and they will be too. Many of my young acquaintances make considerably more money than they did last year. So do I: my books are being published, including those that previously appeared only in samizdat or abroad.

The homeless have formed their own party. People from Vietnam, the Soviet Union, Poland and Romania sell their pitiful possessions in pedestrian precincts, in subways, on the fringe of municipal markets. There are more beggars than before, though they are not a commonplace yet. Television news shows footage of soup kitchens.

My Western acquaintances observe the changes with expectancy, in a friendly but cool manner. We have become more interesting, but also more boring. Yesterday we were still the socialist alternative to capitalism – not attractive, perhaps, but at least a cautionary tale. Then the fiction that there was a rational alternative to liberal democracy could no longer be maintained. As the years passed and we fought for our freedom, we turned into no more than the dunces in the schools of capitalism and liberal democracy. We used to be the Western fringe of the East, more developed than the centre. Now we shall be the Eastern fringe of Western Europe, more primitive than the centre. One frequently hears that all that forty years of Communism were good for was to allow Hungary to drop a few places in the statistics league table: behind not only Italy, Spain and Finland but also Portugal and Greece. It hurts to notice that our skills and knowledge are unsatisfactory – that, judging by international standards, the worth of our individual or collective personality is not what it used to be.

World Bank credits have been granted, and His Holiness the Dalai Lama has arrived in Budapest. We are granted a look into the new Official Residence of the Prime Minister which displays a restrained elegance, and where every object was Made in Hungary. I think also that we will turn into something odd that cannot be described using either the Latin American or the South Korean model. It will continue to be called Central European. Both grotesque and unpredictable, characteristically the odds favour breach, failure, defeat, but the opposite of all this is also possible. Those who were left out before, the dissidents, are present in Parliament and at embassy receptions.

What attracts me, as a novelist, is precisely that something is happening. This society makes itself, restructures itself, reformulates itself. The life of many has become more interesting; new options present themselves. Hungarians are realists, pessimists rather than dreamers. They know that things will be pretty tough for a while, and then they will ease up again. The mood fluctuates: one day prospects look all right, by the next everything looks in a mess again, and then the whole thing turns out to be not so dreadful after all. Passionate changes of mood go with facts that are not all that fatal. An apocalyptic mood and black humour go well together, and with a sort of simple-minded faith that things will turn out all right after all somehow, that we've survived worse before. All that coexists.

The country works, even in the interregnum; the institutions will survive a further dose of amateurism; they'll get by without central instructions. The spirit of conciliation has risen again since the elections; the victors crane at the jump and are beginning to be aware of the difficulties if their parties in Parliament depend on each other. The government party cannot go on for long escalating or even continuing the propaganda campaign against the liberals; populist conservatism cannot be self-confident while arguing against Western liberalism. Showing offence just will not do as an answer in the long run. It is indeed difficult to put into words what being a conservative means in Hungary in 1990, unless it is something like grandfather's silver fob watch. What is there to be conserved in politics? The authoritarian and paternalistic tradition in politics of which Communism was just one – particularly churlish – variant?

It argues against apathy that so much can be done. A golden age for promotions. *Gründerzeit.* All you need is an idea, however foolish it may seem. More adventurous businessmen keep coming from the West, and the Mafia too – everything that is in the air. I don't know whether it is all that good to be part of world society, but I know all right that being out of it is not good. Present political organizations exist because they are wanted and they were created. Proof exists that one can want something and do it.

Both the West and the Soviet Union would be pleased if the situation in Hungary consolidated. They cast a kind eye from both directions; they would rather be supportive than show *Schadenfreude.* They do not want to be overconcerned with our business, but are curious how we'll manage by ourselves. A multilateral foreign policy strategy is in the offing in Central Europe; it is better to depend on many than on one. The country endeavours to complement and counterbalance contacts with Austria and Germany by Latin Europe and North-West Europe, America and South-East Asia. Czechoslovakia and even Poland want to join Italy and Yugoslavia, Hungary and Austria in an Alps and Adriatic Alliance which is still a dream rather than a reality. Co-operation and association are imaginable at all points of the compass. Firms, towns, regions, act on their own and look for contacts, be they amongst neighbours or in distant lands. The future of the country is still undefined; nothing has been decided.

Maybe a growing number will ask for a Central European integration to replace the vanished Habsburg Empire which had its own place and function between the German Reich and Russia. Democratic federalism is still needed in Central and Eastern Europe, as a disciplining and pacifying principle, or nationalist conflicts will be honed to an intolerable edge. The whole region, East Central Europe and Eastern

Europe, would be too large a bite and too tough a nut for the Western
European Community to swallow. Nor, I imagine, would this particular
north–south zone be overkeen to be the back yard of Western Europe,
as Latin America is the back yard of the United States.

Last year the people of the region displayed a fair amount of
sovereignty. The desire for autonomy, the energy, and the inventiveness
of Central Europeans may hold a surprise or two in store yet. It is
something of value in itself that the fate of the country has not been
decided, that people are curious about their future, that both the past
and the future concentrate their minds.

The country showed a certain political maturity. The Communist
Party handed over power in a civilized manner, there was no violence of
any sort, the various political forces work together. Everybody wants to
be European. To say that you are not is certainly not praise. What is
European taken to mean in Hungary, and in the whole region? It implies
respect for the individual, equality before the law, enforceable legal
rights, reliable-quality work, a multicultural society, complex identities.
Hungary wishes to pass the European test.

There is nationalism, but it does not openly supersede democracy.
Anti-semites exist, but they do not declare themselves as such. What is
of the essence is strengthened national sovereignty. Soviet troops will
probably leave the country by the summer of 1991, and the Republic of
Hungary will be neutral when it comes to military matters. National
solidarity in support of Hungarian minorities in limitrophe countries is
confined to European norms, to basic human rights, the basic rights of
individuals and communities. National solidarity prompts Hungarians to
desire democracy in the whole region; hence in their own country as
well. No one has a ghost of a chance to consolidate a new authoritarian
regime. The race is wide open on the political scene, there is no
charismatic candidate for the post of dictator. The electorate rejected
the demagogues. The country works, and at the time of writing it
manages without firm political leadership. I don't know what tomorrow
will bring, and that means we are not bored.

Why is the West interested in the eastern half of Europe? There are
many sober reasons, but also a more poetic one. Perhaps it is looking for
an ideal. It is interested in the metaphor of the lad in the fairytale, going
from prison to the Castle, clad in morality, and on foot. In the idea that
the spirit can overcome material force; that the truths of the realists
came to nothing; that trumps were part of the hand of the utopians – or
rather, the modern idealist. Eyes brighten face to face with this new
Judaeo-Christian parable: that moral determination proved decisively
powerful and victoriously resisted financial inducements, pressure and

threats. It is worthy of attention that a victorious defensive power is present here which perhaps consists of no more than the declaration by a Minister of Religion that he will not be moved from his chair of his own free will: let them drag him away, but he will no longer be guilty of the sin of obeying evil.

After so much materialist realpolitik, which is able to articulate strength only quantitatively, as so and so much power of destruction or accumulated capital, it is in the last resort a moving experience that this gentle stubbornness, this behaviour worthy of an intellectual, should snowball and act as the fuse starting revolutionary change; that a bearing and thinking that does not look over its shoulder should be a historical force. This recognition opens a new chapter in thinking about what it means to be European.

People freed themselves from a dominant paradigm and created another for themselves. A new sensibility appeared which manifested itself in many shapes and political schools of thought. In any event, it was capable of producing the dissolution of the dictatorship. It did not stop there; it also knows how to organize a party and how to take its place in Parliament, in boardrooms and in the academies, and makes its presence felt even there. It skips on, using us as its tools – us who are prone to get stuck in the style of a decade. It employs an ever-novel idiom, it just loves to change the terminology. Sometimes it looks like a religion, sometimes like a philosophy; here an image, here a cloak; but it never gets stuck. It walks the path of impossibility, always bending the parallel blades of Ideal and Reality towards each other, uniting fire and water. Man feels most tempted by the impossible. You can tell by its tracks that the impossible walked this way, that it happened. We are able just to live the religious life without any sort of mumbo-jumbo, without suspending our sense of humour or our hedonism – as players in a game, so to speak.

I think the essence is the anthropological experiment which will perhaps fade away but is still alive. Perhaps there is such a thing as a nameless and invisible religion which is personal in the first place. It has no organization, canon or congregation, it has no badge or symbol, anyone can participate even without being aware of it; at the most they have a faint suspicion. There is no need to chatter about it, one must live it. Life itself can be a religious activity; life as an experiment. It would of course be a bore if the only care a man had were to maintain himself, if he were preoccupied merely with his egotism and self-pity, if he only nursed his traumas, if he transcended nowhere and nobody. This religion demands nothing extraordinary, only the ordinary, the genuine. Nothing extreme – only, let's say, that childlike gaiety with which Adam

Michnik could make history in Poland. It was not he who told me this story but the writer Tadeus Konvicky.

If I remember correctly, in 1983 or 1984 there was already considerable pressure on General Jaruzelski, Commander in Chief of the State of Emergency – who really did not enjoy the role of Head Prison Warder – not to keep the general staff and advisers of Solidarnosc behind bars any longer. Jaruzelski was, however, aware that he would undermine his own rule if he simply released these hardened freedom-makers. They would not stop but continue, prison had no effect on them; they would take apart the domination of the Party State Army! The Church then acted as a mediator and they came to an agreement. Everyone would be released from prison if they went abroad and gave their word as officers and gentlemen that they would not come home to stir up trouble before five years were up. The aristocracy of jailbirds was invited to dinner in a château where, sitting at a round table, they would all discuss the President's proposed deal. Would there be agreement between the regime and the imprisoned opposition? Everyone accepted the invitation to the château, with one single exception. Emissaries were sent to him, good friends; before they had even entered his cell he called to them: 'I know why you're here; don't bother to come in!' They would have fêted him in the capitals of the West.

Michnik insisted that he be released not as part of some deal but simply, normally, legally, considering that he was innocent and that this was his basic right as man and as citizen. One can deal with the government only as an equal partner, and he was not equal while he was in prison. When the others heard that Adam was not coming, they felt ashamed and changed their minds: if he was not going, neither were they. They kept to the code of the Republic of Polish Nobles. And truly, within a few years, military power became untenable. The released prisoners continued their work of making freedom where they had stopped. Once, after the Round Table talks and the election victory, Michnik, as a Senator, called on General Kiszcak, the Minister of the Interior and head policeman.

Kiszcak: 'Allow me, Mr Michnik, to congratulate you on your electoral success and to express my regrets for all that happened. I know that my subordinates in the Ministry of the Interior caused you much trouble.'

Michnik: 'No problem, General; let's talk instead about how we will turn Poland into a democracy.'

Michnik knows no demons. Other men do not have to be feared or hated. It wouldn't do for a lucky player to show that he despised the unlucky one. I take Adam Michnik, like Václav Havel, to be a modern idealist.

These days the West is most familiar with their names, but there are many such unselfish modern idealists, less well known and anonymous. The experienced observer recognizes them; there is a fire in them that drives them beyond personal interest – well beyond, as if they saw something, as if it were an axiom for them that freedom is the due of every man, and that I am not free as long as my neighbour is not. It is difficult to escape the responsibility of thinking with others, searching for what is true and what is not. These examples, the combined stories of various dissidents, indeed conceal a guarded morality which allows its wise old teachers to laugh heartily at everybody and everything.

Could Europe be a suitable way out of our individual and national misery? An escape into a larger space? From our small world into a larger world that can still be surveyed? What is expansion into Europe if not self-multiplication? The worship of Europe could also be the introverted attention of a multicultural continent, a receptivity to uniqueness, an anamnesis addressed to a limitless common past. It is here that the special talents of Europe show up best. Others do no worse in high technology, but Europe still does least badly when it comes to memory. One could mention the inward-turning Eros of Europe, which springs from the worship of differences. It is, after all, only what is different that is in possession of erotic magic. One could mention domesticated dichotomies as the special characteristics of Europe. Antinomies, dualities, paradoxes and ambivalences form the skeleton of European thinking. A transfer into conscious time is effected since historical time can offer absolution for conflicts, wars, tragedies, with its own unpredictable ironic responses. Time after time there is a way leading to the future from the traps of the present.

The grace of fate has once again extended a great temptation to mortals who question the future and know nothing of it: the chance of overconfidence in the eastern half of Europe – as if we imagined that we made history, knowing why we did what and foreseeing how it will all end up. I seem to remember that this kind of hubris always leads to a fall flat on one's face: pride before a fall. It has been said, surveying the new Eastern European elite, that historians are making history, which is better, of course, than semi-literates being at work. The truth is that historians don't know either – or rather, no one knows how. All the paradigms and comparisons are abstract and imprecise. All the forecasts are fiction. Those who endeavour to speak with authority turn out to be both boring and untrue.

European non-violent civic politics was born in the midst of the dictatorships as a modest and marginal force. Tolstoy, Gandhi and

Martin Luther King proved to be sound advisers on questions of methodology. Words are a most powerful force. A society that does not fall apart under the effect of free speech can be called firm and consolidated and deserves to be looked after. In the eastern half of Europe the demand for democracy was joined by an idealism which is modern but does not lack a past. Some of these idealists also believe in God, but there are other idealists who do not.

In the western half of Europe, democratic capitalism is a *donné*; its presence is less likely to give rise to idealism than its lack. In the Soviet Union it is still reckoned a courageous heresy to come out in support of free private enterprise; in Hungary it has not been so for a year or two; in Sweden nothing is more natural. The opposite would be irrational nonsense. It is difficult to be enthusiastic about something that is self-evident. What would I, if I were a Swede, think of the eastern half of Europe turning democratic and capitalist? Perhaps I'd feel like a husband whose wife is loved by someone else after a twenty-year marriage.

The spirit of democracy flies to places where they are in love with it, where they are ready to sacrifice their lives to it. A Romanian woman told me in Hungarian that on the day of the revolution she sewed her identity card into her overcoat, in a waterproof pocket, to make it easier to identify her corpse; then she prepared her two children's tea and went out into the Main Square, where the crowd stayed on their feet, although there was shooting. 'I am a sober-minded female,' this Romanian lady said. 'I am not usually up to foolishness, but on that afternoon it was absolutely clear to me that that was the time to proclaim freedom and to break through the wall of fear.' That day a great many people made up their minds at the same time. A revolution is truly a mystic congruence. This otherwise sober Romanian lady, and many of her companions in the new and humble democracies of Europe, are indeed in love with the ideal of basic human rights, since their biographies are catalogues of insults and injuries. There is much talk of human dignity – yes, they speak of it precisely where, until recently, humiliation was the rule.

The West has spent a great deal on military defence against the East – that is, on the Cold War. The aim was modest: to hold up the Russians, make them stay behind the Iron Curtain. The Eastern European dissidents were reckoned to be a destabilizing factor within the Yalta structure, the more so since they judged the strategic aims of the West to be insufficient. What they wanted was to disperse the Soviet empire from within, not just to erect barriers to its expansion. The way things look now, this job will be accomplished by the end of the century. Dreamers have proved sober realists. There is no doubt whatsoever that so far non-violent liberation has cost a great deal less than the Cold War. That is something worth thinking about.

# 5

# Revolt in Our Time:
# The Triumph of Simplistic Ideology

## *J. K. Galbraith*

The events of the last year in Eastern Europe, building on earlier change in Poland and the Soviet Union, have, not surprisingly, nurtured a major economic discussion. Some of this has been eminently sensible; rather more has been aberrant to the point of mild insanity. The aberration extends to both sides of what was once the Iron Curtain or, in more recent symbolism, the Berlin Wall. We need a name for it; it can, I believe, best be denoted Simplistic Ideology.

The Simplistic Ideology that extensively interprets these events pictures a starkly bi-polar world: on the one side Communism, on the other capitalism. Each exists in an unadulterated form. Now, reversing all Marxian prediction, capitalism is triumphant. Communism having failed both economically and politically in Eastern Europe, the countries once so afflicted will now make their way to the capitalist nirvana – as will, if more gradually, the USSR. The prospect is a blessed improvement in economic life combined with the freedoms that we enjoy in the West. Interim pain and shock are possible and perhaps to be welcomed; 'Shock Therapy for Poland', a recent *New York Times* headline proclaimed. There is no question, however, as to the ultimate reward.

The prime essential is that the transition to capitalism be complete, and this view is being advanced in both East and West. Lecturing on these matters in Budapest last autumn, I was questioned severely by a Hungarian journalist who was distressed that I had not mentioned Friedrich Hayek as a guide to needed reform. Did he not offer the most workable economic and political model? My interrogator was visibly depressed when I replied that it was a design we in the West would not ourselves care to try. The risk would be very great – greater than even our most ardent free-enterprise ideologists would accept if actually in office.

In the last century when Marx wrote, and continuing on into this century and the years of the Great Depression, the survival of capitalism in its original and ideologically exact form was very much in doubt. There was a highly unequal distribution of power and income between employer and employed, and society was made up of a few rich and many poor. Workers were discarded without income when unneeded. There was cruel exploitation of notably vulnerable groups, such as women and children. The perils of old age and illness without income were extreme in the new industrial towns – though many were spared them by early and exhausted demise. There was the deeply conditioned discontent of farmers. Most threatening of all, as Marx foresaw, were the recurring economic crises or depressions that swept millions into unemployment and deprivation.

From all this came anger and alienation and for many the strong feeling, perhaps the near-certainty, that the system could not survive. But the welfare state mitigated the hardships and the cruelties of pristine capitalism. Trade unions were legitimized and exercised countervailing power. And the Keynesian Revolution gave to the state the responsibility, however imperfectly discharged, of smoothing out the business cycle and limiting the associated hardship and despair. The prevention of mass unemployment and the assurance of economic growth became the prime tests of government competence. So the system survived.

Meanwhile, changes in the structure of capitalism rendered obsolescent even the term 'capitalism' itself. There came, in the words of the late James Burnham, the 'Managerial Revolution'. This denoted the passage of power in the modern great industrial and commercial corporation from the provider or possessor of capital – from the capitalist – to the professional management, the managerial bureaucracy. Given the specialized knowledge and experience required in the operation of the modern large enterprise and the diversity and complexity of its tasks, the capitalist or, more often, his questionably competent or committed descendants were pushed aside. In no country did the managerial bureaucracy exercise the same motivated resistance, even hostility, to the claims of its labour force or those of a civilized society as had the primeval capitalist. Here, as from the welfare state and from Keynes, came a solvent for the old anger and antagonism (and for many primeval capitalists the righteous pleasure) in primitive class conflict.

Let us be clear. What the countries of Eastern Europe see as the alternative to socialism is not capitalism. Were it capitalism in its classical form, they would not for a moment want the change. The alternative they see is the modern state with a large and indispensable mellowing and stabilizing role for government.

Mr Reagan and now Mr Bush in the United States and Mrs Thatcher in Britain have enjoyed power in these last years only because earlier and effective *public* action has made a majority of their citizens economically comfortable and secure. In consequence, as with comfortable and secure people over the centuries, those citizens are self-protective in mood – conservative. Had Mr Reagan or Mrs Thatcher sought to restore the austerities, insecurities and cruelties of pure capitalism – an intention that Mr Reagan, in his innocent way, regularly avowed – neither of them would have survived in office. Their debt for their survival, sadly unacknowledged, is to what an earlier generation did to modify capitalism and to what they themselves were kept from doing – or undoing – in office.

## The Nature of East European Socialism

The capitalism to which the Eastern European countries seek to escape bears little relationship to the Marxian model; neither do the economic and political structures under which they have lived and visibly suffered in these last decades. Socialism, as it matured, had a task that Marx and Lenin did not foresee: the production of consumer goods in all their diversity of styles, designs and supporting services. That was the model set by the non-socialist world, and with it a centralized planning and command system could not contend. Nor, in general, could it contend with the special problems of agriculture, an industry that functions well only when blessed by the self-motivated energies of the individual owner and proprietor (or some close approximation thereto). It requires, in less agreeable terms, the exploitation by the individual proprietor of himself and his family. Except as people might be rescued from what Marx was pleased to call the idiocy of rural life, agriculture played little part in his thought and not a great deal in Lenin's.

A further and greater misfortune of advanced socialist development was in close parallel with the advanced capitalist experience: the increasing and eventually overriding role of organization, of bureaucracy. As the modern great industrial firms – General Motors, General Electric and Exxon in the United States; Shell and BP in Britain – develop a large bureaucratic apparatus, so also and much more does mature socialist production – much more because in this system the producing enterprise is united in greater or lesser measure with a supervising and controlling ministry. The result is a truly massive organizational structure; by some counts the bureaucracy of the USSR numbers thirty million inhabitants.

The basic characteristics of great organization, massive bureaucracy, are common to all systems, all cultures. There is, first, the ineluctable effect of age. Individuals, we accept, decline in effort and initiative with the passage of years, but so also does the bureaucratic establishment or enterprise. Accordingly, with the passage of time socialist ministries and enterprises matured and passed on into an intellectually sterile senility. As also, let it be noted, did US Steel, the once-great British automobile companies and now, many avow, General Motors. There is also the further tendency of great organization to proliferate personnel; nothing so measures bureaucratic significance and prestige as the number of one's subordinates. Nothing so eases bureaucratic life as having willing subordinates who spare one thought and action. The most common of all questions in a bureaucracy is: How many people does he have under him? The result is the cost and immobility of a great and persistently growing mass.

But most important of all, bureaucracy defines its own truth. We see this currently and with exceptional clarity in the United States. Our vast military establishment, like the State Department and the intelligence agencies, are now struggling to preserve the sense of need and urgency which, for so long, served stable thought and expanding budgets so well. Some have spoken out in open regret over recent change that might mean diminished budgets and painful thought. The Deputy Secretary of State Mr Lawrence Eagleburger, perhaps our leading current exponent of institutional truth, recently regretted the passage of the Cold War – 'a time', he said, 'of remarkable stability in international relations'.

But the Western commitment to bureaucratic or institutional truth has been less than that of the Eastern European countries. In the West inconvenient thought and its consequences, however deplored, could not, to the regret of many, be suppressed. The justification in the United States for our present scale of military expenditure is now being sharply questioned. There has even been official talk of reduced budgets, the reductions so far suggested being, alas, in previously planned increases. Officials and scholars whose minds, books and lecture notes are also committed firmly to the threat of Soviet expansion have recently been reduced to expressing their concern over Soviet ambitions in Nicaragua, El Salvador and Ethiopia. Not even General Noriega in Panama could persuasively be called a Kremlin agent.

The hold of bureaucratic truth was far more unrelenting in the socialist world, extending its reach comprehensively throughout society. As I have noted on another occasion, the aged men who headed the East German government could not have lived in total innocence of what was happening in that country. The better level of life in West Germany was disastrously visible on television. The secret police almost certainly reported rumblings of discontent from below. (Intelligence agencies, we know, regularly report what their masters wish to hear, but they could not have been that incompetent.) The reality, however, could not be accepted. Bureaucracy enforces its truth not least on those at the top. Theirs was to see, with surprise, the eventual explosion.

So, to summarize: capitalism in its original or pristine form could not have survived, but under pressure it did adapt. Socialism in its original form and for its first tasks did succeed – but it failed to adapt, and thus nurtured an oppressive and repressive political structure. Having shed this last, how does it now adapt?

## The Road Ahead

Two things will be clear. First, those who speak, as many do so glibly, even mindlessly, of a return to the Smithian free market are wrong to the point of a mental vacuity of clinical proportions. It is something we in the West do not have, would not tolerate, could not survive. Ours is a mellow, government-protected life; for Eastern Europeans pure and rigorous capitalism would be no more welcome than it would be for us.

Equally to be avoided are those who see, out of short-run shock and hardship, the promise of prompt economic betterment. In this view the hardship itself is therapeutic. Out of suffering must come good. Elements of theology intrude here: self-mortification is the path to righteousness. The citizens so afflicted will not be as easily convinced as are those who, from a distance or from positions of some personal comfort, see virtue in hardship. And the political consequences are far from attractive. This is a moment of great and welcome liberty in Eastern Europe. It would be tragic indeed were liberty there to be identified with unacceptable economic deprivation. I would especially urge against any prescription of hardship from Western capitals, including Washington. There is little to be said for a therapy that we would not wish to suffer at home.

Were I counselling the Eastern European countries, I would, indeed, urge the release of less urgent consumer goods and services to the market, along with the productive resources therewith required. I would also urge loans from the state banks to facilitate this process, and any necessary steps to accommodate banks to this purpose. There should be no hesitation, as now in the Soviet Union, about having a private employer–employee relationship. This is a relationship, however identified with capitalism, that millions have survived and enjoyed.

I would be more cautious and gradual in releasing basic foods, rents and health services to the market. Here hardship and suffering would be acute and, it should be recognized, this move would involve action that the capitalist countries, as they are still called, would find unacceptable. All the major industrial countries now heavily subsidize their agricultural production. In consequence, farm prices are generally higher and/or consumer prices lower than they would be without such government intervention. All industrial countries also take special steps to provide lower-cost housing; capitalism does not anywhere automatically supply good inexpensive shelter. Health care also is satisfactory only where, effectively, it is socialized.

I do not urge that prices to farmers be kept low; that is a serious past error. I would urge recognition of the fact that all current capitalist practice combines higher prices to the farmer and lower prices to the consumer than the classical free market provides. If in a transition period some rationing continues, I would think that the least adverse of alternatives.

As to the characteristic large producing firm, one would urge that, indeed, it should be released from ministerial supervision. And in response to market demand it should be responsible for its own operations, with management and workers enjoying the rewards of good performance. This means that it should be free to set its own prices and bargain with similar freedom for production requirements from firms similarly released to the market. Loans should be available to finance innovation and expansion, and – a difficult matter – the penalty for miscalculation and failure should fall on the defaulting management.

It does not seem to me greatly important where ultimate ownership resides. In the capitalist world this is normally with stockholders unknown to the management. It would make no decisive difference were it the state – as indeed in many cases it is. What is important is that the producing firm, no less than the individual, should be the expression of its own personality, with the reward of its own success and the penalty of its own failure.

There has been much talk of moving to convertible currencies. This reflects an equally Simplistic Ideology. What is – or would have been – far more important is the immobilizing of accumulated currency surpluses within the country. The persistent and damaging tendency of socialism in the past has been to supply more money than goods. These funds make market liberalization identical with inflation, as currently in Poland. Anyone holding spendable money above a certain amount should have been required, through a currency conversion, to hold it off the market in long-term interest-bearing bonds. This would seem still to be a plausible design in some of the other socialist countries, including the USSR.

I advance these suggestions with caution: on the great problems of conversion and change the socialist countries are, as I have noted, now in receipt of more Western advice than they can possibly use or should ever contemplate using. I read of a recent American mission to the Soviet Union that urged the adoption there of the gold standard in support of a fully convertible rouble. This would, admittedly, be welcomed by the few who would immediately be in full possession of all the gold. Otherwise it is a fair reflection of much of the advice now traversing the one-time Iron Curtain.

## The Role of the West

On one step there should be no hesitation: Western countries and Japan must come promptly and generously to the assistance of the countries now in the process of liberalization. This is the moment of need: freedom must not be seen to have a heavy economic price. Debt service should be suspended, as Jeffrey Sachs, with whom I perhaps differ on the effect of shock therapy, has widely urged. Nor is this a time for lectures from the IMF on austerity. The affirmative help in grants and loans should not be confined to capital goods; it must extend generously to food and consumer goods, the areas of most serious past socialist failure and thus of present need. Let there be no hesitation in providing support to the requirements and even the modest enjoyments of life. These, not plants and machinery, are of the most immediate importance. Needless perhaps to say, these countries should be accorded relief from past capital charges; this, assuredly, is not the time for assigning resources to the financial errors of the past.

The resources are available in the West, for one consequence of these last months, which is visible with a clarity that cannot be resisted by even the most ardent Western exponents of bureaucratic truth, is a diminished military threat with its resulting claim on public resources. It is the most obvious and elementary of steps that some of the resources so freed be used to ease the transition to a world of greater economic success, political freedom and military security.

I do not minimize the reluctance to be encountered here. Bureaucratic truths supported by the economic self-interest of a vast weapons industry are still strong. When I urged these matters in Washington before our Senate Committee on Foreign Relations in company with administration officials recently returned from Poland, I heard much of the advice that might be given to that country. The particular reference was to 'institution-building'. That has the advantage of being wonderfully inexpensive, but it also has the highly probable disadvantage once again of being advice that we would not accept for ourselves: the triumph of Simplistic Ideology once more. As to more substantive help of the kind just mentioned, there was a short reference to 'budget constraints'. Budget constraints are not thought to be similarly decisive where something as remote from reality as anti-missile defence – Star Wars – is concerned. Or the Stealth bomber, the sacrifice of only a few of which would pay the cost of greatly expanded economic aid. Here is bureaucratic truth, as distinct from reality, in its starkest and, alas, also its darkest form.

Nothing would be more disastrous in the West than a return to the economic order envisaged in early capitalist doctrine and still celebrated by its more devout theologians. The system has survived only because of its capacity, in a liberal political context, to adapt. Similarly, adaptation, not a dramatic descent to primitive capitalism, is now the necessity in Eastern Europe and the USSR. It is an untrod road; it cannot be negotiated by adherence to rigid rules. It requires, alas, the painful processes of thought. This has in all economic ages been resisted, as it is being resisted now. There is, sadly, no alternative. Eastern Europe and the Soviet Union are now experiencing one of the greatest moments in their history. That moment is also ours.

# PART II

# Looking Back on 1989

# 6

# Speaking My Mind

## *Milan Šimečka*

(March 1989)

Each time I have switched on the radio in recent weeks and worked my way up and down the short-wave bands, I have caught the name of Václav Havel, pronounced in every possible language. Fortunately it is not a tongue-twister like certain Czech names that lend themselves to mutilation – *à la* 'Kohoot' (Kohout), 'Vachulik' (Vačulik), 'Hnyoopek' (Chnoupek), and so on. Nowadays, Václav Havel's name crops up in speeches by presidents, prime ministers, and other leading politicians. It is pronounced with enormous urgency by a number of public figures, artists and academics from around the world. That in itself does not particularly surprise me: it used to happen even in the past. What matters rather more is that the name of Václav Havel has now roused thousands of people to organize petitions here in Czechoslovakia, and even provoked many to reconsider and reappraise their own attitudes. The official media may well vilify this man, but they can no longer ignore him. On Sunday, I was listening to a quiz programme from Vienna in which an eighteen-year-old schoolgirl was asked to name a 'persecuted Czech writer'; she gave the correct answer – with feeling.

However, above all the clamour surrounding his name I can hear Václav's own voice saying: 'The last thing I want to do is to appeal to people and tell them what to do. I've no wish to say the sort of things they want to hear so as to win them over. That's what politicians do. I just speak my mind. I say how I see things around me. When it turns out that what I say appeals to someone else, and that other people see things the same way, that's fine, friends, that's really fine. But even if nobody did, I'd still speak my mind.'

Perhaps Václav Havel will forgive me for paraphrasing him instead of quoting from one of his books. I was trying to convey his actual manner of speaking, one devoid of any agitational tone. Instead, his voice seems to be directed inwards, towards a constantly operating powerhouse of ideas. Havel's distinctive attitude towards unalloyed political activity found its most precise expression in a number of his essays, particularly 'Power of the Powerless', back in 1978. In essence it is a non-political approach to politics, a constant striving to confront politics with 'other' – that is, normal – thinking.

From his earliest years, Havel observed politics with the mistrust it deserved. It never ceased to fascinate him, though. In order to enter it he had to find a way in that didn't stink of blood and stupidity. He worked at it with his own characteristic intellectual doggedness, while also drawing inspiration from Patočka and his interpretation of the *Lebenswelt*. Life in truth and non-political politics are not new concepts *per se*: in the European tradition such a stance can be traced back to Socrates and the Stoics, as well as to the lives of the saints (albeit not to the same extent). Solzhenitsyn and one wing of Eastern European dissent also upheld truth as that which was most strikingly at variance with the surrounding spiritual climate of immorality and lies. What Havel did was to expound the individual assertion of an authentic vision of reality, undesigning behaviour and an unassuming insistence on the truth – and to do so in a brilliant, stylish and witty fashion; set in a clear historical context and tinged with a certain Czech irreverence. I read 'Power of the Powerless' all those years ago with enormous pleasure, and I know there were many people who found within its pages relief from the depression caused by the stultifying inertia of public History and the apathy of the silent majority.

None the less, I had my reservations about Havel's reasoning. Having been schooled in political science, and convinced that I knew a great deal about the sorts of stimuli that rouse the popular masses, I regarded his appeal to truth as something rather exclusive. I observed the silent majority stuffing themselves with food amidst our stagnation, and even throwing bread to the swine. At that time I was working on a building site, and I'd ask my workmates how the idea of life in truth appealed to them. The answer they gave me was rooted in the centuries-old experience that truth was like politics, something for the gentry, and that ordinary folk had always been swindled and taken for a ride. It had always been that way, they told me, and always would be. Havel has shared my experience: after all, he once worked as a brewery labourer, and the brewer in his one-actor *Audience* is precisely the sort of person who doesn't want any bother – particularly not with his own conscience. So why is it that Havel stubbornly maintains an attitude that bears the stamp of detachment from the people?

One spring, shortly after Havel's release from prison, he and I received an invitation from friends to visit them in southern Moravia. The sole motive for the trip was to give us a chance to relax and enjoy ourselves for a while. One night we were sitting in a wine cellar. It wasn't very warm down there, so we kept our coats on. As we sat there like the Famous Five, it wasn't long before we were chatting away happily. Probably we should have stuck to discussing human life and its trans- mogrifications; instead, I started an argument. I aired for Havel's benefit all my reservations about making truth the pillar of a political programme. As a test, I placed him in the hypothetical situation of having to explain to ordinary people the object of our strivings. I shared with him the depression that regularly overcame me when I took the morning bus to work and had to look at the sleepy, ill-tempered faces of my fellow passengers. I explained how I pictured the consciousness of those people, immersed in the mundane trials and tribulations of their private histories. I told him I couldn't imagine how one could win over those scowling faces for the plain and simple truth, how one could overcome the nation's decline, demoralization and spiritual sloth.

Havel replied that he never suffered from my kind of depression since he refused to argue in terms of political manipulation: canvassing people, persuading them and making them promises. All he had ever done was to tackle his own personal problem. He did not offer 'life in truth' as a political commodity. Having no desire to be manipulated himself, he had no intention of manipulating the consciousness of others – 'I just speak my mind'. I retorted that every truth was open to question from its very inception, and that people's image of reality was formed not by his plays but by the degenerate mass media. That wasn't important, he said. He didn't think in terms of the masses: individuals were what mattered. And on we went, back and forth in the same vein. When I finally hit the hay in the small hours, I decided that I still retained 60 per cent of my reservations.

And lo and behold, the years have sped by and there is Havel's name out there on the main street coupled with a loud clamour for truth. It was in the name of truth that thousands of people decided to risk being beaten or soaked to the skin. After Havel's arrest, other people signed a petition because they felt insulted by the lies our mass media were pumping out in every direction. And the amazing thing is that most of them were employed in the kind of institution from which one can most easily be sacked. It is as if, all at once, everyone feels like speaking their mind. And that's fine, friends, really fine.

I have been following the tide of events over the past months with excitement and emotion. Could it really be that people in the Czech lands find the lies so unbearable that at last they have started to take the perilous path of rebellion? It occurs to me that, contrary to the accepted notion of unchanging causes of social movement, an uprising has germinated within the stagnant public life of our country, motivated by the esoteric need for truth and by people's yearning to speak their minds – a phenomenon unknown to the political science textbooks. Though long suppressed and geared solely to survival and the securing of personal well-being, the national consciousness looks as if it is beginning to react to that appeal for truth issued nearly fifteen years ago – to Havel's exclusive and intellectually demanding appeal for people to take their leave of the post-totalitarian scene. Can it be that people have found the humiliating habit of not speaking their mind too much of a burden to bear any longer?

Havel is in prison, but his name is increasingly on people's lips in this country. It is coupled with the first sign of change we have had here in twenty years. This change, though rooted in non-political politics, has also spilled over into mainstream politics because the regime has to come to terms with it in some way, and the hapless and ham-fisted way they are going about it is sickening to watch. The power of the powerless has become a political reality. As a result of this shift, Havel has acquired a status to which he never aspired. After all, he has never done anything in his life that can properly be described as politicking. He has never promised anyone tax cuts, never took a stance on economic reform or self-financing, never criticized the shortage of toilet paper, never pointed out the shortcomings in 'supplier–consumer relations'. He has certainly not said a word about the 'supply problems' that give the Establishment so many sleepless nights because it believes that only shortages of consumer goods are capable of shaking the regime.

People who have never read any of Havel's plays, let alone his essays; those who know him solely from a couple of radio interviews and the slanders about him spread by the official press, must have the impression that, apart from the freedom to speak one's mind, Havel really has nothing to offer them in terms of the political wares that have traditionally swamped politics. He has won the attention of those whose suffering is largely ethical, those who are distressed at our status in Europe and horrified at the thought of our country hitting rock bottom. And so, for the first time in many years, people have stood up in defence of an intellectual, and in so doing have taken a stand against the debasement of reason and the crass stupidities that are held up for public admiration.

It is unlikely, however, that this would have happened if, in his years of effort to revive common sense, Havel had invested only his vision of the world, not himself. The worth of an idea is always greater when its protagonist is prepared to suffer constant persecution and years in captivity because of it: people surmise that there must be something special about the freedom to speak one's mind if Havel is prepared to go to prison for it. None of Havel's friends and supporters would have thought it at all amiss if he had never gone to Wenceslas Square. For him, though, it flows logically from his concept of indivisible freedom that he should go and face the blows that fall on others. Maybe he thought his presence on the Square might protect those others. Maybe he wanted his reputation to serve as a kind of shield – that is one of the morals of his play *Protest*. Who knows whether he even considered the possibility that he might end up in Ruzyně Prison, where he had been so many times before? It was, however, a possibility that ought to have occupied the minds of those who ordered his arrest, trial and conviction. The trouble is that they are no longer capable of reasoned thought: they are happily burning their bridges lest they be tempted to stop and consider the consequence of their actions, or even change their minds. They are driven ever onwards by dark forces of self-destruction.

I don't know if Havel has heard about the wave of protest sparked off by the ill-disguised vindictiveness of his absurd prosecution. He probably knows something of it, though he cannot be fully informed. Perhaps he has heard enough to know that the power of the powerless has again received a boost, and that people are relishing the opportunity to speak their minds once more – thanks to him. When Havel gets out of prison I'll have to let him know that I have demolished a further 20 per cent of my reservations about his lack of concern for sociological tenets – leaving only 40 per cent. My wish, of course, is for him to return as soon as possible to a transformed Prague, in whose streets he will encounter more and more people who have discovered with amazement the joy and relief that comes from speaking one's mind.

*Translated by A.G. Brain*

# 7

# Conversation with Christa Wolf

## Aafke Steenhuis
### (December 1989)

Over the next little while you're going to hear many people here saying: we've lived here for forty years and it was all for nothing. I won't be saying that. My life hasn't been wasted, it's been very intense, so I have a large treasure-box of experiences.

I drive through East Berlin in a taxi, along the broad grey avenue called 'Unter den Linden' and through old working-class districts, until we stop by a couple of large, dilapidated but stately villas in a park. High plane trees, lime trees. It's starting to snow.

The conversation takes place in the bay window of Christa Wolf's study where there are cane chairs, a round table, flowers. Gerhard Wolf, her husband, brings us coffee and smiles. She looks beautiful: a lively face, greenish-brown eyes, dark hair. A clear voice. She turned sixty this year, but there's something girlish about her. I've known her for a few years. When a mutual friend introduced us, I asked her for an interview. She agreed to do it, but it kept being postponed: 'I'm not going to be in Berlin for a few months. But we will manage to get together some time.' 'Christa Wolf is seriously ill, she can't come to the phone. She won't be able to do anything for quite some time.' 'I wanted to have our conversation this year, but then I looked at my diary and thought about my writing plans, and so now I want to console you with a date for next year.'

Christa Wolf was born in 1929, in Landsberg on the Warthe river, which is now in Poland and called Gorzow. Her father had a grocer's shop. In her collected essays, entitled *The Author's Dimension*, she talks about how when she was young she never met a soul who was opposed to Hitler, and that she had difficulty, after her sixteenth birthday, learning to say '*Auf Wiedersehen*' instead of '*Heil Hitler*'. At the end of the war she fled westwards with her family. She describes that terrible journey in her novels *The Quest for Christa T.* and *A Model Childhood.* In 1949 she joined the SED (the Socialist Unity Party, ruling party of the GDR for forty years). She studied German and history, met her husband Gerhard in 1949, worked as a publisher's editor, published articles, and began writing stories and novels. She has two daughters. Her first appearance as an author was with *Moscow Novella* (1959), followed in 1963 by *Divided Heavens.* Almost all Wolf's novels since the subtle *Quest for Christa T.* (1968) are similarly structured: the central figure is a reflective woman whose memories, thoughts and questions shape the book. Christa Wolf digs deeper and deeper into the past, and also into her everyday surroundings.

*A Model Childhood* (1976) analyses the fascination and confusion of a youth spent during the period of National Socialism. *No Place on Earth* (1979) explores the thought processes of the Romantic poets Heinrich von Kleist and Caroline von Günderrode, who withdrew from society, disillusioned, just as Christa Wolf herself felt she was an outsider in the GDR at that time. *Cassandra* (1983) is about the mania for destruction displayed by two peoples at war with one another, the Greeks and the Trojans – and simultaneously about the perils of the Cold War, between East and West. *Accident* (1987) describes the day she heard about the 1986 accident at Chernobyl.

*Sommerstück, (Summer Piece)* written in 1989, describes life with friends in the country after the political situation in Berlin has become unbearable. 'This is what pains me: the fact that like everyone else I've grown accustomed to never doing just exactly what I want to do. Never saying the precise thing I want to say. So that, without realizing it, I probably don't even think what I want to think any more.' The book has implications far beyond the stifling East German atmosphere. It gives a sense of the emptiness, the aimlessness, of our entire culture. 'I see our outlines dissolving. We don't seem destined to acquire firm contours. There are so many things we've tried out, just to find our feet, so many skins we've slipped into, so many rooms we've sought shelter in.'

Christa and Gerhard Wolf have been part of the critical opposition in the GDR since the end of the 1960s. In 1976 Christa protested when the poet and singer Wolf Biermann was deprived of his citizenship and other writers (including Gerhard Wolf) were expelled from the Writers' Union. And in the past few months, during which the country has been shaken to its foundations and the old power structures are crumbling, Christa Wolf has been speaking at demonstrations and writing appeals and articles for the newspapers.

There is a key question in *A Model Childhood,* put by a Communist to the central character's mother, who was unaware, during all the years under Hitler, of any evil. She meets him, in concentration camp garb, on the flight westwards in 1945. He identifies himself as a Communist, whereupon Nelly's mother asks: 'Communist? But just because you were a Communist they didn't put you in a concentration camp!' To which he replies: 'Where on earth have you all been living?' ['*Wo habt ihr bloss alle gelebt?*'] After the war, people put up with the authoritarian Communist structures in the GDR for forty years before beginning to liberate themselves from them. Can one ask the same question now: Where on earth have you all been living? Did Christa Wolf think things would go the way they have?

**Christa Wolf:**    The speed and also the nature of the changes, initiated by the people on the streets – I don't think anyone in this country saw that coming. I certainly didn't. The thing is that in the last few years we felt more and more depressed and despairing because we could see what a dead end the system was being manoeuvred into by the mulish rigidity of a leadership which was quite simply failing to read the signs. And there were more and more signals. The situation became increasingly inflexible in every area of life. There was a rising crescendo of strong criticism from below, from the Party ranks as well. It was clear that all this must lead to change at some point, but I don't think anyone really had any idea of the form this change would take.

The question you quote, 'Where have you all been living?', is a question one can indeed put here. To give you an example: yesterday I got a letter from a woman worker who has always been in the Party, and now she's in despair, she just can't believe what's happened. She writes that she never knew about all that [referring to the corruption, the diversion of hard currency for arms sales, and so on, by top politicians and SED officials], that she always did her best, and was honest and true. I believe her. I wonder whether the signals sent for a long time now by literature, for example, never reached her.

**Aafke Steenhuis:**    Does the fact that people in the GDR put up with Stalinism for forty years have something to do with the war?

**CW:**    My generation identified very strongly with this society, and from very early on, because we were forced in the forties into an intense and radical confrontation with the fascist past. That process created a very strong bond with this society, a society which was of course being built by anti-fascists, as people here always phrased it so beautifully. This bond remained as strong as it did because we had no alternative. The Federal Republic with Adenauer and Globke: it was impossible for me to live there. Of course the Federal Republic has changed, and my relationships with people there have changed too. But we still held on to the hope that forces would emerge here which could succeed in making the core of the socialist dream come true. Of course our hopes were higher in the first few years. Those hopes were dashed in 1968 when the tanks rolled into Czechoslovakia. That was an existential shock for us.

What happened in the twenty years that followed was sometimes better, sometimes worse, but in the final analysis the old Stalinist structures and ways of thinking became entrenched. And yet there are an astonishing number of people in the GDR who can think very well and very freely. I'm quite sure that fascism, the war, and problems not voiced between the generations all play a large part in these political upheavals. But the nationalism and xenophobia which are coming out now make me feel utter despair, because we know those lines. We've heard them before. And the fact that they're still there, and that they keep reappearing, is just terrible.

**AS:**   Why did it take so long for a broad-based democratic movement to emerge?

**CW:**   It's to do with the fascist past, and also with the division of Germany. Recently one of our theatre directors, Frank Baier, put into words the reason why we have such strong bonds with this state: because as very young people who grew up under fascism, we were full of guilt and gratitude towards the people who had rescued us from that. They were anti-fascists and Communists who had come back from camps, prisons and exile and set the tone of political life here. We felt an enormous reluctance to oppose people who had been in concentration camps during the Nazi era. We did oppose them intellectually. But no mass movement, not even a noteworthy political opposition emerged – people left, or were arrested and thrown out of the country. The division of Germany contributed to this situation, which meant that critical thinkers here were always frustrated.

The core of criticism and resistance crumbled repeatedly. It's only now, since the emergence of a mass movement which is associated with the Church, with young people who are less burdened by such consider- ations and guilt feelings – and above all now that Gorbachev is there – that a large opposition movement has become possible.

We always said, amongst friends: if anything is to change here, it will have to come from the Soviet Union, and it won't happen there. I was talking with some Russian friends about it just recently, and they had to laugh, because they hadn't ever thought that changes would come from them either. But in the Soviet Union it's happening through a revolution from above. For a long time we thought the same thing would happen here, that a group would be formed in the higher echelons of the Party which would introduce reforms in opposition to the old men's stubbornness. But no such group did emerge, and that's why the Party has now collapsed. They failed to make use of the potential for opposition within their own ranks. It was there, but it was blocked. They were too cowardly, and now they are paying the price for it.

**AS:** Could one sense a lot of tension in the GDR over the last few years? Did people feel trapped?

**CW:** People fought for certain freedoms in literature and culture, but there wasn't even a hint of that in the economy or in the political process. The population felt shut in, despite the fact that more people were able to travel to the West in the last few years than ever before. The Party leadership had thought of that as a sort of safety valve. But people didn't want just one finger, they wanted the whole hand. The way people rushed out when the borders were opened shows just how acutely they must have felt themselves to be stuck in a pot with the lid on. Lots of people wanted to get out, wanted really to experience that sense of liberation just by the change of place. In the first weeks people needed to do that. And there was real euphoria then. That's gone now; there's a lot of depression and illness around. People are confused, uncertain, anxious. Many of them earned their living from the old structures. When those disappear, their jobs disappear with them. What are they to do? The people who worked for the Ministry of State Security, for example – they aren't terribly welcome in other jobs.

**AS:** How are you spending your time at the moment?

**CW:** For some time I made a big effort to put certain problems down on paper. I wrote several articles, for example, trying to understand why the younger generation found it so easy to leave, and in such great numbers; why they couldn't identify with their country, and didn't go into opposition either, which is another way of identifying. I wondered: how did they actually feel about their childhood and youth? At school they were forced into a kind of permanent schizophrenia; they didn't learn to think for themselves. I'm still sitting on a committee which is dealing with the security police's violence against demonstrators. Every day I receive a lot of letters, to which I reply. People keep coming to see me, and I go to meetings as well. I haven't had a moment of free time for weeks, at most only in the evenings, but then we watch the news on TV. I haven't seen a single film. I haven't read a book, not even a single line, in weeks. It's totally impossible to read anything literary; it's too painful and at the same time too uninteresting. I can't remember this ever happening before in my whole life ... these really are exceptional circumstances in which we find ourselves; all our thoughts and feelings are totally dominated by this process.

**AS:**   Almost all your books have a reflective woman as the main figure. Her thoughts and recollections structure the work. That's true of *The Quest for Christa T.*, *A Model Childhood*, *Cassandra*, *Accident*, and parts of *Summer Piece*. Why is it that you always end up with this structure?

**CW:**   The funny thing is, whenever I try to write in a different way, it goes wrong. I started to write each book in a new way at least ten times. I'm not conscious of forcing myself to write realistically or objectively or to portray people's lives. When I finally get the feeling that I've found my own voice and my own personal form, it always turns out, when I look at it more closely, to be this same structure. Actually I should know that by now so that I could start writing like that from the start, but it obviously doesn't work that way. I have to go by a very circuitous route before again reaching this thought structure, and often it's a structure of recollection.

Why do I use that form? I think it's because I can discover most about myself that way. That's really why I write: to find out about myself. I come closer to it by a process of association, by trying to become conscious of analogies, by working non-chronologically and asking myself certain questions – although this is of course more tiring and painful. My questions are what structures the book, not events.

**AS:**   That's the way our minds work, isn't it? We carry a thousand things around in our head at the same time.

**CW:**   That's my ideal. It's what I intended when I was writing *Accident*. I wanted to write in the same way as the mind functions. But the book was interpreted, especially here in the GDR, as a plea for or against nuclear power. Dreadful! What I was trying to achieve by the parallels between my brother's operation for a brain tumour and the accident at the Chernobyl nuclear power station was prose structures which come closest to the working of the brain. Of course that's impossible, I knew that too. But that was the problem which really interested me in that book. Of course no one noticed that – well, you did!

**AS:**   What strikes me about your books is the continual transition from everyday details to abstract problems, and vice versa. It seems as if everything is linked to everything else.

**CW:** That reflects my development over the last few years. At a time when grand ideologies became more and more dubious and irrelevant and no longer offered reference points for moral values or moral behaviour, ordinary everyday life became more and more important to me. It also had something to do with the fact that since the mid seventies I have spent part of each year living in the country. It was some time before I realized the significance of daily structures. Several of my books describe a single day, like *Accident*, and the story I'm working on at the moment does too. This story is about the time at the end of the seventies when the security police stood around outside our door all day long. *Summer Piece* [*Sommerstück*] has descriptions of one day in it too.

I've also kept diary-like notes over a period of several years which describe repeatedly the same day of the year. This normal daily routine obviously structures my life and my writing. That has to do with my family, with children and grandchildren. What happens in any one day is important to me. I always try to remember what people say, what was in the newspaper, how a day like that changes in terms of one's feelings. The feelings one has in the morning are different from those one has in front of the TV in the evening. That's very exciting. Everyday things provide a constant in my work, I weave them into my thinking. My ideal is a fabric, a network of thought and action.

**AS:** Your work is also a form of sensual perception.

**CW:** I have managed, with difficulty, to free myself from the snares of theory which I was caught up in during the fifties. I wouldn't have wanted to miss out on studying at university, but it probably cost me years as a writer. It took me a long time to free myself from the ideological concepts which influenced literary studies at that time. Quite simply, I realized that I felt better when I made good use of my senses. At first I had to keep reminding myself of it, had to trust in my senses and simply forget all that ideological rubbish. Now I do it unconsciously; I see, hear, smell, taste, feel, see how people move, and how I move myself ... for that's where it always starts, having a sense of your own body.

You become aware of how tense your muscles are, and although that doesn't make the tension go away, at least you realize *why* you've become so tense. Does the name Feldenkreis mean anything to you? He's a fantastic neurophysiologist. His observations have opened up whole new ways of seeing, feeling and thinking for me. He says that

people's bodies reveal their state of mind and their psyche, as well as
their outward appearance and their sensuality. This is an insight I have
also found in the German Romantic writers. The Classical period,
particularly where Schiller is concerned, was based more on ideas and
ideology.

**AS:**  What is special about your style is its linking of association and
analysis. Isn't it difficult to combine those two forms of expression? The
writer Nathalie Sarraute, for example, refuses to analyse. She says that
would cause a reduction instead of a wealth of words.

**CW:**  I think it's a question of feeling with one's thoughts and thinking
with one's feelings. Thoughts and feelings are not separate from one
another; every thought is seeped in the feelings I am living through at
that precise moment in time. When I'm depressed I think differently; I
draw different conclusions when I'm in a euphoric mood.

**AS:**  But thinking and analysing are different, aren't they?

**CW:**  Yes, one thinks all the time, but not always analytically. For me
it's like this: I'm often in a confused mood which I find agonizing. I feel
really glad when I – I can almost say when I find a formula for it, which
allows me to recognize and name the mood. Abstract formulations are
important to me.

If, for example, I have a writing block, it's nearly always because –
although this too is something I realize only with hindsight – I find it
hard to acknowledge certain things about myself. And once I find the
courage to overcome this reluctance and to express the insight, it's really
easy to write. Heinrich Böll once said to me: sometimes you write a
whole book in order to conceal a single sentence in it. But if I shy away
from that or try to evade it, then I can't write. Then I can throw the lot
away.

**AS:**  Can you give me an example of that kind of block?

**CW:**  It was very clear in the writing of *A Model Childhood.* It took me
one, or almost two years to write the first few pages. I started afresh
thirty-six times; sometimes I had already written ten, sometimes fifty
pages. It was the time it took to get so close to that child – in other
words to me – to find that special tone of voice, that particular way of
writing. Of course I came up against a lot more barriers and blocks
within the book, but in the beginning it's nearly always the same.

**AS:** But you can feel pleased about a block like that too, can't you, because then you know that now it's serious and that you've reached the point where you can get on with it?

**CW:** But when you're stuck in it, you are in total despair, because you don't remember that something important is going to grow out of this. You can't depend on the fact that you'll get through it again this time. You are completely blocked afresh each time, you feel it's quite impossible for you to write. And if it isn't like that, if you aren't stuck in the block, with all your dreams in utter despair, then it's no use to you. It's simple: one mustn't have any idea of the way out – and you don't. You think this time you're never going to write another line. I really have to wring out every insight from myself. I always get there via all kinds of experimental phases which take me miles away from what comes out in the end. Years can go by before I realize what I really want to say. My husband usually knows what it is a lot sooner, but that's no use to me.

**AS:** Doesn't he say anything?

**CW:** He usually mutters something, but he's reticent ... and it isn't nice for him either when I'm in such a desperate phase. I'm sure he knows it will pass, but I don't. He tries to tell me it will, but I can only feel that that's an insult. I'm putting it too bluntly now. This mode of behaviour has gradually, over time, become such a habit that he waits a long time before he says straight out what he means.

**AS:** *Summer Piece* is about a block like that, isn't it? The main character, Ellen, has come out of a difficult winter. In a Mecklenburg village, she gradually loses her sense of paralysis and her creativity returns. It's also possible to read the book as an idyll with menacing undertones. I heard that you worked on it for a long time, and that its final form emerged only at quite a late stage.

**CW:** What *Summer Piece* describes are my experiences in the years following 1975. Life in the country, surrounded by my friends – it was all new to me. It was something many people experienced during that time because it was clear that politics in our country would not tolerate any critical participation. That became clear after Wolf Biermann lost his citizenship, and after the reaction to our protest. The question was whether we could stay in the GDR. I was undecided for a long time. In fact we toyed with the other option, that of going. Quite honestly we didn't know where to go to. We didn't feel any other country offered a real alternative. And on top of that, I'm really only interested in this country. The sharp friction which sparks off productivity is something I only experience here – for all the rebuffs, the self-doubts and the despair that come with life in the GDR.

There were other reasons, more personal ones: I would never have left without my daughters, but they had their families and their lives here. And I still had my father, who died this year. And the fact that lots of people wrote to me saying that I was needed here played a large part too. I realized that I would have to put myself in difficult and morally dubious situations, and that's something I often found hard.

I guess it's possible to understand from my books how my inner liberation came about. I still know precisely the time and the place when it became clear to me that I would have to leave the GDR if I couldn't free myself completely from all the dependencies which would hamper my thinking and writing. I also knew that I wouldn't be able to achieve this overnight and that one way of doing it would be to *describe* the process of freeing oneself, and this was something I couldn't have done if I had suddenly upped and left. It really was like that – that whilst I did still feel a bond, I no longer felt dependent. That's why the situation in our country at the moment isn't so painful for me as for others. I felt the pain much earlier. I felt the sharpest pain in 1968, and then again in 1976, when I realized I still had hope. I was in a bad way for months at that time.

*Summer Piece* is an amalgamation of many summers. I wrote *No Place on Earth* and *Cassandra* during the same period. Behind them all lay the friendships and the togetherness which are described in *Summer Piece*. Many people in the *GDR* at that time retained their integrity and liberated themselves mentally in groups like these. Many people see the book as describing a part of their own lives.

I was very hesitant about publishing it, because it's my most personal book. And I had reservations because of my friends, even though I have altered them all in the book and have added quite a lot which is fictitious. I wondered whether the story could be misread as an idyll, whereas in reality life here was very hard. I had to be forced to publish it. It gets harder with every book.

**AS:**  The form is unusual: it's very autobiographical. You describe yourself from within and simultaneously, in the third person, your friends too. The mixture of reality and fiction is complicated.

**CW:**  That's right, it is. The stylistic device of letting people speak from within was something I added only later, because I wanted to do them greater justice. I didn't want to judge them from the outside, but wanted to explain them from within themselves.

**AS:**   But if you describe someone from the outside, you describe only what you see. If, on the other hand, one claims to be able to describe friends from within as well, isn't that a bit arrogant? Did you discuss this with them?

**CW:**   Of course, yes, and they reacted very differently to it – some with great tolerance; others couldn't accept it. But the internal description is continually reflected and broken up by the others' perspective. There's a sentence in the book which says that we would be able to do justice to the times only if everyone could give their own view of them. That's true for Sarah Kirsch, who has written about the same summer in *Allerlei Rau* and *Rückenwind (Tail Wind)*.

The strange thing is that even friends in Italy said that they experienced precisely the same things at that time. It's as if European countries are communicating tubes, so that ever since the war, or probably for even longer, we have had similar experiences.

**AS:**   How did you come to write *Cassandra*? After you had dealt with the German wartime past in *The Quest for Christa T.* and *A Model Childhood,* and after your work on the German Romantics with *No Place on Earth*, you became absorbed in ancient Greek history.

**CW:**   That had to do with the circumstances at the time. We feared a nuclear war, and the annihilation of our civilization. I wondered: Where do the roots of these destructive forces in our civilization lie, forces which lead ultimately to self-destruction? I went further and further back. Actually experiencing Greek landscape in the flesh and seeing the old sites was decisive: I had the location for my story. I was looking for a metaphor for a woman's reaction to that kind of destructive society. Cassandra and Troy provided the models for it.

**AS:**   Mary Kaldor has recently finished a book on the Cold War: *The Imaginary War.* It was a game, an imaginary, dangerous game. Alva Myrdal, the Swedish peace and conflict researcher, also wrote that the two superpowers, the USA and the Soviet Union, needed one another. The one needed the game of threatening to wage war in order to expand the capitalist economy; the other, in order to hold its empire together. This threat disciplined and oppressed millions of people, but it was all a fiction. Your book also portrays the reason for the Trojan War, Helen of Troy's abduction, as a fiction. Helen isn't even in Troy.

**CW:**  You know the great danger still is that the controllers of the patriarchal system need mechanisms to externalize their internal splits, and their inability to feel and love. Many men are capable of feelings only when they are being destructive. This is a terrible insight which is continually repressed, by me as well. I keep having to remind myself – even in the current developments – how fundamentally destructive our civilization is, and that it's terribly difficult, but none the less absolutely necessary, to reduce this destructiveness.

**AS:**  Does destructiveness arise when people don't have the courage to be themselves?

**CW:**  Where did it begin, men having to be heroes? Being a man is, of course, a misfortune – or it was until recently. Young men today have other possibilities to identify with, and they are taking them up too. But until recently men had to choose some form of heroism, whether as factory manager or as strong worker. That meant they had to suppress part of themselves. But that's something people don't forgive themselves for. They try to make others like them so as to be able to live with themselves.

**AS:**  Does destructiveness also have to do with the fact that people live for such a short time? That in order to give their lives some meaning they want to control others and the future?

**CW:**  That can be a motive for it, but the suppression of feelings, especially in men, seems to me to be the key thing. They feel they are being themselves only when they are destructive. It's a tragedy for soldiers, for politicians, and even for many artists. There too destructiveness and necrophilia reign supreme. It would be revolutionary if men could learn to find their security in gentle feelings.

I'm also wondering whether, in the committee investigating the violence against demonstrators, we couldn't try to bring together young policemen, who are of course ashamed of themselves and don't understand their own actions, with the young people they mistreated. They belong to the same generation. I think something like that will have to happen. How can you bring confrontation to an end? By getting to know each other. Then you'll get differing opinions about one another, not on the basis of absurd enemy images which one has had drummed into one, but on the basis of mutual acquaintance.

**AS:**  Do you keep a diary?

**CW:** Funnily enough, not in these last weeks. Usually I do.

**AS:** What is the connection between writing a diary and your literary writing?

**CW:** Writing a diary is often a form of preparation for literary writing, and it's also a form of arguing with oneself in order, for example, to clear blockages. I often spontaneously formulate something in my diary which then helps in writing fiction. Of course the diary is also a memory store for details and recollections. The diaries are important most of all because from them I can always draw reminders about how I was feeling in a particular year.

**AS:** You were young when you had your children. How did that influence your writing?

**CW:** I can't answer that very well, because I can't imagine a life without children. They were just always there. When they were still small, there was a strong sensual influence. I experience a great deal through touch and smell. I notice it now again with my grandchildren: how many unexpected situations they produce, how it keeps one alive. Perhaps no one has taught me so much as my two daughters, who often made me think things over. For me children are the foundation and the ferment of my life. I've never understood Simone de Beauvoir and her total rejection of children because they supposedly disturb the development of the intellect.

**AS:** Many women writers are childless: the combination is difficult.

**CW:** Yes, it is difficult, I know that from women colleagues too; all of us have shortchanged our children a bit. But I always worked to the limit of my strength, I couldn't have done more. Perhaps I should have done it differently, should have spent more time with my children, as my daughters do with their children now. For our generation in the fifties and sixties, relationships were subordinate to work and politics. That is taking its revenge now. The children of those parents who were not able to build up a real relationship with them at the time are the young people who are now leaving the country.

**AS:** You've been with your husband for forty years?

**CW:** Just a minute, is it really forty years? Yes, you're right, it's true. We met in 1949. Are you asking how that can still work?

**AS:** You don't write about sexuality.

**CW:** I don't feel the need to ... I feel the same way about it as Ingeborg Bachmann, who said that it's something which is between two people. I don't know ... we were always caught up in arguments, criticism, actions; our young years were occupied with all that, and those were the things which I felt the need to express. The other, love, sexuality, was always there, as a background we took for granted ... and I also have a degree of reticence about getting too close to my intimate life.

I don't know what Gerd would say, but I need him as a partner very much, not just because of the security, but above all because he knows me so well. Because I can have arguments with him about what I'm writing with the security of knowing that he doesn't intend to destroy me. When you publish a book you always get destructive attacks. But when you've got an exchange of opinions with someone who is often very critical but is nevertheless someone who you know wants you to express yourself as completely as possible, that's a great source of happiness. Our daily life is never boring, it's a constant endless conversation. And then there are the children.... I don't think I'd be alive today if it weren't for these people. There have been quite a few critical moments.

**AS:** In *A Model Childhood*, as well as in *Accident*, you wrote about your brother. Brothers are a literary theme which recurs frequently with women writers – with Marguerite Duras, for example. Do brothers provide the possibility of in-depth reflection about men? Fathers, lovers, sons and brothers are the most important relationships a woman has with men. But you don't have any sons.

**CW:** I've got two grandsons now who have taught me a great deal about men, about little men! I often have to laugh at them. I didn't set out with the intention of writing about my brother so as to be able to say something about men. I took the topic from the area of my own experience. But later on it seemed like a chance to write about a man who is close to me but also very different from me. I have an ongoing argument with him. We still have a close bond and mutual affection, despite all our differences of opinion, even our political differences. I find it wonderful to write about someone who is very different, who questions me and often fills me with aggression, but is not alien to me. I have never been able to write about anyone I hate.

**AS:** Do you think women writers have made a special contribution to literature?

**CW:** That's a question which is always difficult to answer.... I think that women give more of themselves. I have a sense that the literature of our century is hampered by something Ingeborg Bachmann calls 'illness', men's illness. You can even call it a curse, a disaster which is not their fault, but consists in men finding it so difficult to acknowledge their feelings. It seems simplistic for me to ascribe the difference between men's and women's literature to this ... although I must say, in parenthesis, that I often find women's emotional outbursts frightful ... those unadulterated, unreflective and unformed explosions of speech.... But on the other hand, perhaps they have succeeded in preserving something ... a faith in subjectivity which possibly helps and is of use to everyone, male authors included.

*Translated by Barbara Einhorn*

# 8

# Warsaw Diary

*Lynne Jones*

### Monday 2 October 1989

I have acquired a room in Warsaw, or rather three connected ones, plus a front door with four locks. It is in a pre-war apartment building in Ochota. The district is poor but neighbourly. There is a church at the back with a tree-filled yard. My street has a general store, greengrocer, bookshop and a number of specialist shops selling the sort of things you know you will need one day but not right now: dog leads, parts for televisions, sanitation equipment, felt slippers. There is also a tailor, a rarity in Warsaw these days, according to my friends. Communism provided little opportunity for the skilled artisan.

Giedymin is quite wrong. There are plenty of poor people here. I see them all the time: the old lady standing next to me in the queue at the grocer's in tailored coat and velvet hat, who found six hundred zlotys (five pence at current black-market rates) too much for a piece of cottage cheese; the old man who rummages in the bins behind the apartment building. They have pale, lined faces; their clothes are 'good' but worn. They creep around the edges of this society with none of the assertiveness of their counterparts in London or New York. These aren't bag-ladies or schizophrenics, just elderly people finding it hard to cope.

### Thursday 12 October

Anna Niedzwiecka rang and told me about the boycott of military classes at the university. These classes are compulsory if the student is to graduate, and include a large amount of ideological instruction. The

99

boycott started in Krakow and has extended to Warsaw and Gdansk. There is some friction between the organizing groups: NZS (the independent students' union) has less radical demands than WiP (Freedom and Peace), which would like the classes abolished, not just reformed. The boycott so far has been very successful: students hate the classes and are happy to stay away. Anna said I would find her on the picket. When I got there, three students were folding up their banners. They had forgotten it was Army Day and classes were cancelled anyway. So they sent me off to the anti-militarist demonstration being organized by anarchists in the city centre. It wasn't difficult to find. There is a pedestrian shopping area opposite the Forum Hotel where a woman sits inside a brand-new car selling lottery tickets to eager buyers. Small caravans decorated with orange and yellow light bulbs, and the words 'Supermusic', 'Cassettes' in gold lettering, blare out their latest offerings. Private food stalls sell German coffee, Swiss chocolate, cartons of fruit juice, bananas, oranges and nuts – all for zlotys, all at a price.

In this setting the spiky-haired, black-clad young demonstrators stood out like crows at a banquet table. After a speech through a hand-held megaphone we moved off down Aleje Jerozolimskie, black flags flying, drums banging and trumpets blaring. Some three hundred demonstrators occupied the full width of one of Warsaw's main streets with police cars at front and back, bringing the traffic to a seemingly unirritated standstill. 'We don't want a compulsory army.' 'No Warsaw pact, no NATO.' Two young soldiers joined in briefly until they were removed by their colleagues. The demonstrators marched to Parliament, where a number of them pulled out their military passbooks and ceremoniously burned them in front of an uninterested gold-braided doorman. No one else was around and the demonstrators seemed uncertain where to go next. But after circling restlessly, they moved off to the ministries and the army prison, ignoring police directives to 'Please walk on the pavement'. Impossible to conceive of this a year ago – either the police protection or the indifference of passers-by.

## Monday 16 October

Gosza has been asked to be an adviser to Solidarity trade union on 'Women'. 'I think they felt that a "perfect" trade union should have a women's section,' she said. The initiative had first come from the International Confederation of Free Trade Unions, which wanted to help women organize in Poland. 'The realization that there *is* a problem is a step forward.' Her idea was to create small working groups in each region who would focus on whatever issues interested them: working conditions in the textile industry, ecology in Silesia. They could then demand political representation in each region's authority, hoping both to make their problems visible and to influence the politics of the union as a whole. They had been promised financial assistance: the problem was, would women themselves be interested? 'Most women simply don't see themselves as exploited even when they're working night shifts at the meat-processing plant here, carrying thirty-kilogram loads, way above the norm.'

Not everyone in the region was happy about the project. When Gosza and some friends who were in the local teachers' union had gone to ask for a room where they could meet and have coffee, Bogdan Borus-zewicz, Chief of Gdansk Region Trade Union, had exploded: 'I suppose you would like to see men giving birth to children next!' He saw no point in a separate women's organization, and although Gosza had carefully avoided the word 'feminism' in order not to discourage him, had shouted that no 'Western feminist fashion would be followed in Gdansk!' Gosza had retreated upstairs to the national offices, where they had told her not to worry. She could organize at national level first and perhaps Boruszewicz would come round.

Adam wanted to go down to the university. The boycott of military studies had spread to include Gdansk and he wanted to try interviewing some of the military teaching staff for *Gazeta Wyborcza*. To our surprise they were delighted to talk to us. If someone had told me, even a year ago, that I would be sitting at a long table under a crownless eagle and a picture of desert warfare, while two army officers informed me that they taught their students about four kinds of pacifism, I wouldn't have believed them. Apparently, they told us, there are the Christian Gandhians, who don't mind serving in the army if necessary; the 'aggrieved', who are against the authorities but will defend themselves; Humanists and 'Integral' pacifists, who are END pacifists; and 'total refusers'.

'What is END?' I asked, astonished to hear it being taught about in Gdansk University's military studies curriculum.

'Oh, a Western anti-nuclear group that is now very political. We don't evaluate it, we just inform them as best we can. We have a lecture – "Bringing up People for Peace", but the problem is that in Poland people just don't discuss this subject,' said the senior officer.

He had nothing against conscientious objecting but argued that no society had completely rejected the idea of training its intelligentsia to be military-minded. It was necessary for the defence of society. As Marshal Sternakowski said to the Polish Senate, 'It's very negative for young people to have a negative view of the army.' There was no question of political indoctrination. They taught: 'Methods of defence in Poland's

history and the present, the structure of present forces and the obligation to defence of the nation.' 'I've often thought the teaching of
military history to young ladies was unnecessary, but it is needed for
people going to be officers. I ask them after each training if they feel
indoctrinated. They laugh at the idea.'

As to the boycott: 'It's not a spontaneous boycott, it's organized by
NZS, who support Solidarity, but we don't try to convince them one way
or the other.' Indeed, they themselves had pinned up the demands on
the noticeboard – unfortunately they couldn't show us as someone had
taken them down again. 'It's not up to us, but the Ministries of Defence
and Education. They are discussing the matter. In my thirty years'
experience as an army officer, the army has always been in the hands of
the nation, which decides what it should do. The army is here to be
ordered about, you know.'

'How do you respond when students ask you about the role of the
army in martial law?' I asked.

'The 1792 constitution said that each nation must defend itself,' the
senior officer began.

'We're talking about the use of the army against its *own* nation,'
Adam interrupted.

'Martial law was a political decision; every army must do what the
government says.'

'Some Polish officers recently criticized the invasion of Czechoslovakia as a mistake,' I said. 'Do you think that officers might begin to see
martial law as a mistake?'

There was a long pause, then the senior officer, looking grave, spoke
again: 'I think it's very bad when an officer tries to come to political
conclusions. He should stop being a soldier. There's no place on earth
where a soldier can make political decisions; he has to follow orders.' He
added, more cheerfully, 'I'm an optimist, and don't believe there's any
place in Europe where armies will have to make this sort of decision
again.'

'But hasn't unquestioning obedience led to some really appalling
crimes? My Lai, the Holocaust . . .?' I asked.

'There are specific laws for these situations. In your country some
personal dramatic decisions have to be made – Ulster, for example. I
don't think British soldiers like having to pacify a strike. It's very similar,
our soldiers have to follow orders. The army is a centralized institution
and one has to be loyal.'

'Loyal to whom? Country or government?'

'Country, of course.'

'So could there be a situation where loyalty to country might require a
decision to act against the government?'

'Oh, I don't think that could happen in this country,' he smiled.

It was time for us to go, but the junior officer was very anxious that we should understand what very good relations they had with their students. 'We know these rumours of negative selection, jokes that we're not capable of other work, that we would do anything to keep our cushy jobs and obstruct the boycott. It's not the case!' He looked very upset. 'Every teacher is evaluated for their intellect! Besides, I've been a student myself at this university for nine years. I understand students, I think like them.' At the end of every year they received flowers and a book dedicated to them from all the students – this years Miss Polonia herself had signed. 'We've seen the students have to make very dramatic choices, young ladies crying because of having to choose between loyalty to Solidarity and their private interest.' He shook his head regretfully. We were being escorted out past the picture of soldiers crouched behind camouflaged artillery, popping out of tanks, firing missiles and an incongruously placed poster advertising a 'Solidarity song book: Songs for Street and Home'. Both officers bowed, heels together, kissing my and Gosza's hands. Out in the courtyard Adam shook himself: 'Flowers! Miss Polonia! Don't they realize students want to pass their exams?'

## Wednesday 18 October

'Women' seems to be another of those currents rumbling under the surface. In fact, women have constitutional equality in Poland. But harsh economic conditions, a traditional approach to family life and a powerful Catholic Church combine to create a quite different reality. Most women do not choose whether to work or not: it is essential to generate enough income to support the family. Meanwhile, shopping, cleaning and childcare are still very much their responsibility. So 'emancipation' is equated with a doubly heavy workload and 'feminism' with a kind of foreign craziness, totally irrelevant to their situation. All the political structures – Communist Party, former opposition and now the new government – are predominantly male.

But recently things have begun to change. This spring the Church proposed that abortions, performed for any reason, should become a criminal offence, with both woman and doctor punishable with three years' imprisonment. Sex education is non-existent in schools (a reasonable textbook was recently withdrawn under pressure from the Church). Contraceptives are a scarce resource unless you have the hard currency to buy 'anti-baby' condoms at Pewex shops. Abortion is therefore seen as a necessary evil by many women, and it is the Church's initiative that appears to have kicked the beginnings of a women's movement into life. Two thousand people demonstrated in Warsaw in the spring, various women's self-defence leagues were established around the country, and although the proposal was shelved, the groups have continued to function.

The Warsaw Feminists have been in existence as a discussion and support group since 1980, but the abortion issue and the new political climate have made them decide to be more active. When I got there four women in their thirties were sitting round a table in a pleasant kitchen, looking and sounding very much like Western feminists: concerned whether to meet in the afternoon so that women with babies could come, or in the evening so that working women could. They were also planning a demonstration for 12 November. An American woman had rung and asked them to support the 'pro-choice' demonstration on the same date in Washington. The women saw this as a good opportunity to raise the abortion issue again, as they felt that the Church's proposal might well be revived by Catholic deputies in the new Parliament. They were a little anxious as they planned to picket the US embassy; no one had demonstrated outside these sacrosanct premises before.

They also planned to register as a legal association. This meant finding a treasurer. 'Not that we want a formal hierarchy or anything,' Ivanna explained, 'but we need a place where people can meet and we can keep materials accessible.' The group had other concerns: violence against women – 'There's no data, but we know it's an enormous problem just from considering the high rate of alcoholism in this country,' Jola said – and pornography: 'It suddenly seems fashionable to have lots of pictures of almost nude women all over the newspapers,' she added. Officially pornography is forbidden.

They were mostly professional women: a psychologist, a translator, university teachers. Jola echoed Gosia's view that working women didn't see themselves as particularly exploited: 'They have often organized together, but paradoxically, it sometimes appears to be in support of their own exploitation.' She told me about women working night shifts at Warsaw steel works. This is illegal under international regulations. The management decided to move them to day work. The women organized a protest, pointing out that while they were paid less than men doing night work, they were paid more than women on day shifts. The hours gave them a chance to be with their children and besides, 'they had worked the shifts for so long that they didn't need much sleep'.

## Saturday 4 November: Poznan

Today I participated in a 'historical event'. This was how Elzbieta's friend Basia described Poland's first national feminist conference. The Poznan Women's Club had invited women's groups from all over the country to get together and share ideas. Basia, who found Poland so sexist she had moved to Amsterdam, had returned especially for the occasion.

Three men and about fifty women, mostly professionals in their twenties and thirties, had gathered in a small seminar room. The men were a surprise to me; also to Basia. 'How can a feminist group be 30 per cent men?' she asked as a stocky man from an organization called 'Profemina' introduced himself as their representative.

'We don't use the word feminism,' a woman from the same group replied. 'Our priority is to fight for women's right to conscious motherhood.'

'You implied in the article you wrote in *Polityka* that you were only a women's group,' a journalist from Krakow said sharply. 'You should have made it clear.'

'And what has anticlericalism got to do with feminism?' a dark-haired woman asked a smartly dressed, moustached man from the 'Anticlericalist League'.

'We're against the Church hierarchy – you should support an anti-Church movement because there are quite a number of national organizations forming now that will organize against you,' he replied. He had an aggressive manner that contrasted with the women's more tentative approach. Having, along with the other men, placed himself squarely at the front, he now had to turn awkwardly to speak to the women behind him.

'But we want to go in quite a different direction; we want the Pope to be our friend,' the woman said.

'We're not against religion, we're trying to interfere inside the Church,' he replied.

'Sounds like the Ministry of the Interior to me. It's up to the Church to decide its own way of organizing,' another woman said.

The discussion moved on to other familiar topics: whether to organize a women's political party or not: yes, 'because we want influence'; no, 'because we don't want either sex ruling the other', 'our main concern is to raise consciousness, we need a socialist movement, not a party'; whether to work separately from men or not: no, 'because issues like ecology affect us all, we need to change men'; yes, 'because working separately is the only situation in which we can understand the stereotypes that oppress us'; how to propagate 'another model for women's lives apart from that available in traditional Polish family life'.

At lunch time two women from 'the Women's League' arrived, saying that a radio announcer that morning had expressed anxiety at the conference 'degenerating into gossip'. It showed no danger of doing so. There were talks on patriarchy, pacifism, the silence about women in Polish history and philosophy.

By tea time, however, the man from Profemina was feeling frustrated. First of all, he felt he had not had as much time to discuss his views as women; secondly, women were being very impractical, failing to discuss 'concrete proposals' like 'bulletins', 'campaigns'. 'Don't treat us instrumentally,' Elzbieta responded. 'First, we simply want to find out how each of us feels about things.' She wanted to know about 'the Women's League'. Gosia in Gdansk had also expressed anxiety about the women's League, organized by the Communist Party after World War II 'in order to appear progressive': 'They had no independent political influence at all. Their main activity was to organize excursions to places where one could buy otherwise unavailable consumer goods.' Gosia was concerned that, recognizing women as a political force, they would make use of this to revitalize their own organization. Profemina, for example, was heavily influenced by the Women's League. 'Women don't understand that Profemina is not an authentic women's organization at all: men take all the decisions.'

Now Elzbieta was asking: 'Are you here just looking for support for the Women's League, or are you reforming yourselves?'

'We want to take the Women's League where it has never gone before,' a blonde woman said, sounding rather like Captain Kirk on the *Starship Enterprise*. They were reforming themselves; of course it would be easier if more feminists came into the organization. Moreover, in the struggle to protect a woman's right to abortion, unity was needed. Darek, one of the men, agreed: 'We should ignore our differences and work on this urgent issue together.'

'It might be politically necessary,' Suzanna from PPS-RD[1] argued. 'This feminist association is very elitist and the Women's League has a representative in every factory. They could activate working women.'

'Could they,' said a woman called Magda, 'after forty years of doing nothing? Who will listen?'

'I don't want to collaborate with an organization with which I have only one point in common,' said Elzbieta.

The Women's League woman shifted her ground. 'We're not so much feminists – we have a Christian approach,' she said, somewhat surprisingly. 'Most Polish women go to church and won't enter a feminist movement.'

'It's not a question of making all women "active feminists" but of making sure they have the right to choose their own way of life,' another woman replied.

At this point positions became rather confused. Darek and the man from the Anticlericalist League pointed out that the Church was 'a military organization that required a militant struggle to combat it'. Elzbieta responded that while she had problems with the Church, she was a Christian and she thought Darek sounded like a Stalinist: 'It's utterly mistaken to attack it this way.'

'The Church is a political institution that needs to be dealt with politically,' said Suzanna firmly.

'But you can't ignore the fact that it provides a social and moral context for people's lives, particularly Polish women,' responded Elzbieta, sounding suddenly rather like the women from the Women's League.

'Enough!' Basia called. 'Time to go.' The man from the anticlericalist group wasn't happy; he wanted the last word: 'You feminists will never succeed in Poland if you don't join us! Why? Because you are against patriarchy, that is your problem.'

Western stereotypes simply do not apply in Poland – not just because words like left, right, socialist, feminist, Catholic don't match their Western counterparts, but because they don't describe unitary phenomena. It's hard, for example, as a woman to get to grips with a Church that seems both to liberate and to oppress: on the one hand providing essential physical and intellectual space for the opposition in its buildings and publications, supporting pacifists, reaching out in dialogue to the Jews; and on the other also appearing to support militant, nationalist, sometimes racist thinking. On the abortion issue it has made things very simple – it is not a question of a woman's right to make autonomous decisions regarding her body; the fetus is a human being from the word go. Abortion is murder, full stop. I have Catholic, pacifist friends in Torun WiP who with logical consistency combine campaigns against abortion with those against militarism and violence. They also believe that 'tolerance is the foundation of a free people' and therefore quite happily coexist in a network with 'pro-abortion' activists.

When we got home, exhausted, Elzbieta turned on the radio: 200,000 people demonstrating in the GDR. The biggest demonstration so far, demanding free elections and better travel laws. There is a Polish–Czech solidarity meeting in Wrocław and thousands of Czechs have been stopped trying to cross the border to attend. Thousands have also succeeded – by travelling to Poland through East Germany. The Czech embassy has denied any knowledge of events at the Polish border.

The radio went on to report the break-in to the PPS (Polish Socialist Party) flat in Wspolna. Suzanna had told us that morning that on Friday

evening, after the Zarnowiec demonstration, a group of men with sticks
had beaten up two women who opened the door to them. One was still
in hospital. Staszek and others from Krakow WiP ran after the attackers
and caught two of them. The radio was now reporting that these were
both seventeen years old and from 'good' schools. They told the police
that they had gone to that flat because 'they had heard Communists
were there'. The police are investigating. 'Welcome to democratic
politics,' Suzanna had said that morning. Elzbieta was pacing around the
room. 'Sometimes,' she said 'I just can't stand facing this "very historical
moment in Poland". I'm fed up with it. I would like to live in a boring
country where the radio talks about boring problems!'

## Sunday 5 November: Wrocław

Elzbieta was not so fed up with historical moments that she didn't want
us to get a 5.30 a.m. train to Wrocław to meet the Czechs and go to a
seminar, 'Central Europe in Tumult: between Totalitarianism and
Commercialism'.

'You missed the best bit!' Jan Kavan (from Palach Press in London)
told me when we arrived. He was almost dancing on the spot with glee.
'Just incredible, Krýl and Hutka playing in the Teatr Polski, six
thousand young Czechs shouting "Long live Havel", they wouldn't let
him stop. I thought they were going to march out of the theatre and start
the revolution immediately in Wrocław.'

In the lecture theatre, the Czechs, serious young people in denims
and leather jackets, were listening to Ivan Svitak discussing the problems
of a Common European Home. 'Are we going to have a closed elitist
society? What about Bulgarians, Estonians, Lithuanians, Ukranians?
What about "Gastarbeiter"? The Communists screened people
according to class origin. Will we do it according to geography?'
Another historian stressed the problems of difficulties between peoples:
the Polish–Hungarian co-operation against Czechoslovakia before the
war; Polish–Lithuanian, Hungarian–Romanian antagonisms. Jiri Pelikan
suggested that 'each nation should build its own house first and perhaps
look later for the common roof', and also emphasized the need not to
forget social justice: 'Many Poles are crossing the Czech border to buy
the bread and butter which Polish democracy does not guarantee them.'

It felt a little different from the previous day, sitting in a beautiful
baroque hall with the plaster forms of a variety of philosophers staring
down at us. Whatever else happens, it is clear that our future 'Common
European Home' will be run by men, at least at the outset. I listened to a

moving letter from the Czech philosopher Šimečka saying his utopia was quite modest: 'not a market economy, but just the ability to attend a meeting with friends without wondering how many policemen are around, or to be able to take a slow, second-class train to Wrocław'. Then I walked around in the cobbled streets, watched Czechs queuing to get into a small second-hand bookshop, bumped into Radek, who was bubbling over at having a new daughter, in perfect health; and came back into the lobby, where Adam Michnik was having an emotional argument with a Russian who wanted Christianity and to hang all the Communists.

'The only way to democracy is compromise; look at Spain,' Adam Michnik said.

'I would put their names in the paper, announce their guilt, try to pay back the humiliation they caused. It's not a question of those who win against those who lose. Did Nuremberg stop anyone?'

He took up the theme again that evening in a final speech: 'When I hear the call for another Nuremberg process, I warn you, from the perspective of a man who has been a prisoner. Those who know the taste of prison bread and have heard the voice of a prison officer don't wish the same on anyone, even their enemies.' And he went on to speak to the Czechs about Poland's part in the 1968 invasion: 'I must say that we are guilty, and we should not try to find historical justifications for our presence in the guilt. I repeat once again what we have been repeating since 1968. Yes, we are guilty, and we are very sorry.'

'We are a frustrated country,' a Czech man said at the press conference. 'We have the strongest democratic tradition and now we are the last to change. We have no tradition of open revolt, but we would make the most of democracy if we had it.' On the train back to Warsaw I asked Jan Kavan what he would do if the situation changed. 'Give me twenty minutes to pack my bags,' he replied.

## Tuesday 7 November: Warsaw

Kostek Gebert is back from the 'What's Left' conference in Florence. He tells me he handed round a questionnaire: 'Socialism is a Bloody Waste of Time: Agree, Disagree?' All the East Europeans – Miklos Haraszti from Budapest, T. Kostek, Pavel Bratinka from Czechoslovakia – except Boris Kagarlitsky from the Soviet Union agreed. All the Western Leftists disagreed. Kostek thinks Poland is heading towards social revolt. 'People feel betrayed. What started as a movement of ten million people ended as a compromise between elites. The choice was to negotiate with illegitimate authority or sit it out, hoping that authority would be swept away by the winds of history. The Solidarity leadership didn't want that because of the side-effects. Surprisingly, so far, negotiation has worked – I don't think it can in the long run. A substantial part of the population is not going to continue to accept a contract made up in their name but behind their backs. They wanted a free country; what they got is free prices,' he said, quoting one of his own articles.

He saw the root of the problem as the nomenklatura: 'It's a criminal Mafia, who are actively working to destroy this country. A free market makes no sense unless their backbone is broken, nor will this government get real political support. The demise of the nomenklatura means the demise of Communism.' He didn't feel the government were doing enough: 'Their power base is at local level. The central nomenklatura is competent and secure, but locally it's corrupt and inefficient. They could be sacked overnight.' The solution was to have proper local elections as soon as possible. Then 'give the local authorities final say in the authorization of private enterprise, allow them to clamp down on ecological problems, give them control of the local police (who still regularly beat people up); and the situation would change overnight, without spending a cent or involving the IMF.'

It was rather similar to what Leszek Budrewicz, chief information officer for Solidarity trade union in Wrocław, had been saying to me two days earlier. He too felt that people needed something more concrete than just being told the economic changes were necessary. 'They can't keep repeating "it will get better" when for 30 per cent, mostly young people, it's going to be a catastrophe. Kuron [Minister for Labour] offering free soup makes people laugh. We know the economic situation is terrible, but if you can't give bread, at least show people that something has really changed.' Leszek's solutions were: don't have [Prime Minister] Mazowiecki on TV looking just like the Communists, shaking people's hands, flowers from children and so on – have him arguing, discussing things; don't put privatized industry straight into the hands of the nomenklatura just because they have money and it avoids conflict; and have the local elections in spring, not autumn as Lech Wałęsa was suggesting.

'They couldn't reach agreement on this issue at the Round Table and the question now is: Where is the greatest danger?' Kostek continued. 'Do you compromise with the Communists on this to get other reforms, provoke a few idiots in Krakow and hope people's endurance holds out? Or do you tackle the Communists head-on like John Wayne? In my opinion the first option is bullshit. The second' – he shrugged – 'the Peasants and Democrats could obstruct and bring the government down – so we would have open conflict and polarization on both sides. But if we are going to have a social explosion anyway – the question is: Which side of the barricades do we want to be on?'

Kostek, as David Warzawski, was instrumental in KOS (an underground opposition network called the Committee for Social Resistance) opening up a dialogue with the Western peace movement, in particular END, in the early eighties. Strange to sit talking with someone to whom you have been writing anonymously for years.


## Wednesday 6 December: Warsaw

I succeeded in thoroughly irritating Adam Michnik this morning by putting to him the accusations of the 'Left' and the 'Right' that the current parliament was an 'alliance between the red and the pink', and that parts of the OKP[2] were 'elitist' and determined to hang on to their monopoly of power.

'Idiotic! In every country you have people with crazy ideas.' He made a twisting gesture with his hand. 'Unfortunately, Poland is not free of them. Everyone now has far more opportunity to organize than before the Round Table.' We were sitting in Adam's tiny room at *Gazeta*, with its window on to the chaos in the outer office. Our chairs were crammed between three desks and a table. Adam had chosen the time, but he was combining it with reading three newspapers.

'The government has been confirmed by the majority of society,' he continued. 'It is not simply an anti-Communist vote. If they had wanted other candidates or parties like Moczulski, they would have voted for them. There is a "national consensus" at the moment, bearing no resemblance to the "consensus" described by Macierewicz. *Gazeta* published an opinion poll yesterday showing that "us" is now "Government, Sejm, Senate, Church, Solidarity", while "them" is "PZPR, ZEL, SD OPZZ, police and army"[3] ("TV is somewhere in the middle"). At the beginning of the year, "us" was just Church and Solidarity.' So this would appear to bear Adam out. And yes, the consensus was 'healthy' and 'necessary' in a country 'building democracy'.

'The longer it exists, the longer chance we have to move into democracy without civil war.... In my view the pre-war structure of multiparties will not be rebuilt in Poland now. The parties that are going to occupy the political scene will be those founded and grown from the new reality.... A new form will emerge from all the structures that are organically constructed in the body of Polish society – Solidarity is such a movement.' The problem was that while the 'social base' for such a movement existed, it had not yet apparently 'gained an awareness of its power'. He saw the citizens' committees as the basis of this new 'movement' – not party – 'It's a dirty word in Poland and we are trying to avoid the social trauma connected with it.' If people in the committees didn't like the idea, they could leave and form their own parties. No one prevented them.

It all sounded very reasonable. The problem for me is that it would seem a great deal easier to get political support for an idea that already has a power base – in established structures like the trade-union and local citizens' committees and in a friendly press – than for one that must start from scratch, just as the only parliamentary candidates freely elected were those endorsed by Lech Wałęsa. Of course, one could argue that the Solidarity movement *earned* that power base through its own courageous struggle in far harder times. But the real test of a group's commitment to democracy must be its ability, once in power, to share resources that give access to power – like funds and media space.

'Anyone who wants to can found a newspaper,' said Adam, but he did not have to finance his own; while a Green Federation friend told me he would love to start one, but simply didn't have the means.

'Why was *Gazeta Wyborcza*'s column for differing opinions abandoned?' I asked.

'It stopped being interesting. How often can one read about Soviet tanks being based in Poland, about Jewish masons and economists being responsible for all our problems, or that our paper is anti-Christian and anti-Church? Actually I think we should reintroduce it, but I don't have a clear editorial idea.'

'And what about social movements? Do they contribute to democracy?'

'They have some positive tendencies, but they can be very destabilizing.' At this point we were interrupted by Helena and a small entourage carrying documents relating to the breakdown of some relationship with the Italians. A lot of people in the office were talking at once. Adam leapt to his feet, waving his arms, shouting. However, he knew someone, who knew someone, and it would all be sorted out.

We offered to go, but Adam wanted to finish his point about social movements: 'For example, this mess about the Lenin monument was very negative.' (The statue of Lenin in Nowa Huta, Krakow, had been set on fire by a crowd of demonstrators on the day before Mazowiecki's visit to the Soviet Union. Debby had told us that the Soviet ambassador was *very* upset. The protests were still rumbling on.)

'Is that just because it was a violent protest?' I asked.

'No, if the government is legal you must act legally,' Adam insisted. 'If it is regarded as illegal by society, then all kinds of protests are justifiable. You cannot demonstrate against Pinochet and Allende in Chile in the same way. We have a government based on social agreement, and there are legal ways available.'

'But non-violent civil disobedience is sometimes the only way a minority can express its view even in a democratic society.'

'And what are the limits of the anarchization of society?' He jabbed his finger at me. 'Supposing you want an abortion; that is your legal right, and you come to the hospital and it is occupied by women from the Catholic anti-abortion movement? What then? Hm? What will you do? What are the limits of protest?' He nodded triumphantly and, after kissing my hand and smiling charmingly, rushed off to deal with the Italians, so I had no chance to reply that my limits were the use of violence. That in my experience, when minorities had strongly held views that were outside the social consensus, expressed in a country's legal statutes, they didn't usually choose between 'action' and 'restraint' but between 'non-violent and 'violent' action. I would rather those against abortion choose non-violent occupation than hate mail and death threats; and I would prefer fascists to sit down in the street to burning down synagogues. The former actions offer the possibility of dialogue; the latter maim and destroy – that is what counts.

Non-violent action still seems to be toppling heads of state. Today is Wednesday: it must be East Germany – Krenz has resigned first as Party leader, now as head of state. Too many booing crowds. Honecker is under house arrest for corruption and the Czechs are threatening another general strike if more suitable candidates are not proposed for the new government. Unlike the Poles, they are not going to accept a Communist Minister of the Interior or Defence. It's extraordinary how the time frame for change speeds up in each country....

## Notes

1. Polish Socialist Party – Democratic Revolution: a splinter group from the Polish Socialist Party.

2. The OKP is the Citizens' Parliamentary Club. It consists of MPs and Senators elected from the Solidarity list in the June 1989 elections.

3. PZPR: Polish United Workers Party (PUWP), headed by General Jaruzelski; ZSL: United Peasant Party; SD: Democratic Party; OPZZ: official trade unions.

# 9

# The Lessons of 1989: An Exchange between Anthony Barnett, Timothy Garton Ash, Neal Ascherson and Barbara Einhorn

*Anthony Barnett:*

## EASTERN PROMISE

It is important not to be naive. The world is still full of brutality and oppression. Its power structures feed the rich and destroy the planet. The simplicities of Manichaean class politics may be behind us, but the jealous priority of existing privilege retains its grip. It would rather destroy where it still can than allow us emancipation from its past.

None the less, something profoundly important has changed. After 4 June came 9 November. Tiananmen presumed the continuation of the Cold War. Instead, the Cold War is over. Even the liberation of Tibet is now conceivable. Alongside the determination to survive, there are at last grounds for hope. Political power is changing. For the first time, it seems to me, it is possible to be political and honest. That is, to be practical – to have a real rather than symbolic effect – without 'selling out'.

Today, power can be truthful and truth can be powerful. This is what has changed. Can be, not is. Obviously, I do not include the American presidency, while the Soviet presidency has existed for less than a month. But the impact of the green movement, once scorned for its naive, apolitical approach (and in a much smaller way that of Charter 88); and above all the success of Lech Wałęsa and Václav Havel in Eastern Europe, suggest a new possibility: the realization of democracy in ways that are more than the manipulations of public opinion through plebiscitory, opinion-poll elections.

Havel, as a spokesperson for Charter 77, was one of a group who wrote in support of Charter 88 when it was first published. When he was here, several of us went to the Czechoslovak embassy to present Charter 88 to him. The last time I had been there was in 1968 to shout my protest, outside in the road. Now it was still a protest, but one registered from inside. For me, this means that the successes of the East show that something has also changed here in the West.

But according to Tim Garton Ash, it has not. Garton Ash has taken on a near-official status as the Anglo-American interpreter of Eastern and Central Europe. He has just published a brilliant reportage on the revolutions of Eastern Europe (*We the People*) and at the end he asks: What can the East European 'enthusiasts bring to the new Europe?' His answer: 'If I am right in my basic analysis, they can offer no fundamentally new ideas on the big questions of politics, economics, law or international relations. The ideas whose time has come are old, familiar, *well-tested* ones.'

I have italicized the staggering complacency of Garton Ash's presumptions about the West. Perhaps it is related to the steady quality of his observations on the East. Beautifully recorded across the sweep of changes in very different countries, *We the People* is an outstanding act of political witness. It is also thoughtful. He sees how the one-part regimes of the Warsaw pact were, for all their declared 'internationalism', founded upon a bovine nationalism rather than a developed cooperation. This allows Garton Ash to defend the new regimes of Eastern Europe from the complacent charges so rapidly levelled against them in our media. The new governments in Prague, Warsaw and Bucharest are far more internationalist than their predecessors, even if the nationalism they do express is more open.

1989 may have been the Springtime of Nations, Garton Ash observes, but it was the springtime 'above all, of citizens'. In this way, he offers us the best characterization of the transformation he has observed so well. But what does it mean in his view? It means that the peoples of Eastern Europe 'have offered us, with a clarity and firmness born of bitter experience, a restatement of the value *of what we already have*, of old truths and *tested models*, of the three essentials of liberal democracy and of the European Community as the one and only, real, existing Common European Home.'

This is dangerous stuff. We are far from one reàl Europe. The EC itself is hideously undemocratic. NATO is a superpower construction that, thanks to Washington, will not commit itself to no first use of nuclear bombs. The rise in fundamentalism is in part a response to the violent exercise of Western supremacy in the Third World. In these circumstances, the way Garton Ash refers to but fails to write down the 'three essentials' is revealing. For if by this he means Liberty, Equality and Fraternity, who could write that we already have them? They may be old truths, but they are hardly existing, let alone *tested,* ones.

It is important to insist that the West's notion of 'normality' triumphed over the East wherever the separation of word and fact was absolute. The revolutions there – from above in Russia and from below in the countries once subservient to Moscow – have been, as Garton Ash says, revolutions of the truth. This is not simply a matter of people being able at last to say what they think, or to express their religious beliefs without fear, or even of their dropping the pretence of official lies. This is far too intellectual a view of truth.

Truth is also material. It is about being paid properly, shops with food in them: this also is a form of truth. Travel is another. What kind of self-development is possible if this is forbidden? Yet this is what happened to young people in Eastern Europe. Their countries were a prison. Both commodity and liberty, freedom to travel is a right to see for oneself; without which there cannot be truth. That is one reason why the destruction of the Wall was such a joy. It does not follow, however, that we in the West live in the best of all possible worlds: the appalling conclusion of Tim Garton Ash's valedictory column as foreign editor of the *Spectator*. Ironically, such an attitude preserves the example of Eastern Europe. To conclude, as Garton Ash does, that 'the combination of strong government with real democracy which is our system – with all its faults' is the best there can be, because the others that have been tried are worse, vindicates the West by contrast with the East. It therefore takes *that* unspeakable system as the base measure of our possible future. It builds Brezhnevism into our politics, not only to justify the denial of further improvements but also to defend existing privileges.

Under capitalism, and the political systems we have inherited, there remains a grave separation between truth and proclamation, between the announcement of our freedom and its reality. In London, Havel repeated the theme of his major presidential addresses. We have *all* been compromised by the past; we have all internationalized silences and dishonesties. Freedom is for others as well as ourselves, but it is hard to tolerate and difficult to carry out – especially in power. And the moment he feels that he must sacrifice his views for office, he will resign.

Here is an alternative 'conviction politics'. The first contrast is in the eyes. Thatcher's pulsate with will, refuse irony, vaporize dissent. Havel's swing away at the end of his sentences. He leaves those whom he addresses to make up their minds for themselves. In a famous aside, Thatcher admitted that she was in favour of consensus, provided that people agreed with her. Havel believes in people's right to diversity.

Garton Ash says that he senses, in his frequent trips across the

Continent, that the real divide is between those in the East who 'believe in Europe' and those in the West 'who have Europe'. We do not 'have Europe', Timothy. Together, East and West, we might. The basis for this achievement will be the classic traditions (including socialism) that have remained alive here in the West, but are now being spelled out with new clarity in the East. But the diversity, democracy, citizenship which this demands are from from achieved. The revolutions in the East challenge us to make good the promise of the liberty we have preserved. It will be hard to bring the 'old ideas' to life: for women as well as men; for the minorities without whom the economic machine of the EC would halt; and even for the nationalities, from Catalonia to Scotland, which are as yet unrepresented at Strasbourg or Brussels.

The 'springtime of citizenship' does not present us with an alternative model, a new utopia, or an opposition to Western power. That is true. They propose something more subversive: that the West should realize the values it proclaims. Charter 88 has begun to spell this out: a democratic second chamber, a constitution that safeguards and protects minorities, even a Bill of Rights. Sign it, Timothy Garton Ash: don't be a subject, be a citizen!

## *Neal Ascherson:*

# BIRDS OF AN EAST EUROPEAN FEATHER RISE ABOVE THE EARTHBOUND WEST

When the wind of history blows,
The people, like lovely birds,
Grow wings. Meanwhile, trousers
Flap round the ankles of nerds.

The eastward sky is full of lovely birds at the moment, veering and soaring and squawking in many tongues, as the nations of the Soviet empire ride the wind at last. Here in the West, however, there is a sound of trouser-flapping. The verse, which is my own awful translation from a ballad by Konstanty Ildefons Galczynski, is about earthbound people who cannot rise to an imaginative occasion: 'ugly birds who can't fly'.

There's no doubt about it: the Western response to the 1989 revolutions has been earthbound – partly because many people have got no further than 'what's in it for us?'

A tidal wave of cowboy investors, loan sharks, asset-strippers and carpetbaggers is already submerging what used, laughingly, to be called 'the socialized sector' of the East European economies. Another wave of grizzled old looters, their suitcases stuffed with fifty-year-old title deeds and share certificates, is about to surge over urban housing, country castles, nationalized factories and sequestrated estates.

But the response of Western thinkers has been a bit earthbound, too. Their first worry is that their own fixed ideas might be blown over by the great wind and chipped.

If the thinkers are in the conservative band of the spectrum, they generally agree with Mrs Thatcher that the East has rebelled in order to become part of the West; these nations bring no subversive or new ideas with them. If they are on the socialist sector of the horizon, however, the thinkers will argue that social democracy has actually been fortified rather than discredited by the revolutions and that President Havel is more at home with the signers of Charter 88 than with the diners of 10 Downing Street.

All this broke out in polemic the other day. Anthony Barnett, who is co-ordinator of Charter 88 and an associate editor of *New Statesman and Society,* had a go at Timothy Garton Ash. The target was Garton Ash's new book, *We the People: the Revolution of '89.* The book is shrewd and vivid, and Barnett praised it as 'an outstanding act of political witness'.

But he was enraged by its final judgement: that the revolutions

offered no really new ideas but 'offered us ... a restatement of the value
of what we already have, of old truths and tested models, of the three
essentials of liberal democracy and the European Community as the one
and only real existing Common European Home'.

Barnett called this 'staggering complacency', and he belaboured
Garton Ash's 'appalling conclusion' that we in the West lived in the best
of all possible worlds. Each man, I don't doubt, finds the other
unbearably arrogant. But each, if he listened, could hear the trousers
flapping in the wind of history. This is an argument between Westerners,
while the birds whirl overhead.

For most of the last twenty years, most opposition groups in
Communist Europe struggled towards 'old truths and tested models'
visible in the West. Garton Ash lists their 'three essentials': multiparty
democracy, the rule of law, a social-market economy. And those groups
were accordingly dismayed by upsurges in the West which seemed to
challenge those models.

In the 1980s, Solidarity conspirators choked with disgust as Polish
television showed anti-Pershing demonstrations in Frankfurt. Today, I
am certain, dissidents in Tirana and Peking are writhing as their
television gloats over our poll-tax riots.

But this is simply the East's mistake about the West. Almost all
protests and challenges are part of the dynamic of those 'social-market
economics' which the East admires; very few of them these days
threaten the Western systems with a serious alternative. Here, I think, is
the error in Tim Garton Ash's one-dimensional, static view of the West,
which contrasts oddly with his understanding of historical process in the
East. He is aware of Polish and Czech readers and hesitates to betray
their dream.

And here there are echoes of another, older argument between
Westerners about how we should live up to the courage shown by
opposition movements in Communist countries as they battled for 'our'
ideals.

One side – the right-wing side – claimed that the only decent
response was to close ranks in the fight against Communism, to support
any increase in NATO weaponry, to renounce 'carping criticism' of
knights of Western civilization such as Ronald Reagan. But the other
side argued that the best service they could do for Charter 77 or
Solidarity or (earlier) the Soviet dissidents of the 1960s was to exercise
the liberties which those embattled democrats did not have. And that
meant contesting, protesting, demonstrating.

This was not a favour which East Europeans always appreciated. I
remember a young Polish woman who returned from Holland to visit
her parents in Warsaw after many years. On the first day, she criticized

American behaviour in Vietnam and was thrown out of the flat. There was no room for grey in those black-and-white decades. As Father Popieluszko used to put it: 'It's either the thousand-year-old Polish religion of love, or the alien Bolshevik doctrine of atheism and hate.'

But one of the reasons that there was no room for ideological grey was, precisely, the morally grey area in which most people lived. Communism was hated not least because it gave most of its subjects good reasons to hate themselves.

If that period is over, there's no time to lose in educating the publics of Czechoslovakia and Poland and Hungary and Romania: they have to study the gap between rhetoric and reality in our part of Europe, and they have to grasp – so that they can exploit it – the economic and political pluralism of the West.

They can hear that capitalism means one thing in London and quite another in Frankfurt, or that neo-fascism is thriving in France, or that Christian Democrats despise British Tories so much that they will hardly sit on the same benches.

And, after all, the East did bring new ideas. Back (one more time) to that precedent of the revolutions of 1848. Liberals in Britain saw the upheavals in Bohemia or Hungary, in Paris, Berlin and Vienna, as only a grasping for 'old truths and tested models' – in those days constitutionalism, press freedom, free trade, an extended franchise, and so forth.

But we, with hindsight, can see that the 1848 revolutions were also throwing new and untested ideas on to the shore of history: 'modern' nationalism based on race, a concept of dictatorial populism, an awareness that there was such a thing as an urban working class whose notion of justice might be quite unlike that of a patriotic lawyer or journalist.

So it is this time. The future is staring us in the face, if we could only see it. I think that 1989 caused a European mutation, introducing a new gene. It is carried by all these Forums, even though they will probably wither away in the next year or so. It is about self-managing societies, about the decline of state authority, about a new kind of power-sharing deal between the wealthy and the producers of wealth, about the rise of nationalities and the fall of nation-states.

That wind, even when the lovely birds have come to earth again, will blow our trousers out of shape.

# Timothy Garton Ash:

# TELL ME YOUR EUROPE AND I WILL TELL YOU WHERE YOU STAND

Returning from three weeks abroad in a continuous argument – an argument called Israel – I find that I have been attacked at home. The attack comes from Anthony Barnett in the *New Statesman and Society* and the polemic is so gentle, so courteous and thoughtful that in Israel it would certainly be taken for a eulogy. It calls for a response none the less, because the questions he raises are important.

Mr Barnett takes issue with the conclusions of my book, *We the People*, that the East European revolutions 'offer no fundamentally new ideas on the big questions of politics, economics, law or international relations', but rather 'restatement of the value of what we already have, of old truths and tested models, of the three essentials of liberal democracy and the European Community as the one and only, real, existing common European home'. This, says Mr Barnett, is 'dangerous stuff, because 'we are far from one real Europe', the EC is 'hideously undemocratic', NATO is a 'superpower construction' that will not renounce first use of nuclear weapons, and our own institutions are far less democratic than they should (and pretend) to be. My 'presumptions about the West' betray 'staggering complacency'.

There are two issues here. The first is whether there are in fact any major political ideas, structures, forms of leadership, action or association emerging from Eastern Europe that are so new and good that we should at least consider their possible applications in Western Europe or Europe as a whole. The second is our judgement of what we already have in Western Europe, and how that judgement is affected by the East European revolutions.

I have spent much of the last decade looking for new ideas, forms and examples in Eastern Europe. In the early 1980s I actually thought I had found a new ideological synthesis – yes, a third way – in the programme of Solidarity in Poland. It was therefore not from any ideological prejudice, and not with any *Schadenfreude*, that I came to the first conclusion Mr Barnett quotes. This conclusion is empirical, not ideological. It seems to me a fair generalization – and of course all generalization implies simplification – about what people have actually written, said and done in Eastern Europe over the last year. I would still very much like to find those new and desirable ideas, and look closely at all suggestions, but I must compare them with what I actually see on the ground.

Anthony Barnett writes that the impact of the green movement in the

West and 'above all the success of Lech Wałęsa and Václav Havel in Eastern Europe, suggest a new possibility: the realization of democracy in ways that are more then the manipulations of public opinion through plebiscitary, opinion-poll elections'. Mr Havel, he muses, 'suggests an alternative "conviction politics". The first contrast is in the eyes. Thatcher's pulsate with will, refuse irony, vaporize dissent. Havel's swing away at the end of sentences. He leave those whom he addresses to make up their minds for themselves.' Now whatever your opinion of Mrs Thatcher's eyes, this is hardly the stuff of a serious argument. As for Lech Wałęsa, I would like to supply Mr Barnett with a small anthology of Mr Wałęsa's comments about democracy over the last few years. If he thinks Mrs Thatcher is authoritarian.... The serious issue, of course, is not the personalities but the systems in which they operate.

Writing in the *Independent on Sunday*, Neal Ascherson, who has been hunting the new in Eastern Europe for not just ten but more than thirty years, with marvellous eloquence and sensitivity, gently chides both Anthony Barnett and myself for being too earthbound in our responses to these revolutions. Then he takes off into the clouds: 1989, he says, 'caused a European mutation, introduced a new gene.... It is about self-managing societies, about the decline of state authority, about a new kind of power-sharing deal between the wealthy and the producers of wealth, about the rise of nationalities and the fall of nation-states.' In another article, in the *New York Review of Books*, he describes the Lithuanian Sajudis movement as a 'typical example of the new "forum politics" that has emerged in the 1989 revolutions: its commitments are to the market as a dimension of political liberty, to the revival of civil society and the shrinkage of state power, to a Europe of federated nationalities rather than nation-states'.

There are items on these lists that are so much of the clouds, cloudy, that they are hard to discuss (what on earth is this 'power-sharing deal', for example?); others are debatable (one might also describe what has happened in Eastern Europe as the *revival* of nation-states); but the most remarkable thing about most of them is just how familiar they are. The market as a dimension of political liberty? Rolling back the frontiers of the state? A Europe of federated nationalities? This is the central stuff of West European political debate over the last decade. That was precisely my point. The emphasis on the notion of civil society is, perhaps, distinctively East-Central European. But again, in *practice*, East European countries have a vast distance to travel before their civil societies will be as developed, or their state apparatuses as reduced, or, for that matter, their nationalities as federated, as they are in some West European countries – although, I hasten to add, not in all.

Yes, the sight of pinstriped know-alls fanning out across Eastern

Europe ('Our experience with privatization ...') is hard to take, especially since they *don't* know it all, because the problems of de-Sovietization are unique. For myself, I would much rather be among the doubting seekers who still feel there may be things to be learnt as well as taught. Indeed, I think there are: but not about how to run an economy or organize a polity. And I think to describe our democracy as 'manipulations of public opinion through plebiscitary, opinion-poll elections' is as wrong as it would be to paint it as the immaculate conception. One lesson Václav Havel does have to teach us is responsibility in the use of words.

Anthony Barnett goes on to suggest that, having supported Charter 77 and the cause of democracy in Czechoslovakia, I should now support Charter 88 in Britain. Curiously, I think he has a point, although it is not exactly the point he thinks he has. One effect of the end of the East–West political and ideological divide in the centre of Europe (an economic divide remains) is to make the smaller differences between West European countries seem relatively more important. Take away the Berlin Wall and you are left with the English Channel. Another effect is to reduce the distance between Left and Right. Perhaps contrary to first appearances, 1989 was not a triumph for the Right. It was a triumph for the liberal centre; if a liberal centre can enjoy anything so risqué as a triumph. It does not make things dramatically easier for Mrs Thatcher and dramatically more difficult for Mr Kinnock: rather, it sets new challenges for them both.

Those challenges are increasingly defined by, and in terms of, Europe. It is no accident at all that Michael Heseltine's book is called *The Challenge of Europe.* Tell me your Europe and I will tell you where you stand. Now if one looks closely at Charter 88 one finds that in its efficient rather than its dignified part, to use Bagehot's distinction, it is also very much about Europe – but not, as its name wrongly suggests, about Britain and Eastern Europe. Rather, about Britain and Western Europe. Indeed, it says: 'Today the British have fewer legal rights and less democracy than many other West Europeans.' And most of the things it specifically demands – a written constitution, proportional representation, more freedom of information, a different distribution of power between national, regional and local government – can be found in other West European democracies. (Of course one could make another list of things that we have, and they do not.) Historically speaking, Charter 88 is a most untypical document of the Left, because it refers only marginally to an idealized past, and hardly at all to a utopian future, but rather to real, existing alternatives: in fact, to those West European 'tested models', my reference to which provoked Anthony Barnett's indignation.

Since the refusal of proportional representation in Britain has denied a serious chance to the European alternative presented by Liberal or Social Democrats, one has to look for the European alternatives inside the Labour and Conservative parties. Increasingly, Conservative differences are expressed in terms of different visions of Europe. This is progress. If the Charter 88 ginger group can contribute even a little to a corresponding Europeanization of the Labour Party, it will have done the state – or should I say, society? – some service.

# Anthony Barnett:

## REPLY TO GARTON ASH

Timothy Garton Ash finds Charter 88 a strange kind of left-wing document. It is not left-wing at all; Britain is a right-wing country. I appreciate his perception of the Charter as effectively European. By the same token its radicalism stems from the backwardness of the 'United Kingdom of Great Britain and Northern Ireland'.

Likewise, Mr Garton Ash's response to my article in *New Statesman and Society* fails to see the main point. I agree that the transformation of Eastern Europe is due primarily to a series of citizens' revolutions: thus they do not present us with any alternative models. Instead, I argue, 'they propose something far more subversive: that the West should realize the values it proclaims'.

This is something Charter 88 calls for when it says: 'To make real the freedoms we once took for granted means for the first time to take them for ourselves.' Yes, we in the West, including *New Statesman and Society*, have the ideas. It is the fact that Mr Garton Ash perceives Western liberalism as being a reality, tried and tested, that I find staggeringly complacent.

Thus, in the month when it is revealed that half a million British a year are subjected to surveillance, when the poll tax becomes unsupportable and the Scottish convention is ignored, though it may prove the harbinger of Britain's Lithuania, Mr Garton Ash suggests that we have nothing to be taught 'about how to run an economy or organize a polity'. Try telling that to Cardboard City.

On one point I am corrected. I was wrong to place Lech Wałęsa alongside Václav Havel if the former's views are so anti-democratic as to make Mrs Thatcher's seem benign. I should have known better, and can plead only one extenuating circumstance.

Mr Garton Ash writes: 'I would like to supply Mr Barnett with a small anthology of Mr Wałęsa's comments about democracy over the last few years.'

But whom have I been reading on Poland over the last few years but Timothy Garton Ash. Why didn't he tell us long ago that Mr Wałęsa is such an appalling anti-democrat?

Or did I miss something?

# Neal Ascherson:

## TWO WINNERS FOR EACH LOSER IN EUROPE'S NEW PROMISED LANDS

I want to come back to this argument about what is happening in Europe after the revolutions of 1989: I mean the triangular argument between Timothy Garton Ash, Anthony Barnett of Charter 88 and myself. Our ball is still in the air, and today it's my turn to throw it.

This is what has been said so far. Summing up his book *We the People: the Revolution of '89,* Garton Ash said that the upheavals produced few new ideas but, instead, sought 'old truths and tested models' in the West: multiparty democracy, the rule of law, a social-market economy. Anthony Barnett attacked this view as complacent: the West, and the European community were much less democratic than they pretended. I suggested that the new democracy in the East mimicked neither traditional leftism or traditional rightism in the West, but might instead be generating a quite new political mutation. Last Thursday, in *The Independent,* Garton Ash retorted to both of us. He said, roughly, that Barnett was wildly exaggerating, and that if I could see something new and non-Western in 'forum politics', he could not.

But it's time to move the argument on. So far, it has been about what is on the surface. It has concerned itself with politics and personalities: what sort of President does Václav Havel make? Is the Romanian regime infected by the Ceausescu past? Can Sajudis in Lithuania hold together under Russian pressure? Is Leszek Balcerowicz, the Polish Finance Minister, a Thatcherite or a 'Kohlite' in his economics?

Now I want to ask a much more old-fashioned question about these liberated societies. Who is really doing what to whom? Who are the winners in Czechoslovakia or Poland, and what sort of people will the losers be? Tim Garton Ash writes that 1989 was not a triumph for the Right, but rather for the 'liberal centre'. If so, who is central in Hungary, and who is peripheral?

At one level, the 1989 revolutions were in everyone's interest (except for those of secret policemen and the thickest Party hacks). Freedom arrived: to travel, to read and write, to speak, to organize. Fear departed: fear of political vengeance, of informers, of police violence, and Soviet tanks. After that, though, interests begin to diverge. The real beneficiaries of 1989, in the medium to long term, are unmistakably the 'intelligentsia' in the broad sense of the word: the highly educated, the cultural and technical creators, the well qualified, the professionals.

The revolutions consist of two stages. First comes the securing of national independence and internal democracy; then the reform of the economy towards a market model which is decentralized and based on private property. As soon as this kind of reform became safe to discuss in private – which means almost thirty years ago – it became obvious to the first 'dissidents' that there would be losers as well as winners. In the late 1960s, before the Prague Spring, private discussions of economic reform centred on the need to substitute managers chosen for their expertise rather than for their Party loyalty. After that would come the break-up of central planning, and then the introduction of market forces into the 'socialized sector'. (Privatization, if not unthinkable, was still unmentionable in those days.)

This 'empowering of the qualified' was obviously going to help the whole of society. An economy run by trained experts with open minds would improve everyone's lives. At the same time, it was obvious who would get first gulp at the jam in the sandwich. The qualified, or the intelligentsia, would at last be able to use their own talents, would earn decent money, gain access to privileges, and begin to acquire political power. The philosopher Leszek Kolakowski in Poland had already shown that economic reform was impossible without freedom of speech and without an end to systematic lying about basic data. These hard-won crumbs of civil liberty, too, would first benefit those whose profession was communicating and imagining: the journalists, the writers, the film-makers.

And, of course, it was also seen that the working class might well be the losers – even if only temporarily. Reform would mean an end to primitive Communist equality. It would bring steep wage differentials, rewarding skill and penalizing its lack. It would close inefficient factories. It would set up great insecurity, as unwanted labour trekked around seeking new jobs. It would oblige workers to work. It would increase consumer prices – though back then the colossal push of liberated prices towards hyperinflation was not foreseen. It might (the voice would sink to a mutter) involve some unemployment.

Was this to be seen as a transfer of power from one class to another? Here, classic Marxist–Leninist terms didn't fit. The working class might be hurt by the process, but they plainly weren't in power anyway: they were the serfs of the political bureaucracy. Were the intellectuals and technocrats a class? They didn't fit the model of a 'bourgeoisie' with property, but neither were they a white-collar proletariat (that badge of rank so popular in the 1960s).

Yet the 1989 revolutions have enthroned a new social group, whatever name we give it. In 1980, it was a workers' movement – Solidarity – which broke through and gave European Communism a mortal wound: the Polish intellectuals were merely advisers to Lech Wałęsa's strike committee. But a few months later, as the trade union held its first regional elections, the manual workers (like the women) proved very reluctant to stand for office. They preferred to vote for schoolmasters, poets, professors. Today, the parliamentary party which has finally emerged from the union is overwhelmingly middle-class and learned. Poland's government is almost a Professorate.

At the moment, class or group interest is not dictating people's day-to-day political behaviour (with the exception of the peasantries). The Polish workers, bearing the brunt of a horribly painful reform programme, still back their Professorate. In most Eastern European countries, the ethic of social unity which arose in the revolutions is still dominant. But we can't expect that unity to last. It's fair to argue that the market economy will eventually make life better for most people – if it succeeds. But not for everybody. Hungary was already a 'two-thirds: one-third' society – a nation like our own in which two people do better but one person does distinctly worse – before 1989. Czechoslovakia will go the same way. Poland and Romania will be lucky to achieve as good a proportion of gainers to losers.

So, in the end, there comes the question of who will represent these losers – unskilled workers, small peasants, pensioners, the unemployed, the single parents, the poor in general. Once, socialism or social-democracy would have drawn them into its net, but that wing of politics has weakened to insignificance.

The prospect which I most fear is that the new poor will be target and constituency for something very different: the nationalist, populist, authoritarian Right. The 'liberal centre' of the new prosperity would be surrounded – besieged, even – by something which was not liberal at all. And the politics of hatred are also, unfortunately, a well-tested Western model.

## Barbara Einhorn:

## 'NEW ENEMY IMAGES FOR OLD': THE 'BOYS' DEBATE' AROUND TIMOTHY GARTON ASH'S *WE THE PEOPLE*

The 'peaceful revolutions' of autumn 1989 in East-Central Europe have precipitated confusion and self-doubt amongst Sovietologists and the Western Left alike. The total negation of all that the East European people have known for the last forty years was equated with a rejection of any form of socialist project; indeed, the term itself has been rendered unusable, at least for the moment. But this does not necessarily mean 'a restatement of what we already have' in terms of Western-style 'liberal democracy', as Timothy Garton Ash would have it. Rather, it implies a need for a total rethink not only of the way we talk about East-Central Europe but of the very concepts and even language we use to describe politics in both East and West.

The one point on which Garton Ash, Barnett and Ascherson all agree is that the politics we are now witnessing in East-Central Europe signify the end of the old Left *v.* Right style of politics. Anthony Barnett questions, however, whether this represents the triumph of 'liberal democracy', and Neal Ascherson suggests that the politics of East-Central Europe is an entirely new mutation, symbolized in the 'Round Tables' of the GDR, Poland and Czechoslovakia. In other words, what we are seeing is neither the mere negation of the Left's ideals along with the rejection of existing or state socialism nor a triumph for 'liberal democracy'. Rather, it is a rejection of Left and Right dogma in favour of a kind of issue-based consensus politics.

Garton Ash is at his best, as other reviewers have already pointed out, as a brilliant observer of the day-to-day, minute-by-minute events and decision-making processes of the remarkable revolution of autumn '89. His phrase about 'the flap of turning coats' ('turning necks' is the German term for them) is quite uniquely apt as a description of the shabby and at times pitiful personal manoeuvres as bureaucrats try to secure a new footing, and everyone seeks to justify their long-standing opposition credentials. In this context the centrality of language becomes very apparent, for it is in their vocabulary and their didactic style that the old guard betray themselves. Garton Ash is right on the mark when he speaks of the importance of words, describing the revolutions of '89 as a search for a new language. This is also why it is inappropriate to describe what is happening in terms of traditional Western categories.

Christa Wolf, the GDR author widely regarded as the best living author writing in the German language, has written repeatedly since the early 1980s about the devaluation of concepts such as 'democracy' and 'freedom' through their misuse by politicians and the media. She experienced a 'nausea' at words used to describe the arms race or nuclear power. She has written that the radioactive clouds of Chernobyl 'knocked the white cloud of poetry into the archives'. More recently, she felt inspired by the witty and inventive slogans on the posters of the Alexanderplatz demonstration of 4 November. Maybe language could be regenerated, could break the bonds of bureaucratized jargon; maybe 'the language of dreams' could be rediscovered through creative popular wit. Such is the pace of history that many in the GDR opposition already look back on the moment of hope in the autumn with nostalgia. They feel that the transition has gone too fast for there to be any chance of articulating the self-determination they had dreamt of for their society.

The need for a new language is more than ideological or idealist; it reflects the fact that reality itself has been turned on its head by the events of autumn '89. Before the Wall fell, rare plant and bird species thrived in the 'death strip'. Since it finally crumbled, the 'death strip' is being used as a cycle track, but will the plants and birds survive? Similarly, we find ourselves in a kind of no-man's-land, no longer the strip across which two superpowers confronted each other but symbolic of the historic moment between the way we used to talk about East-Central Europe and the need for a new language to conceptualize the changes.

Is Garton Ash right, for example, to assume that what East-Central Europeans mean by 'democracy' is the West European model of multiparty parliamentary democracy? This may be what many of them believe. But on the one hand there is genuine ignorance of what democracy means in practice in the West; and on the other, 'democracy' is not a unitary system. It has very different connotations across the British political spectrum, not to speak of what it means for West German Greens or Christian Democrats.

In the changing reality of East-Central Europe, contradictions and paradoxes abound. Only when doctors in East and West Berlin began holding joint seminars did one realize the full enormity of the fact that they had not been able to share research findings for almost thirty years. The Cold War border through the heart of this city had by force of circumstance become accepted as 'normal'. Now what was unthinkable becomes mind-bogglingly normal – crossing the Wall for a cup of coffee on the 'other side' with a GDR friend recently returned after being expelled to the West only two years ago for peace movement activism. Berlin is, after all, one city. Yet a short taxi ride across the city to

attend the first joint East–West Berlin lecture on women reveals
incomprehension and the lack of a common language, because life
experiences really did diverge.

While Garton Ash is an acute observer with considerable understanding of the people and the processes, he fails to acknowledge
sufficiently contradiction and difference in the new political structures.
In the GDR, for example, groups like New Forum, Democracy Now or
the Initiative for Peace and Human Rights, who initiated the 'autumn
revolution', far from being thrust into power like Civic Forum in
Czechoslovakia or even Solidarity in Poland, are having – with prominent exceptions in the persons of Foreign Minister Markus Meckel and
Defence and Disarmament Minister Rainer Eppelmann – to learn to live
with the fact that they will continue, in the radically altered new
circumstances, to form the opposition. Indeed, in the rush towards
unification they are rapidly becoming marginalized. Yet their understanding of democracy, arising out of their experience as opposition
social movements, is something we in the West could perhaps learn
from.

To some extent, Garton Ash's preoccupation with Western liberal
democracy arises from his focus on predominantly male opposition
intellectuals and on Solidarity, also a very male-dominated organization.
Indeed, all three men involved in this debate underestimate or ignore the
influence and role of women in the revolutions. Whilst it is true that this
role was considerably smaller in Czechoslovakia or Hungary than in the
GDR, this remains a glaring omission. Old men declaim and boys climb
statues in Garton Ash's Hungary; individual male personalities take
centre stage in his favourite theatrical metaphor. Women, however, have
purely walk-on parts.'Pretty girls' pant for Havel's autograph or bring
him another bottle of pink champagne. 'After a fortnight of revolution,
wives and children are complaining.' A female student makes an
incomprehensible speech in Prague (the only case where a woman
speaks at all); 'a girl' presents flowers to a sadly anachronistic female
singer.

Garton Ash's sparkling and sensuous account, which comes alive
precisely because of its anecdotal immediacy so that one is drawn into
and lives the tension and excitement of the smoke-filled atmosphere at
the Magic Lantern Theatre, sometimes tends to deteriorate in this
respect into an account of 'famous men I have rubbed shoulders with'.
There is token reference only to the leading role of women such as
Bärbel Bohley, Ulrike Poppe or Vera Wollenberger in the GDR peace
movement of the early 1980s and the opposition movement of autumn
'89.

Neal Ascherson does note that women stand to lose from the current changes; indeed, he highlights the issue of losers in a future 'two-thirds:one-third society'. For women the apparent openings of the autumn have already turned into new/old forms of closure. Abortion and reproductive rights are threatened by the Catholic Church in Hungary and Poland and the notorious paragraph 218 of the West German Constitution in the GDR; women are the first to be made redundant – after all, they are unreliable workers, taking extended maternity leave or sick leave to care for ill children; firms struggling to survive see the closure of crèches and nurseries as an obvious saving; or the state removes subsidies from childcare facilities, forcing women in Poland to give up their jobs for financial reasons.

The failure to perceive the role of women reflects a general inability on Garton Ash's part to acknowledge the role of new social movements in the 1980s, except for Solidarity. Undoubtedly the opposition figures of the 1970s pioneered the notion of 'civil society', and Solidarity pioneered the role of autonomous self-organized movements in opposition to oppressive governments. But outside Poland, it was in fact new social movements like women's, peace and green groups which translated this idea into reality. And whilst Garton Ash does acknowledge that non-violence was the autumn revolution's first principle, he fails to recognize that this principle emerged from the independent peace movements in those countries. Particularly influential groups in this respect were the Women for Peace in the GDR, themselves influenced by Greenham and other peace and women's movement groups in Western Europe, and the Independent Peace Association in Czechoslovakia, in which women also played a central role. Even in Poland, where the principle of non-violence was pioneered by Solidarity, it was the young peace movement Freedom and Peace which transformed the concept from a political tactic into a guiding principle.

For this reason, Anthony Barnett is right to point to the influence of the green movement. The most urgently pressing problem to emerge in many of these countries and written in as a priority to the political programmes of every party and opposition group in the GDR, for example, is the grave environmental damage perpetrated by the *ancien régime*, ranging from air and water pollution to dying forests and the decaying historical heritage in the form of dilapidated housing stock.

These new social movements had a threefold impact: they provided the individual actors of the autumn revolution, and were responsible for the non-violence of demonstrations and the non-hierarchical structures and direct political style of the Round Table discussions. This new political style, centring around the dissemination of new ideas as opposed to the wielding of power, is what is new about the revolutions of '89, what they have to offer us in the West.

It is in the area of issue-based politics – around women's or environmental issues – that the best counter to chauvinistic nationalist tendencies is to be found. As Chernobyl proved once and for all, Europe
has no boundaries: radioactive clouds pay no heed to Iron Curtains or to
any other divide. And on the positive side of the balance, there is a great
opportunity to build on the bloc-transcending work of the European
peace movement in demolishing enemy images throughout the 1980s,
work which was very influential for the 'peaceful revolutions' of autumn
'89.

All the same, it would be wrong to over-romanticize the new social
movements. Garton Ash portrays students on the Charles Bridge
waiting for the 'King of Bohemia', Havel. This is the politics of
adulation, of a passive population unused to wielding power and waiting
for the 'heroes of the revolution' to do it for them.

Another major problem is nationalism. Garton Ash draws on
Orwell's distinction between nationalism and patriotism, implying that
what we are observing is patriotism, legitimate love of one's country, as
opposed to nationalism, an exclusivist sense of identity. Understandably,
the fake, externally imposed international solidarity of state socialism
has given way to a legitimate drive for national (as opposed to regional)
self-determination. However, it is also the case that 'we the people'
turned out to be nationalistic in the sense of prejudiced and ready to
indulge in racial or ethnic hatred, and in some cases violence. In the GDR
there have been manifestations of anti-Semitism and violence against
visiting Vietnamese workers, as well as Polish street traders. In Poland,
there is hatred of the Germans and the Russians and black African
students are beaten up. Hungary has seen an attempt to confine gypsies
to a ghetto in Miskolc, and in Romania there is discrimination against
Hungarian and German minorities. The search for post-Cold War new
enemy images – which produces old and well-tested ones – is far
advanced.

It must also be a matter of concern that most of the new governments
in East-Central Europe are concerned with their relationship with
Western Europe to the exclusion of all other foreign relations. They are
preoccupied with the danger that they may become 'the Third World' in
Europe, and they vie with one another for admission not only to the EC
but to the perceived 'goodies' which West European economic models
have to offer. Garton Ash is right to observe that 'the free market is the
latest Central European utopia'.

What is strikingly absent from this new form of Cold War ideology –
that is, the continuation of an exclusive East–West focus (with some few
exceptions in the statements of the Greens, PDS, and New Forum in the
GDR, or Havel in Czechoslovakia) – is concern for the global impli-

cations of change in Eastern Europe: rather, there seems to be a generally accepted as well as generally unspoken assumption in those countries, that, for example, the inferior goods they produce which will not stand up to competition on the (West European) market, not least military arms, can be offloaded on to Soviet and Third World markets. This is already happening in the case of Polish textiles and shoes, and there will undoubtedly be more examples to follow. Countries in the 'two-thirds:one-third world' are rightly concerned that European Community aid might be diverted to restructuring East-Central European economies.

Hence I share Neal Ascherson's worry about those who lose out in the economic transformations of these societies falling prey to the 'politics of hatred', to 'the nationalist, populist, authoritarian Right'. This makes it all the more important for social movements in both East and West to join together in rethinking concepts like 'socialism' and 'democracy' in order to articulate a new internationalism, based on the need for globally socially just trade and economic policies, a demilitarized world, and a worldwide federation of decentralized civil societies – a kind of global 'democracy from below' on the well-tested model of the 'detente from below' practised throughout the 1980s across the Cold War divide in Europe by END.

# PART III

# Welcome to Europe

# 10

# Good Morning Europe!

## *Mient Jan Faber*

Security policies in the nineties will differ fundamentally from the policies of the Cold War. This may sound rather obvious, but the period of transition will not be easy, especially since many politicians prefer to work with institutions and categories inherited from the past. Both 'East' and 'West' – you see, even I make use of outdated categories – are used to a status quo based on nuclear deterrence; the two antagonists developed their respective security policies largely as each other's mirror-images. All their ideas and plans were carried out in the Cold War framework, the only one available. Now, in 1990, everything has changed. The Cold War is over. NATO and the Warsaw Treaty Organization (WTO), the main European political players for such a long period, are either in disarray (WTO) or faced with the necessity of developing new functions and corresponding strategies in order to survive (NATO). The European landscape can no longer be characterized as two blocs along with some neutral and non-aligned countries. Neutrality has lost its meaning anyhow, because it cannot exist without a policy of equidistance *vis-à-vis* two competing political entities.

Probably sooner rather than later, security policies in the nineties will be derived from the newly emerging power configuration in Europe. The common wisdom in the West is that NATO will remain, but in a different form: more political than military in its approach. The forward defence system, in which national units from several member states stood shoulder to shoulder defending the East–West demarcation line along the river Elbe, will be dismantled and replaced by multinational units and far fewer soldiers. In Western Europe the centre of gravity of security policy – and of military power as well – will steadily shift from the United States to the European pillar in NATO, which in the end is likely to turn out to be the European Community (EC).

Indeed, the EC will probably become the main actor in Europe, not only economically but also politically. In a rather traditional way we are going to witness the rise of a new superpower: economic integration joined by monetary integration and completed by political integration. Intensive discussions about the future role of the European Political Union (EPU) in security matters are taking place already. And consensus is growing: the EPU will indeed become the European pillar of a newly defined Atlantic Alliance (NATO +). Step by step the EPU will gain greater influence on security arrangements in Europe, in agreement with the USA and due to the decline of the Soviet Union. The end of the bloc system in Europe probably marks the beginning of a new era in which Europe will be dominated by a new power: no longer from 'over the ocean', but from within. 'Business' as usual.

There is a big difference, in terms of political power, between the EC and the former socialist countries, including the Soviet Union. The EC is the product of a historic process over more than forty years, which began with the introduction of the Marshall Plan that forced Western countries to co-operate. The former socialist countries in Central and Eastern Europe, on the other hand, have to start from scratch. One by one they liberate(d) themselves from the Leninist political system, and with more or less success they are now introducing a pluralist society with a market economy. Confronted with the enormous task of building up a completely new system – in social-political terms – one can hardly expect them to bother that much about security alliances. Their first concern is getting rid of the old one, WTO.

It is interesting, however, to note that the Czechoslovakian government in particular is spreading the idea of a pan-European security system, based on the Helsinki Accords of 1975. Also, the likely-to-be-short-lived GDR government is showing a lot of interest in this idea, as will become clear from the discussion I had with Defence Minister Rainer Eppelmann, which I describe later in this chapter. But can we really speak of a security system? Or are the ideas on a pan-European security system primarily an attempt to establish a new consultative mechanism in Europe? A framework in which the member states of the Helsinki Accords can meet regularly and develop particular instruments for the verification of arms agreements and the resolution of disputes? However useful such a system may be, a security system in Europe is quite a different thing: it involves the control of armed forces. Despite serious criticism of NATO – the massive rallies against the modernization of nuclear weapons in the first half of the eighties – modern post-war experiences did convince majorities in the Western world that a collective security system must be based on an integrated military structure. To return to a situation of national armies contradicts the process of voluntary integration in which Western Europe is currently engaged, and could re-create painful and harmful memories of the pre-war situations. The ultimate advantage of an integrated military structure is that national armies are chained and put under a common political authority; they are thus no longer able to move either forwards or backwards. In other words, such a structure creates a rather good system of international military stability among member states.

Of course the Soviet Union strongly advocates the idea that now, after the end of the Cold War, both NATO and the WTO have lost their original functions and should wither away side by side into a new pan-European *common security* system. The notion of common security also dates back to the beginning of the eighties, when it was promoted by the Palme commission, the West German SPD (Social Democrat Party) and the East German SED (Socialist Unity Party) i.e. the Communists. In reaction to 'the new Cold War' of that period, a security concept based on defensive military structures and an institutionalized dialogue between East and West was explored. Indeed, it was a useful and creative approach for re-establishing military and political detente. But the concept was a logical product of the ruling bi-polar system which today no longer exists. The original initiative for the CFE (Conventional Forces in Europe) talks constituted an explicit implementation of common security. In the meantime, the common security concept has tended to degenerate into a system of national security concepts. In the talks, the emphasis has shifted from a bloc-to-bloc approach to a policy that has become increasingly focused on the achievement of (upper) ceilings for national armies and foreign military presence. The Soviet fear of a strong reunified Germany dictated this emphasis, which clearly emerged from the so-called 'two-plus-four' negotiations. The difference between what was East and what was West is starkly evidenced by the fact that Germany will become a full member of NATO. The WTO will have to wither away all by itself, for obvious reasons: it is extremely difficult to find a modern rationale for an alliance so shaped by oppressive Soviet and Communist policies of the past. A more institutional Conference on Security and Co-operation in Europe (CSCE) could become a natural way for the East European countries to internationalize their own security concerns. For NATO countries, however, it is unlikely to be more than an additional body for international deliberations: definitely of some use, but equipped neither to replace nor to suspend NATO.

Nevertheless, this does not mean that everything remains the same and NATO can go about its business as usual. Politically speaking, NATO has to adjust its policies and strategies much more to the demands put forward by the rise of the EC as a new political and economic superpower than to the decline of the Soviet empire. NATO, at best, can help to manage the latter. In the final section, I will clarify this point. But first I would like to share with you the concerns and ideas of a personal friend of mine, Rainer Eppelmann, who became GDR Minister for Defence and Disarmament after the free elections of 18 March 1990. Of course, his world-view is determined by his (geographical) place in history and differs rather sharply from mine in some aspects. Even though I am very sympathetic towards his ideas, I am also sad to say that it seems rather unlikely that his utopian policies will be realized.

## Talking to Rainer Eppelmann

The last time I met Rainer Eppelmann was in 1982. Invited by the CDU-Ost, I spent a couple of days in the GDR. (The Christian Democratic Union, then a so-called bloc party subordinated to the Communist Party, is now by far the strongest party in the country.) On a sunny Sunday morning, after going to church, the Deputy Minister of Church Affairs [*Kirchenfragen*] Mr Kalb, received me in his house for a 'social' chat. While enjoying his coffee and cake, he took the opportunity to warn me about some 'figures' in the GDR who suffered strongly from a 'profile neurosis', as he put it, and would be better off in a psychiatric hospital. When I asked him whom he referred to, he mentioned the names of several of my personal friends, in particular Rainer Eppelmann, a pacifist priest from East Berlin. From that moment on, his coffee no longer tasted so good and I was quite relieved when I was able to leave his apartment a little later. Although the CDU people who accompanied me tried to control every step I took in Berlin, I succeeded in getting rid of them. So that afternoon I sat down with Rainer Eppelmann and we talked about the situation in the GDR, the churches, the peace movement, the arms race, the future of Europe, and so on. Later that evening, I went back to West Berlin. A few days later the GDR authorities made it clear that I had enjoyed my last visit to their country: they declared me to be one of their state enemies. For Rainer and myself this was an additional reason to sign a personal 'peace treaty' in which we promised each other we would continue to work together in solidarity for peace and justice.

In May 1990 we finally met again, this time at the guesthouse of the Ministry of Defence, some 40 kilometres outside Berlin. He introduced me to three high-ranking military officers, including Admiral Hoffmann, Eppelmann's predecessor and now 'merely' his Chief of Staff, his three state secretaries – all veterans of the East German peace movement –

and his speech writer and personal adviser, a teacher of philosophy and religious studies from Hanover. Although everything had changed, at the same time nothing had changed in the way Rainer Eppelmann behaved. In a strict but informal way he asked us to sit down and to start an open discussion about the future of Germany and about European security. And so we did. Old soldiers, stalwarts of the former regime and young ex-*Bausoldaten*, who had been harshly oppressed by the former regime, entered into a passionate debate, while Eppelmann informally presided over the two-hour session, occasionally jotting down an interesting new idea or perspective in a little notebook. He himself believes that the GDR will have a role to play in the security field as long as there is no comprehensive European security system. The GDR could become a kind of bridge between East and West, he argued. But how? I asked him. Isn't the GDR considered to be a lame duck, on the brink of absorption by West Germany? 'Even if the GDR has no juridical status, there will be a GDR for some time to come. The history, experience and political culture of the GDR will leave its stamp on the whole of Germany, and especially on the East German *Länder*,' Eppelmann answered. This may be true, but mainly in the socioeconomic field, because many East Germans are condemned to live in very poor conditions for many years to come. But Eppelmann insisted that the GDR's most important consideration should be not to let the unification of Germany exclude the Soviet Union from a future European security system. And Admiral Hoffmann added: 'My friends in the Soviet Union ask me, are you still friends with us? And I want to tell them, yes and you will get more friends.'

Okay, let us follow your point, I said. What kind of military-security options do you see for the GDR, in order to fulfil this bridging function? According to Eppelmann and his people, the problem comes down to what to do with the *Volksarmee*: 'The situation is that there are two armies, one in NATO and the other in the Warsaw Pact, while Germany is uniting politically.' They all agreed that absorption of the *Volksarmee* into NATO was unacceptable. The GDR might join NATO in a political sense, but could not join it in a military sense, for it had to satisfy Soviet security concerns. They outlined three possible options for the military status of the GDR:

1.  The *Bundeswehr* is part of NATO, the *Volksarmee* is neutral;

2.  There is one German army, belonging to both alliances, NATO and WTO;

3.  The *Bundeswehr* is in NATO and the *Volksarmee* is in the WTO.

Theoretically one can conceive of more options – for instance one army and a neutral Germany – but Eppelmann considered this impracticable: 'The three options mentioned are attempts to cater to the demands and expectations of everyone: the GDR, the FRG, the EC, and the Soviet Union. We have put them all into the melting pot.' He went on to say that each of the three options more or less provides for a bloc-free Germany – that is, a situation in which Germany agrees to all sorts of legally binding treaties with both NATO and WTO, thereby showing that it is willing to contribute to the creation of a pan-European security system.

Eppelmann himself favoured the first model – the *Bundeswehr* in NATO and a neutral *Volksarmee*: 'This is the most realistic approach.' But is it really a road to a European security system? I doubt it very much. Will it not be seen as a face-saving model for the Soviets, lasting only the few years in which the Soviet Union is expected to pull its troops out of the GDR?

It was quite remarkable to see how Rainer Eppelmann was trying to define new political concepts – in particular that of the GDR as a bridge – while at the same time doing his utmost to stick to Western approaches and to devalue proposals made by the Soviet Union but unacceptable to NATO. For instance, he rejected the idea of transforming both NATO and the WTO into purely political alliances, arguing that NATO might transform itself into a political alliance, while the WTO would dis-integrate even more rapidly: 'That means that there will be only one alli-ance which would have little interest in coming to an agreement with the Soviet Union in constructing an all-European security system. Moreover, several former members of WTO will rapidly move towards NATO.' But isn't this already a reality? The WTO is disintegrating and Hungary and Czechoslovakia are sending out signals which imply that they see their security future as being closely connected with the EC and NATO. 'Maybe we have to establish a kind of political brake,' responded Eppelmann. Asked whether he really meant to say that Germany had to sustain the ongoing existence of the WTO he nodded vaguely, as if he too felt that this was somewhat too much to demand.

A demilitarized Germany is also undesirable, in his view. It would mean an *Alleingang* (going-it-alone) policy for Germany: 'It would make Germany immensely powerful in Europe and the world, like Japan, because everyone else would be spending large amounts of money on armaments.' I could see his argument, but what is left if he, in line with NATO policies, rejects all proposals the Soviet Union has made so far? 'What about the idea of establishing multinational military units as nuclei of a future pan-European security system?' I asked. He wrote the idea down and a couple of weeks later he launched the proposal to establish multilaterals: Dutch, German, Polish, Soviet units and the like.

But Rainer Eppelmann is not only a Defence Minister, concerned with military configurations. He is probably first and foremost a Minister of Disarmament. With great excitement he outlined for me his utopian vision of a European security system: 'Military forces have been hugely thinned out and are purely defensive, for border control. There are no weapons of mass destruction. There is a machinery for the peaceful settlements of conflict. National conflicts – say between Hungary and Romania – would be settled by pistols, not machine guns. Social justice is an important factor for stability. And this is not only a domestic requirement, it is also true internationally. We need a huge transfer of resources from military spending to aid for the Third World.' I fully agree with him. But how do we develop instruments to achieve these goals?

## To Wake Up as a Superpower

Watching television on 9 November 1989, I hardly realized that it had anything to do with me. The Berlin Wall was torn down and masses of exhilarated people crossed the inner German border, many for the first time in their lives. From now on the East–West stalemate belonged to the past. Many of my 'dissident' friends appeared on TV, celebrating freedom and democracy. And I knew that it would be only a short time before Czechoslovakia, Romania, Bulgaria and even the Soviet Union would join them on the road so well prepared by the peaceful changes in Poland and Hungary.

Waking up the next day, I felt rather uneasy. Where did I live now? The liberation of Eastern Europe would have tremendous consequences, not only for the East Europeans but for us in the West as well. The disappearance of the Eastern-bloc also implies the dissolution of the bloc system as such: simply because it takes two to tango. The philosophy of nuclear deterrence with which I had grown up had suddenly become obsolete. Indeed it has no sense without an enemy right around the corner. The influence of the two great powers which have dominated Europe for so long will diminish, partly because of the ongoing decline of the Soviet Union but also because a united Germany will regain its full sovereignty. The war and post-war agreements concerning Germany between the four occupying powers – the USA, the Soviet Union, France and Britain – are coming to an end. And I slowly became aware of the need to think about the new situation in which I find myself.

What should we think about NATO? Since the mid seventies I have strongly criticized the nuclear policies of the Alliance, because of its growing emphasis on nuclear warfighting capabilities and strategies and its unwillingness to consider seriously the alternative of a nuclear-free world. But warfighting capabilities and bloc confrontation were inseparable; therefore battlefield nuclear weapons are likely to be removed from Europe in the next – say – three years. Parallel to this development, the nuclear vocabulary will change too. Deterrence has lost its meaning and instead, I bet we will talk of 'dissuasion' in the near future. The French nuclear philosophy will probably become commonplace in Europe. A troublesome idea, since the anti-nuclear campaign that ploughed Europe deeply in the eighties had virtually no impact in France.

NATO is looking good these days. People are rereading the founding treaty, which was signed on 4 April 1949. And indeed it is difficult to formulate a treaty which would better fit our security feelings in Europe in 1990. Relieved of its negative record as one of the main upholders of the Cold War incapable of contributing to substantial changes in Europe, NATO can start a second life now with a bright outlook. Of course it will have to change its appearance. There is no place for a flexible-response strategy, based on an escalation ladder ranging from conventional conflict to all-out nuclear war. The forward defence posture no longer makes sense because there is no direct threat, since our former enemies have either become friends or at least good neighbours.

But an even more challenging question is: 'Why not invite other European countries to join NATO?' The Czechoslovakian Foreign Minister, Jiři Dienstbier, would probably accept the invitation immediately. Asked what he thought about NATO, he answered, 'I only have one objection. We are not a member.' Nevertheless, I think he will have to wait for some time before he finds an invitation in his letter box. Nobody in NATO is considering this possibility seriously; there are only some academic discussions around it. But the Soviet Union is the stumbling block. Indeed, assume that Hungary, Poland and Czechoslovakia apply for NATO membership and that NATO would welcome these countries – then what should be done with an application from the Soviet Union?

The EC is in a somewhat different position, engaged in a process of establishing a new political and democratic entity in Europe, a federation of states. As long as the EC sticks to that goal and really strives for more than the creation of a free-trade zone or a 'European Economic Space' – as it is called today – then the size of such a Community or Federation forms a serious restriction. Indeed, it is quite impossible to envisage a situation where the United States of America or the Union of Soviet Republics is a member of such a European Community as well.

In my view, NATO's future is inseparably connected with the developments in the EC. The present debate in and about the Community can be
described as a fight between 'broadeners' and 'deepeners'. Great Britain
in particular is in favour of a Community which is merely a free-trade
zone and, moreover, pursues an open-door policy towards the countries
of Eastern Europe. After a period of adjustment, those countries can
become full members of the EC. On the other hand, the FRG advocates a
deepening of the internal structures of the Community. The Germans
claim that only a strong European Political Union is able to develop a
constructive and promising policy towards the East. They do not,
however, exclude the possibility that in the long run some countries from
Eastern Europe could join the EC. The French position is rather
dubious, as usual. Although France supports the idea of establishing an
EPU as soon as possible, it does not want to give up much of its own
sovereignty. So for France, the EPU has to become an intergovernmental
body, not a supranational entity.

The final outcome of this debate will also decide the future structure
of NATO. If the EC focuses its activities on the creation of an (all-)
'European Economic Space' while sticking to its intergovernmental
features (the British–French option), then, as in the case of Spain,
Hungary, Czechoslovakia and other East European countries may
combine an application for membership to the EC with one for NATO. Of
course, in such a situation membership of NATO is unlikely to entail
substantial military integration, since there is no rationale for this.
Nevertheless one can envisage a situation where some countries co-
operate more closely together in the military field. Common exercises,
the formation of multinational units, the location of foreign troops, and
so on, could still take place as almost autonomous phenomena. Even
where a country – say the Soviet Union – is not prepared or is unable to
join the EC, it can apply for NATO membership. There are, after all,
several other NATO members who do not belong to the EC: Norway,
Iceland, Turkey, Canada and, last but not least, the USA. Now assume
that the WTO is dissolved and Hungary, Poland and Czechoslovakia are
accepted as EC and NATO members – is there any substantial argument
left to refuse a request for membership of the (democratic) Soviet
Union? So this approach – broadening NATO – could even provide the
basis for a pan-European security system! In the end, however, such a
system would be much more than a piece of paper, at least in a military
sense. Of course, it has some political value.

Suppose that the 'deepeners' (the German–French option) win the
debate in the EC, and the EC emerges as a supranational authority,
ideally also involving the further development of democratic rules and
procedures. Then is it likely that the Community (Federation) will begin

to define a defence and security policy. In such a situation, several NATO structures (minus the Americans) might be relegated to the authority of a newly created EC institution. The multinational military units, for instance, can become nuclei of an EC army. Helmut Kohl has stated many times that the Franco–German Brigade, which was formed in the second half of the eighties, must be viewed as a nucleus of a new 'European' army. In this scenario, the units are not independent structures but basic elements in the construction of a comprehensive and integrated military structure for a new sovereign state, the EC. It seems to me very unlikely that East European countries will be invited to contribute to these multinational military units, because that will only complicate the process towards a fully fledged sovereign Community. Of course, serious problems must be tackled during this process. What do we do with nuclear weapons? France's reluctance to give up exclusive control over its own *force de frappe* is as strong as ever. On the other hand, Germany has expressed its commitment to the non-proliferation regime, and will therefore remain a non-nuclear power. In principle there are only two options for solving this difference between France and Germany. The first, which I prefer, is that France (and Britain) dismantles its own nuclear forces, but a second could be the installation of a new EC-level authority which would have final responsibility for the use of nuclear weapons on EC territory. As long as no solution is agreed upon, a murky regime based on America, French and British nuclear policies will be in force, but sooner or later a solution has to be found.

The EC is the cornerstone of the major developments in Europe. Watching Brussels, the headquarters of the Community, one is impressed by the new energy spurring the EC on the road to political union. If Germany continues to stimulate Community integration as a result of its policy of being anchored in the West and active in the East, then we are likely to witness the emergence of a new superpower in the nineties. Is this a good prospect? Of course, it raises many questions, but the alternative is not very attractive either. De Gaulle's vision of a 'Europe of the Fatherlands' sounds rather romantic, but in reality it comes down to a traditional European game: the survival of the fittest. And then the most likely winner will be called Germany.

## Epilogue

Václav Havel says we have to speak the truth, and that means analysing political realities. In this essay, I have tried to spell out what seems to be the most likely future for Europe. I may be wrong. Maybe Western Europe will be able to bridge the gap that divides us from the Soviet

Union. Maybe we will transfer huge amounts of resources to the East, as the West Germans are doing for their fellow countrymen. Maybe Europe will be demilitarized almost completely, so that Rainer Eppelman's vision of 'only border control' becomes true. I really hope so. Nevertheless, I have forced myself to describe what I think is most likely to happen. That is very different from what I would like to happen.

The peace movement and other social movements can function effectively only if they understand and take into account political realities. During the 1980s, we analysed the bloc system and described it in detail. There was hardly any possibility of a breakthrough. We seemed to be condemned to live in a divided Europe for ever. Having understood that, we started to explore alternatives. The most successful alternative was 'detente from below'. We allied ourselves with opposition groups in the Eastern bloc countries. For us and for them, this was a real attack on the bloc system, quite distinct from our campaigns against nuclear weapons.

Today we have to develop a similar strategy. First, we must describe and analyse the new situation. Second, we must develop alternatives. 'Detente from below' has provided a framework for finding answers to address the negative consequences of the new superpower that is probably going to dominate the European scene. The Helsinki Citizens' Assembly can become an important meeting-place where realities are taken seriously and alternatives worked out.

# 11

# New Europe: New Security

*Dan Smith*

The May 1989 meeting of NATO heads of government reviewed the Alliance's strategy and declared that there was no alternative to it 'for the foreseeable future'.[1] By Christmas 1989 it turned out that the future had been unforeseeable. A few days less than a year after that summit, General Vigleik Eide, chairman of NATO's Military Committee, stated: 'The threat from a united Warsaw Pact no longer exists,' and announced 'a fundamental review' of NATO strategy.[2]

The new European landscape does indeed demand a fundamental review. It is no longer possible to treat the people or governments of the Warsaw Pact states as enemies. The immediate task is to design an approach to security which reflects that. The opportunity exists not just to reduce armed forces but to replace a security system based on confrontation with one based on the impossibility of war which is, of course, the surest foundation for security.

The goals of security are, in the broadest sense, to avoid war, to create and maintain conditions for democracy and a reasonable degree of prosperity, and to establish a framework for international collaboration to clean up the mess that has been made of the environment and prevent further damage. Meeting those goals poses several requirements. Ultimately, security will rest on a process of entrenching democratic values and expanding networks of international co-operation. To achieve that, it is necessary to think about politics and policies at the European level rather than in different and often competing national or regional frameworks. More immediately, those goals must be approached by developing specific policies on security and strategy which are appropriate to them.

## The Perils of Conservatism

There are numerous obstacles. After a long period of fixed certainties, many NATO leaders clearly find the greatest merit in the least change. The institutions, policies and philosophies of confrontation are deeply entrenched in North Atlantic politics. This conservatism cannot be simply dismissed. The pace of change has made many dimensions of the new Europe hard to discern. Ambiguity will persist for quite some time, including ambiguity in areas which are decisive for security policy. It is hard to know for sure which elements of the apparently emerging shape of Europe on the first day of 1990 will endure. Amid forgivable uncertainty, conservatism is an obvious first resort.

But it is not only a refuge for the uncertain. It has been repeatedly asserted on both sides of the Atlantic that the USA must retain its strategic role in Europe, albeit with reduced forces. This insistence implicitly reveals official awareness that a fundamental reappraisal of NATO strategy inevitably raises questions about the continuing need for a major US military presence in Europe. That issue has long been taboo; the need has been taken for granted. The much-mooted transformation of NATO into a 'political alliance' (as if it had not been political from its inception) is explicitly seen as a way for the USA to retain a role in Europe.

For the USA, despite the costs at a time when military spending is under pressure because of both the mood of disarmament and the overall federal budget deficit, keeping a leading role in Europe is a necessary part of the administration's effort to retain global strategic leadership. In Western Europe, insistence on continuing to accept US strategic leadership can be traced to three fears: fear that, without the US counterbalance, Germany will predominate; fear that the Western Allies cannot co-ordinate their efforts without US leadership to bind them together; and fear that too much strategic change may spill over into too much political change.

But if the politics of the Cold War determine the future shape of European security, there could be very significant costs and risks. There must be doubts about just how fundamental NATO's self-assessment will be. Plans are well advanced to deploy new air-launched nuclear missiles and to allocate further sea-launched nuclear weapons to the Supreme Allied Commander Europe.

The most immediate cost of strategic conservatism is economic – the burden of maintaining needlessly large forces in an unnecessary confrontation with a non-existent threat. But confrontation may create its own reality, generating hostility and mutual suspicion. For the new Europe will not be free of disputes; the point of security policy should be to ensure that these stay at the level of disagreements and do not escalate into conflict and confrontation. Spurning the current opportunity to create a wholly new security system could instead ensure that serious disputes are expressed in the language of conflict and confrontation. This risk barely exists between the states of Western Europe and those of Central and Eastern Europe. But among the latter, as tensions between Hungary and Romania indicate, the risk is real. Equally, it would be disastrous to renew confrontation with the USSR.

Finally, there is the risk of confrontation with a different enemy. For NATO, focused on the Cold War with the USSR, the central front has been in Europe; the Mediterranean has been the southern flank. But a school of thought has developed within NATO since well before the busting of the Berlin Wall, before the detente of the second half ot the 1980s, before even Gorbachev's assumption of power in the USSR, which sees the Mediterranean as itself a central front. On the other side of a central front, of course, is a major enemy. In this case the enemy is darker-skinned – which makes it easy to sell confrontation in the rising atmosphere of racism – and widely seen as uniformly fanatic. To set out on a course of confrontation with the Arab world could lead, if not to a major conflagration, to a series of small wars and raids which would kill not the Arab dictators but their oppressed subjects, and create a new threat to European security.

It is essential, then, that the vision of a Europe in and for which war is impossible is inserted into the debate about the future of Europe and its security. This is not the time to forget the peace movements' vision of a Europe 'beyond the blocs'. This period is as decisive as the years immediately following World War II. An old order is crumbling and a new one has to be constructed. Great gains and great mistakes are equally possible. To allow the security debate to be dominated by the institutions, philosophies and habits of the Cold War – to let political, strategic and bureaucratic conservatism set the terms – would be the first great mistake.

## Beyond Confrontation

Hitherto, Western European security has been conceived in confrontational terms. But for at least two decades, the proposition that the USSR had aggressive intentions, held back only by NATO and deterrence, has been very dubious. The USSR had become a status quo power in Europe; the idea that, under Brezhnev, it sought to conquer Western Europe was never very tenable. This was more or less recognized by a shift in some NATO thinking, laying less stress on invasion and more on the fear of

154 EUROPE FROM BELOW

blackmail through military means (though what these were was never quite clear).

After Mikhail Gorbachev came to power in 1985, the Soviet threat became even less credible. Official acceptance of this in the West did not come quickly. In 1987, for example, Caspar Weinberger, then US Defense Secretary, spoke of 'a more aggressive Soviet Union under Gorbachev'.[3] In August 1989 the current US Defense Secretary, Richard Cheney, said the Soviet threat had not diminished but grown.[4] Even at the time, such statements looked anachronistic. They implied an instinctive unwillingness to prepare for life without the Soviet threat.

Gorbachev's policies progressed through a decisive effort to improve US-Soviet relations, which had been at their nadir in 1983–85; to breakthroughs in arms control talks in 1987, leading to the Intermediate Nuclear Forces Treaty; to unilateral cuts in armed forces announced in December 1988 and supplemented in the first half of 1989. By the summer of 1989, strategic planning assumptions based on the immovable permanence of confrontation had lost credibility. The *New York Times* a useful indicator of mainstream US opinion, had already declared that the Cold War was over.[5] And in the second half of 1989 came the upheavals in Central and Eastern Europe.

In the wake of Gorbachev's new policies and the events of 1989, the context of security debate is marked by a refreshing absence of the threats that have traditionally concerned strategists. Not only is there no threat of territorial aggrandizement, ideological enmity is evaporating as the Eastern and Central European states become parliamentary democracies and the USSR abandons the Communist Party monopoly of power. Economic rivalry as a source of conflict can be ruled out by creating a web of mutually beneficial economic relations, just as it was in the creation of the European Communities. That leaves military confrontation. This is where the risk of war in Europe has lain in recent years. The danger was that a superpower crisis somewhere else could provide the spark to ignite the powder keg of the European military arsenals. That risk can be eliminated simply by ending confrontation.

The political changes which make such an optimistic strategic assessment possible have created the opportunity to eliminate the numerical disparities in armed forces which have so alarmed Western opinion. Indeed, with the USSR withdrawing its forces from Czechoslovakia and Hungary by mid 1991, the process of eliminating numerical disparities has not waited for the results of the Vienna Conventional Forces in Europe talks. But treaty agreement is also needed, and if doubts about the durability of Gorbachev's position are well placed they suggest that the opportunity should be grasped while it is available. This was apparently one reason why President Bush decided to be bolder on arms control at the 1989 NATO summit in Brussels than he had previously intended. The other reasons were fears about the effects of inactivity in arms control – what *Time* magazine called being 'almost recklessly timid' – on NATO unity and on Bush's political standing in the USA.[6] Ironically, that inactivity had earlier been justified by the same concern about the fragility of Gorbachev's position.[7]

A far less alarmist view of the military balance has always been possible. Pentagon studies since the early 1960s have found NATO forces to be equal to their tasks.[8] This view rests on the inadequacy of numbers as measures of relative military strength. It was put at its boldest in 1987 by the Deputy Supreme Allied Commander of Europe, General Hans Joachim Mack, who said, 'We could handle a five-to-one superiority.'[9] More cautiously, the International Institute for Strategic Studies repeatedly concluded its analyses of the European military balance by expressing concern but judging that 'the overall balance is still such as to make military aggression appear unattractive.'[10]

But this debate is fast becoming of merely historical interest. Alarmists and non-alarmists alike can agree that the cuts being negotiated in the CFE talks will eliminate numerical disparities, whatever their previous significance. So whichever way it is argued, Western European security planning need no longer be so obsessed by the Soviet threat. This makes it possible to do more than simply cut armed forces.

Security based on confrontation contains ineradicable flaws. It is in the end illusory. Often though this was affirmed by political leaders during the detente of the 1970s, they could not find a way out of confrontation. It became a cliché of the communiqués issued by East–West summits to say that political detente had yet to find a military corollary.

It seemed to one school of strategic analysts that part of the reason for the failure of detente then lay in military confrontation itself and the mutual suspicion it created. While Western politicians worried about the USSR's military build-up, Soviet leaders worried about changes in US strategic nuclear doctrine which seemed designed to make nuclear weapons more usable, implying that they could be used aggressively. This school of thought developed new concepts to find a way out of confrontation. Ideas such as 'common security' and 'defensive defence' are based on the insight that security is indivisible and cannot be augmented at another's expense.[11] Their essence is to think of security in terms of partners rather than adversaries, and to adopt military postures which emphasize defensive strength and minimize offensive potential.

This is part of the approach which can now be brought to bear in creating a new framework of European security. It already finds a good deal of acceptance. NATO adopted some of it in the negotiating position for the CFE talks with its emphasis on reducing offensive capabilities. Gorbachev also adopted elements of it in his long-term agenda for conventional force cuts in Europe. It can be summarized as a shift to security without confrontation.

The second part of the approach is implicit in the first, but goes well beyond what the advocates of defensive defence and common security were able to envisage during the 1980s. Then, the task was to find ways to render division less confrontational. Today, division has broken down. As a result, the only framework for security planning which makes any sense is pan-European.

The third element addresses the basis of pan-European security in the long run. What it proposes is a framework of security comparable to the current system in Western Europe.

The security of Western Europe against threats from outside has been endlessly discussed for the past several decades. By contrast, the topic of security *within* Western Europe, with the exception of terrorism, is now hardly discussed at all – and quite rightly, for it needs no discussion. War between the Western European states is unthinkable, but not because of their armed forces. Security between them is entirely non-military. It was not always so. In historical perspective, eliminating the possibility of war between traditional enemies is an extraordinary achievement. No less a goal can be set for pan-European security.

## Security Threats

Despite all of this, we cannot conclude that there are no threats to security worth considering. We should, however, be careful not to treat all potential threats as if they were on a par with the threat long perceived from the USSR, meriting the same sort of response. Recent debate on European security suggests three themes to explore.

### 1. Reform derailed

Perhaps the most obvious threat is that the process of change in the Warsaw Pact states could be derailed. That hardly seems likely to be done by the demoralized and defeated representatives of the old regimes in Central and Eastern Europe. There were rumours of a November 1989 plot in Moscow and Prague, allegedly involving the KGB and Czechoslovakian intelligence, to crush the Czechoslovakian revolution and overthrow Gorbachev.[12] But once Gorbachev made it clear that crushing the popular movements was not acceptable, the old regimes collapsed without a fight – except in Romania.

But there is a great deal of scepticism and concern about the durability of perestroika in the USSR and about Gorbachev's personal position in the face of separatist pressure, ethnic conflict and economic sluggishness. US intelligence studies in 1988 were sceptical about the prospects of perestroika and again, and with perhaps rather more basis, in 1989.[13] In 1990, guessing Gorbachev's chances of political survival became an international pastime. These concerns were shared in the USSR. An *Izvestia* commentary in January 1990 warned that disorder in Azerbaijan and continuing economic difficulties might 'be used tomorrow by people whose main objective is to bring the country back to the policies of the past'.[14]

There are three different sources of pressure on Gorbachev: from the conservative 'old guard'; from separatist nationalism; and from radical reformers impatient at his slow pace and the lack of economic success. Each of these creates a different type of pressure. The conservatives pose the threat of the coup. The separatist movements have the potential to break up the USSR, or at least shrink it. The radicals' growing strength suggests the possibility that as democracy advances, the chance to vote Gorbachev out of office will arise and be taken.

There is an interplay between these different oppositions to Gorbachev. Both radicals and separatists draw strength from the blocking efforts of conservatives and see there further cause for pressing their demands more urgently. Meanwhile, the conservatives' determination to resist and perhaps to strike may be strengthened by each new success registered by both radicals and separatists.

In itself, the replacement of Gorbachev by a democratic process raises no obvious problems for European security. Indeed, the situation in the USSR will be better the more it is possible to distinguish between the prospects of perestroika and those of its initial architect. Equally, in itself the prospect of secessions from the USSR is not a European security problem. The cause for concern, of course, is the conservative reaction to either development, whether after the event or in an effort to pre-empt it. The problem is both that a coup would be a disaster for the USSR and that it is not hard to imagine the new regime taking a much more confrontational approach in security. Several qualifications should be entered, however.

To begin with, despite the evident waning of his popularity, events since 1985 warn against underestimating Gorbachev. He retains a firm grip on the senior levels of the state apparatus and the armed forces. His ability to outflank a coup, nip it in the bud or crush it should not be ignored. In addition, a coup may be less likely than some fear. Though reactionary stupidity can never be discounted entirely, a sane calculation of the costs must dissuade potential plotters. It could not be the relatively painless, essentially administrative type of coup by which Khrushchev emerged from being *primus inter pares* to *primus* in the 1950s and by which he was removed in the 1960s. In today's USSR, such action could have no constitutional legitimacy: Gorbachev was appointed President not by the Party Central Committee but by the Supreme Soviet, where votes are many times harder to rig. The only possibility for a coup is one which involves armed might. Fury within the USSR would create turmoil, while outrage abroad would renew Soviet isolation. The new leaders would take over a state whose population, having had a taste of freedom, would be far less docile than in the years preceding Gorbachev. They would be opposed not by isolated dissidents but by mass movements. They could not be sure that the army would be reliable, that it would be uniformly untainted by radical reformism and separatist sympathies. They would inherit profound economic problems and cut themselves off from the means, both at home and abroad, with which to solve them. They would have no prospect of regaining sway in Central and Eastern Europe. The prospectus for the potential takeover is hardly appetizing.

Were a coup to occur, the most probable consequence would be prolonged chaos amounting to widespread civil war. The new rulers would pose a military threat not to Europe but to Soviet citizens, and would probably attempt to use a new confrontation with the West as a means to legitimate repression at home. Thus, continued confrontation with the USSR would simply play into the hands of the conservatives both after a coup and while it remains a possibility, for confrontation is the only possible legitimation for repression and for a coup. The greatest support to democracy in the USSR lies in opting as far as possible for security without confrontation.

Finally, however the risk of a coup is rated, and whatever its consequences, a clear distinction needs to be made between the USSR and the other Warsaw Pact states. It does not justify continuing to treat them as adversaries. Fundamental strategic change remains a necessity. The question which is raised by the possibility of a coup in the USSR is not whether to develop a new security framework, but how wide its geographical scope will be.

These concerns should be recognized for what they are: speculation about a possibility. It would be wrong to ignore it, but quite mistaken to predicate security planning on the assumption that a coup will occur. That would be the worst case of the worst-case planning which has bedevilled Western European security planning with false fears of a Soviet threat, for it must be stressed that it is in the greatest interest both of European security and of Soviet citizens to include the USSR within a pan-European security framework to the farthest possible extent.

There are genuine problems here: even if, as seems likely, the risk of a coup declines as democracy advances, it is not clear that the USSR sits wholly comfortably within a pan-European security framework. It has huge territory, separate security concerns on its southern and south-eastern borders and, however much progress is made on both democratic and economic fronts, will probably face ethnic conflict and separatist pressure for some years to come. It should not be impossible, however, to come to an arrangement which includes the USSR in the new security framework and thus eliminates confrontation with European states, while at the same time recognizing that its legitimate security concerns are not wholly contained within that framework.

If concern about a coup gives grounds for caution, that is not an argument for standing still. Arms control agreements and a strategic shift to defensive defence remain necessary and possible. They are steps along the way to a non-military system of security. Even moving with all possible speed, it will be some years before a new framework is in place. In that time, questions about the USSR's vulnerability to a coup may be answered. If a coup does in fact occur, these strategic shifts will prevent a new regime establishing legitimacy and will keep relations with it as non-confrontational and as safe as possible.

## 2. Nationalism, irredentism and ethnic conflict

The second source of threat to pan-European security lies in what psychoanalysts might call 'the return of the repressed' – the re-emergence of nationalisms, irredentisms and ethnic conflicts in the Central and Eastern European countries, long held in check by the Cold War and political repression but never disposed of. These conflicts are currently at their most virulent in Yugoslavia, which is not a member of the Warsaw Pact, but there are other national groups which have long suffered discrimination, often with larger groups of co-nationals on the other side of state borders. In current debate, these disputes and problems are wrapped up into the code word of 'instability': the argument is that, against them, NATO must remain largely unchanged so as to be a factor for 'stability'.

However serious these disputes are, they cannot be viewed in the same way as East–West division and confrontation of the past forty years. They do not justify a continuation of the same strategic policies. The idea that, for example, 'demonstrative use' of nuclear weapons – long envisaged as a nuclear option for NATO – would resolve nationalist pressures is not only brutal but laughable. The idea that such pressures could result in a major offensive against Western Europe is merely laughable. To argue against major strategic change because of these conflicts is intellectually decrepit, serving merely to mask some other motive for conservatism.

Such conflicts have to be addressed primarily through domestic politics. Military action can sometimes suppress but never resolve them. Parliamentary democracy may help by providing a forum to express and a means to recognize grievances and perhaps somewhat assuage them. Much depends on the solidity of the new governments and their political maturity. The better they do economically, the more they can claim the support of the people. But similar conflicts in Western Europe – Northern Ireland, Spain, France, Belgium – indicate that neither parliamentary democracy nor relative economic prosperity guarantees a solution. What may help more is a democratic, regional devolution of power. But whatever path is taken, security policy will probably be quite irrelevant to the peaceful resolution of ethnic and nationalist conflicts.

There may, however, be a role for international action to prevent conflicts escalating. If so, it will mainly be diplomatic and directed at mediating territorial disputes. Some interest has also been expressed in the idea of using international peacekeeping forces to keep warring factions apart. Care is needed in approaching this prospect. The conditions for successful peacekeeping operations are strict. All parties to a conflict must agree to the deployment of the forces, which do not conduct standard military operations and are equipped only with small arms which they use only in self-defence.[15] Even when these conditions are met, the record is mixed. The situation would need to be desperate, yet unambiguously amenable to such operations, before the risks were worth it.

## 3. The Middle East

Many have identified a threat to European security in the Islamic countries of the Middle East. This has been promoted in part by US interest in NATO operations outside the area set by the North Atlantic Treaty.[16] In 1981, in his final report as US Defense Secretary, Harold Brown called for Allied participation in US operations in the Gulf region.[17] In the same year, Caspar Weinberger described the region as 'the fulcrum of contention for the foreseeable future'.[18] Preparations have been made to provide indirect aid and fill in the gaps if US forces in Europe are used in the Middle East.[19] US pressure for out-of-area support reached its height when Weinberger described the regional restrictions as 'an outworn geographical tag'.[20] So far, however, NATO has not conducted military operations outside the treaty area; when NATO states sent naval forces to the Persian Gulf in 1987–8, it was done under the aegis not of NATO but of the Western European Union.

Taken at face value, it is hard to see what the fuss is about. A large-scale military response could not deal even with those threats which are said to exist. Not even the wildest fantasist has raised the threat of invasion. The recent acquisition of long-range missiles by some Middle Eastern states, the possession of chemical warfare weapons by Iraq (and possibly, soon if not now, by other states) and its apparent efforts to get nuclear weapons could lead to a threat of retaliatory strikes if there were, for example, European military intervention in the region. But they would not give Middle Eastern states the ability to invade or dictate policy to European states. Deploying large fleets and armies would be unnecessary for defence and ineffective as a response to terrorism.

Behind face value, of course, other questions lurk. Classically, one is access to oil supplies. Military action to secure access – to force a state to sell oil if it does not want to – must always be of dubious practicability and could have no ethical or legal basis. Beyond that is the more general question of imposing the West's will. That, it should be stressed, has nothing to do with the security of the people of Europe and everything to do with the narrow interests of small and powerful groups. But coinciding with those interests, there are those groups – military bureaucracies, industrial interests – which will face dislocation and perhaps worse if the end of the Cold War leads to large-scale disarmament, as it should. Unless prevented, they are fully capable of forging a coalition to direct European arsenals against the Middle East, and of developing a publicly acceptable explanation by focusing on fears of Islamic fundamentalism and exploiting racism.

This temptation to find a new enemy in the Middle East to replace the Soviet threat should be resisted. The real reasons for a strategic shift towards the South, making the Mediterranean the new central front, have nothing to do with security – understood not as a code word for 'power', which is how it is all too commonly used, but as a genuine, legitimate and universal requirement. From the point of view of power, it may be useful to have the capacity to bully Middle Eastern states. From the point of view of security, it is both unnecessary and negative, more than likely to create insecurity, exacerbate existing conflicts and generate new ones.

## Strategic Adjustments

The discussion above can be summarized by saying that it provides no reasons not to pursue the goal of a pan-European non-military security system, and some extra reasons for doing so. The next question is how it would be possible to implement that policy. Though what follows is not an overall blueprint, it touches on the most important shifts which would be necessary.

As the experience of Western Europe shows, a non-military security system does not necessarily mean the absence of armed forces. Some may see the disarmament measures mentioned below as stepping stones towards general and complete disarmament, but in themselves they neither presuppose nor rule out that goal.

The changing times and the nature of the necessary strategic shifts mean that the process of security planning has to change. Hitherto, the centrality of confrontation has led planners to focus on the nature of the threat and how to counter it, with the goals taken more or less for granted. Successive ministerial meetings of the North Atlantic Council have found it important to reiterate NATO's overall goals, but they have not figured much in the details of choosing one weapon system over another; there, assessing the threat has been far more important. This must now change. The aim of a non-military security system on a pan-European scale must shape the details of force planning and arms control, replacing the old focus of the 'threat'.

## 1. Flexible response

NATO's strategic doctrine of flexible response was adopted in 1967. Compared to its predecessor, it gave a larger role to conventional forces and attempted to set a basis of graduated deterrence in which retaliation would be commensurate with the scale of aggression. But it remained centred on nuclear deterrence and the willingness to use nuclear weapons first.

The doctrine has never made strategic sense. Lawrence Freedman put it neatly:

> The attempt to deter conventional aggression in Europe with a nuclear arsenal controlled by a non-European power that is itself subject to nuclear retaliation has never appeared to be an example of political or military rationality.[21]

In similar vein, Henry Kissinger once remarked: '[I]t is absurd to base the strategy of the West on the credibility of the threat of mutual suicide.'[22] Or as Robert McNamara put it, 'One cannot fashion a credible deterrent out of an incredible action.'[23] So overwhelming are those objections that one hesitates to add others, such as the immorality of starting a nuclear war.

Flexible response survived despite its flaws because it embodied a political compromise without which NATO's continued existence might have been in doubt. This compromise was between the USA and its

Western European allies. The latter wanted a clear US commitment to their defence and got it, while the concept of a graduated response allowed the USA to avoid giving the guarantee of automatic nuclear escalation which its allies then sought. The outcome satisfied – though perhaps did not exactly please – all parties.

The compromise grew out of the conditions of the time, both in Europe – it was adopted before Willy Brandt's Ostpolitik had begun, before the first period of East–West detente – and in transatlantic relations. Since then, Western Europe has changed. It will change more with market integration in 1992, more again with the development of new economic relations with Central and Eastern Europe, and yet more again with steps towards political union. When NATO was founded, Western Europe was economically, politically and strategically dependent on the USA. Now it is neither economically nor politically dependent, and continued strategic dependence will be increasingly incongruous and unnecessary in the coming years. Moreover, with its federal budget and trade deficits, the USA's role in Europe is certain to change and diminish.

The doctrine has therefore run its term. The political conditions from which it grew no longer exist. The opportunity to replace it is welcome. The willingness to use nuclear weapons first – and especially the efforts to make that option credible – inevitably appear threatening to the adversary. It has no role in a system of security without confrontation.

## 2. Forward defence

'Forward defence' boils down to NATO's commitment to defend the whole of Western German territory in the event of Warsaw Pact aggression rather than (in military parlance) trading time for space. It has always been possible to understand West German sensitivities about the need for forward defence, even if its tactical merits have always been in doubt because of its strategic rigidity. As the Warsaw Pact disintegrates, however, those sensitivities lose their salience.

Some argue that forward defence should be shifted to the Western Soviet borders. The justification for this is either the possibility of an anti-Gorbachev coup in the USSR, or the impossibility of including the USSR in a pan-European security system, but there are several problems.

The first is that transposing forward defence eastwards from West Germany would not diminish its tactical flaws in the slightest. If anything, they would be magnified because the front line of defence, where so much military effort would be focused, would be that much closer to the potential aggressor's heartland. The second problem is that forward defence both presupposes and sustains confrontation. However execrable a hypothetical future Soviet regime might be, there is nothing to be gained from confrontation if security can be assured without it. Timely arms control can go a long way towards making certain that it can be.

Thirdly, it would mean Central and Eastern European states exchanging one foreign military presence for another. It cannot be assumed that this would be popular. Nor is it desirable: it would sacrifice many of the new openings which the second half of 1989 created. Finally, it presupposes that NATO absorbs Central and Eastern Europe. Expanding one military bloc while the other fades, regardless of the issue of forward defence, would sacrifice new opportunities to demilitarize European politics and banish old fears. It would also increase the risk that relations with the USSR would continue to be dominated by military confrontation.

Political, strategic and tactical considerations thus combine to make the case for discarding another doctrine which has never made much strategic sense and is now unnecessary.

## 3. Nuclear weapons

Replacing flexible response means that most of NATO's nuclear arsenal would no longer have a role. Despite earlier US and British opposition, the 1989 NATO summit accepted West German pressure for arms control negotiations on short-range nuclear weapons, but insisted that the aim should be partial reductions. To keep Mrs Thatcher happy, the word 'partial' was underlined.[24] The shift to security without confrontation makes it necessary to drop the restriction and enter negotiations aimed at clearing Europe of nuclear weapons entirely.

There are many obstacles to this shift. There is a deep psychological attachment to the notion that nuclear deterrence provides protection, and fears about nuclear attack can easily shift from the USSR to new threats such as those in the Middle East. The US administration will try to resist nuclear disarmament going 'too far', for Western Europe's nuclear dependence on the USA has long been one of the major elements of US strategic leadership. In this it will have strong allies in the European Atlanticist Establishment, always ready to exploit blind fears.

Then there are the British and French nuclear forces. They embody a sense of national prestige to a far greater extent than they reflect strategic calculation. Britain's commitment to NATO should have made it unnecessary to have its own nuclear weapons, but successive governments could not abide the prospect of not having these most powerful deterrents. And while fear of the USSR has explained support for NATO having nuclear weapons, the case for Britain having them has been sustained more by imperial nostalgia than anything else except, perhaps, for determination that France should not be the only Western European nuclear power. There is a degree of irony here, since it was de Gaulle's refusal to let the British have that status which led France into its own production of nuclear weapons. But though these forces are political symbols rather than strategic instruments, there is no evidence that they have ever been useful symbols. Nobody has ever been able to show that they aided British or French interests in a specific dispute or negotiation. The symbolism is turned inwards: the weapons make it easier to swallow the bitter pill of a lost empire.

British and French nuclear weapons have no place in a new security system in Europe. Not only is the current expansion of the two states' nuclear arsenals particularly inappropriate; adopting a 'minimum deterrence' posture is also problematic. Minimum deterrence is as flawed as other nuclear doctrines. It is ultimately a threat to commit suicide and contains an inherent momentum towards strategies of nuclear warfighting. It provides no basis for international stability.[25]

Elsewhere in Europe, and especially in both parts of Germany, the pressure to be nuclear-free is growing. But no foreseeable British or French government seems likely to accept nuclear disarmament, at least until Soviet forces are reduced well below the levels currently being negotiated with the USA. The question arises whether the development of a new security system in Europe should wait for Britain and France to grow up and stop seeking a useless prestige through nuclear symbols wrapped in their respective flags. Perhaps the better choice is to move towards a system which will erode the fears on which part of the nuclear obsession is built, using the momentum of nuclear cuts in Europe as a whole to strengthen the pressure for reducing and finally eliminating the British and French forces.

## 4. Defensive defence

The strategic framework into which the abandonment of flexible response and forward defence fits is set by the concept of defensive defence. The principle aim is, to the greatest extent possible, to eliminate offensive capability while retaining defensive strength. All too often, military preparations diminish security because, whatever the intention, they look aggressive to the other side; the point of defensive defence is to avoid that trap.

Theoretically it rests on rejecting the notion that a balance of opposing forces is desirable. It seeks instead to make defensive forces superior to opposing offensive forces. The offensive/defensive distinction is not based on the capabilities of weapons, which are deemed offensive or defensive depending on how they are used. Rather, it is based on the capabilities of the overall force posture. After years of orthodox analysts rejecting this distinction, it was incorporated into NATO's negotiating position and the mandate for the CFE talks.

Defensive defence means abandoning, or at least sharply reducing, those elements which are required for offensive operations. This focuses particular attention on tanks, on long-range strike aircraft and on naval capabilities for sea-borne landings – amphibious warfare. The single key element in Europe is severely reducing the armies' armoured forces. These are the core of any offensive capability. The new force posture would emphasize light, highly mobile and dispersed infantry forces, capable of blunting armoured offensives but incapable of making them.

Because the resulting forces are capable of strong defence, they still provide a military contribution to security, but they do not do so at the expense of any other state's security because they neither contain offensive potential nor imply aggressive intentions. With the aid of arms control agreements, the new posture would involve far smaller forces than are deployed at present. And the absence of aggressive capabilities would create an inbuilt tendency towards further arms reductions.

Adopting defensive defence would lock into place the intention not simply to reduce armed forces but to eliminate the possibility of war between former adversaries. Another element could be to take proposals in NATO for establishing multinational forces – which is different from the practice hitherto of committing national forces into the NATO command structure – and extend them to embrace East–West multinational forces. The existence of joint Anglo-Soviet or Belgian–Romanian brigades would be another way to help create conditions in which pan-European co-operation in other fields besides security would lay the basis for a non-military security system. Defensive defence, with or without multinational forces, is a stepping stone towards that system and a guard against any tendency to find and aggressively confront new or old enemies.

## 5. Arms control

Defensive defence sets an agenda both for replacing current strategic doctrine and for arms control. The reductions negotiated in the CFE talks, though welcome, are a long way short of what is required. To take only the example of ground forces: tanks remain the core component of offensive capabilities and 20,000 for each side is far too many, but that is the scale discussed in CFE. The fact that tanks can be used for defensive operations does not mean that they are acceptable in such numbers. The point is to have forces which can defend but cannot mount major ground-taking operations.

A CFE treaty is the starting point for the arms control agenda, but the CFE talks are not the only means of reducing armed forces. Unilateral cuts by the USSR and other Warsaw Pact states were the mechanism which got arms control going. Further unilateral reductions by NATO states as well can keep the process rolling, with treaty negotiations being built around them. The components of an agenda for unilateral and multilateral reductions include:

a.  At the same time as agreement is reached on a CFE treaty, a mutual declaration against the first use of nuclear weapons.

b.  CFE II: sharper cuts in conventional forces, focusing on eliminating offensive capabilities in the 'guidelines area' for the current talks (the Atlantic to the Urals); on the USSR completely withdrawing forces based beyond its borders in Europe (if any were still left outside them); further cuts in US forces; reducing other NATO and Warsaw Pact forces.

c.  In parallel, negotiations to eliminate short-range nuclear weapons from the same area.

d.  Simultaneously, preparing for the outcome of CFE II and building on the no-first-use declaration; the elaboration in NATO of a no-first-use doctrine; jettisoning flexible response.

e.  Following agreement to remove short-range nuclear weapons; negotiations on the further denuclearization of Europe, the Mediterranean and North Atlantic.

Alongside this process, beginning immediately, other arms control efforts are needed in a wider arena. It is clearly essential to restrict the trade in nuclear technology which provides the basis for nuclear weapons proliferation, to impose much tighter controls on the trade in certain chemicals which make it possible to manufacture chemical warfare weapons, and to find ways of limiting the conventional arms trade. None of these measures is politically possible if the most heavily armed states fail to disarm, and none of them is possible simply by attacking the activities of the states which are seeking to get these weapons.

The problem does not reside only with the importing states but also with the exporters. States in Europe and North America have either provided advanced weapons and weapons-related technology or, in the case of chemical warfare weapons and some conventional weapons (for example missiles), done too little to prevent industrial corporations from providing them. The panic in Europe and North America about military imports in the Middle East is widely and justifiably seen elsewhere in the world as tainted with racist overtones. Only if the activities of the exporters are restricted will it be possible to develop the political alliances necessary to restrict weapons proliferation. Even then the road will be hard and long, because of emergent military industries in such countries as Iraq.

## Institutional Structure

The institutional structure of security is as important to the future of Europe as the policy. The real issue here is what to do with NATO. Like the Warsaw Pact, it is a product of the Cold War; the difference is that the Warsaw Pact barely exists. Its only remaining role is as a clearing house for problems relating to the withdrawal of the USSR's forces from the other members' territories. NATO broke the pattern of peacetime alliances. Its integrated command structure gives it an appearance – though not a function – much closer to the form of alliance previously reserved for war. In this, the Warsaw Pact followed suit.

If it were possible to begin afresh, nobody would propose the formation of an alliance of fourteen European states (counting Iceland and Turkey as such) plus two from North America as the appropriate institutional setting for a pan-European security system free of confrontation. Far less would it be appropriate for it to have an integrated military command structure, in which most of its members participate and which is always headed by a US army general.

Though the USA will have a security role in Europe for some time, it is no more acceptable for it to have a dominant role than for the USSR to have it. But NATO is a vehicle for US influence in Europe. It runs as an effective organization to the extent that the USA runs it; whenever US leadership in NATO has been indecisive, so has NATO. How long that can continue has been a matter of interest for some years now – so long that one may be forgiven for suspecting that it will be a perennial talking point on which no action will be taken. It remains in the USA's interests to lead NATO, even though the task is getting harder as the threat which justified it vanishes, the costs become more burdensome and the political conditions which made it possible disappear. And Western European Atlanticism remains strong.

But the 1989 dispute over the deployment of new short-range nuclear weapons resulted in a compromise in which the US administration lost its two central demands. It had argued for an early decision to deploy and no arms control;[26] the outcome was a decision to delay deciding whether to deploy and a commitment to arms control. The success of the West

German government, under strong political pressure at home, speaking for the majority of NATO governments was richly suggestive of a growing Western European capacity to take over the reins of the Alliance. That capacity has always been stymied by divisions within Western Europe as much as by acceptance of the need for US leadership. If EC economic integration is matched by steps towards political union – however that is defined – it may be that the short-range nuclear issue in 1989 will come to be seen as a breaking point in the USA's NATO hegemony.

Even with reduced US influence, however, NATO remains the wrong institution for a pan-European system. If the response is to argue that NATO should expand to absorb all European states, one wonders why the bother would be worth it. The USSR and several non-aligned states would find such a proposal hard, if not impossible, to swallow. An alternative exists in the Conference on Security and Co-operation in Europe, founded in 1975 and containing thirty-five members, including all the NATO and Warsaw Pact members and all other European states except Albania, which has recently indicated interest in joining.

With a stronger secretariat and the real commitment of the major European states, the CSCE could easily take on new functions. It could begin with a role in verifying compliance with European arms control treaties. It could become a forum for mediating disputes and elaborating new strategic doctrines and security guarantees. At some point, possibly quite soon, it will be inappropriate to negotiate European arms control in a 'bloc-to-bloc' forum like the CFE talks; further negotiations could then be conducted within the CSCE. It is quite possible that new European states will be created in the coming years, from the ruins of Yugoslavia and the fringes of the USSR. A strengthened CSCE would be an ideal place for addressing the security concerns of these fledgeling states.

The CSCE does not have and probably could not develop an integrated military structure. There is no case for one – for a peacetime/ wartime alliance – in the new Europe; it is needed neither internally nor externally. The primary responsibility of the CSCE would be security, not military affairs. The distinction between the two needs to be emphasized, with the recognition that security is a larger and superior concern.

Within the CSCE it is certain that groups of states would want closer consultations with each other. In the case of the EC states appropriate forums already exist, not only in summit meetings but also in the European Political Co-operation structure. One possibility worth considering in relation to the separate issues of whether and how to expand the EC is to begin by opening the EPC structure to wider participation. For the EC to develop a role in European security is both logical – given its probable trajectory – and desirable, since it will necessarily weaken US hegemony. But the distinction between a security and a military role again needs stressing: for the EC to develop a military wing would be the first step towards a new military bloc which is neither necessary nor desirable.

Habit dies hard, however, and it is unlikely that NATO states will soon abandon the Alliance, either formally or effectively. And until a new CSCE framework is fully implemented, it may not be wholly desirable to do so. It is not only on the right that strong arguments are heard, making the case that it is better to have a united Germany firmly anchored in a larger alliance than to have it floating free in Central Europe with a military might to match its economic clout. To that extent NATO may offer an appropriate framework, though if its real role is to control the Germans, one wonders who is going to sell it to them. But that extent is limited: it is possible to conceive of NATO continuing without wrecking the prospects for a new European security system only if its functions become less important, its forces are much smaller, its strategy is defensive defence and its continuation is explicitly interim. After the Cold War, the old goal of the mutual dissolution of both military blocs has become more, not less, relevant.


Ultimately, the evolution from today's incongruous situation, where a military bloc based on confrontation has nobody left to confront, to a system of security without confrontation and then to non-military security will not happen because of treaties, strategic adjustments and institutional change, though it may be expressed through them. It will come about because economic and political relations over a period will make clear to all that no state in Europe has any intention of, reason for or interest in going to war with any other.

The real task of security policy is not to get in the way of that process. It must be based on breaking down barriers of suspicion and distrust, not on entrenching them, and on including the maximum number of partici- pants, not excluding any. The immediate task of the peace movement is to press for the detailed policies needed to express and implement that perspective. The movement stood for a peaceful, nuclear-free and united Europe throughout the 1980s, which began as a period of unremitting arms build-up and deepening hostility. Now Europe is developing in a way which holds out more hope than ever before that it will become a region in and for which war is an impossibility. Powerful opposing forces remain. Though the Cold War is over, a host of political issues have yet to be resolved satisfactorily. But as long as there is strong public pressure for disarmament, optimism is well founded.

# Notes

1. *A Comprehensive Concept of Arms Control and Disarmament*, Press Communiqué M-1 (89) 20, NATO Press Service, 30 May 1989.

2. *Guardian*, 23 May 1990.

3. Speech at the Belgian Centre for Defence Studies, 25 May 1987 (US Information Service, 26 May 1987).

4. 'Cheney Criticizes Cuts in Military', *New York Times*, 24 August 1989.

5. *New York Times*, 2 April 1989.

6. 'Mr. Consensus', *Time*, 21 August 1989; the timidity gibe comes from 'Do-Nothing Detente', *Time*, 15 May 1989.

7. M. Walker, 'Gorbachev reforms threatened' and 'Bush unwilling to bet on perestroika', *Guardian*, 15 February 1989.

8. On studies in the 1960s, see A.C. Enthoven and K.W. Smith, *How Much is Enough? Shaping the Defense Program 1961–1969*, Harper & Row, New York, 1971, pp. 132–42. On a 1973 study, see 'Study Insists NATO Can Defend Itself', *Washington Post*, 7 June 1973. For a survey of the issue through the mid 1970s, see M. Leitenberg, 'Background information on tactical nuclear weapons (primarily in the European context)', in F. Barnaby, ed. *Tactical Nuclear Weapons: European Perspectives*, Taylor & Francis, London, 1978. On the views of the US Joint Chiefs of Staff in the 1980s, see 'Pentagon Study Finds NATO Forces Can Deter Conventional Attack', *International Herald Tribune*, 1 December 1987.

9. Quoted by M. Urban and P. Pringle, 'Assessing the arms divide', *The Independent*, 7 May 1987.

10. For example, picked at random, *The Military Balance 1980–1981*, IISS, London, 1980, p. 115.

11. See *Common Security: A Programme for Disarmament*, The Report of the Independent Commission on Disarmament and Security Issues under the Chairmanship of Olof Palme, Pan, London 1982; on defensive defence, see the Alternative Defence Commission, *Defence Without the Bomb*, Taylor & Francis, London 1983; for a brief survey of the major concepts, see my 'Themes in the Non-Nuclear Defence Debate', in M. Randle & P. Rogers, eds, *Alternatives in European Security*, Dartmouth, Aldershot, 1990.

12. 'KGB–Prague plot claim', *Guardian*, 23 February 1990.

13. M. Walker, 'Why Mr Bush isn't really going KGA', *Guardian*, 25 January 1989 and 'US Unease on Gorbachev: How Exposed is He?', *New York Times*, 10 September 1989.

14. R. Cornwell, '"Izvestia" warns of risk to Gorbachev', *The Independent*, 24 January 1990.

15. *The Blue Helmets: A Review of United Nations Peace-keeping*, UN Department of Public Information, New York, 1985.

16. The NATO area is the territory of member states in Europe and North America, the Atlantic as far south as the Tropic of Cancer, and the Mediterranean. The terms are set in Article 6 of the North Atlantic Treaty of 1949, amended to include Turkey on its accession in 1951: *NATO Basic Documents*, NATO Information Service, Brussels, 1981.

17. H. Brown, *Department of Defense Annual Report Fiscal Year 1982*, DOD, Washington DC, 1981, p. 63.

18. *Statement by the Honorable Casper W. Weinberger Before the Senate Armed Services Committee*, 4 March 1981, mimeo, US Department of Defense, p. 6.

19. See M. Aguirre, 'Looking Southwards', in D. Smith, ed. *European Security in the 1990s*, Pluto, London, 1989.

20. 'NATO row over boundary shift', *Observer*, 15 June 1986.

21. L. Freedman, 'NATO Myths', *Foreign Policy*, no. 45, Winter 1981–82, p. 50.

22. H. Kissinger, 'NATO: The Next Thirty Years', *Survival*, vol. XXI, no. 6, Nov./Dec. 1979, p. 266.

23. Quoted in Enthoven and Smith, *How Much is Enough?*, p. 124.

24. *Comprehensive Concept of Arms Control and Disarmament*, p. 12.

25. I have developed this argument in 'Nuclear Deterrence and Strategic Stability',

*Arms Control*, vol. 5, no. 2, September 1984; and in 'Strategic Defence: Forward to the Past', *Arms Control*, vol. 8, no. 2, September 1987.

26. 'U.S. Rejects Appeal by Bonn for Battlefield-Arms Talks', *New York Times*, 25 April 1989.

# 12

# The European Community and the Challenge of the New Europe

## *Robin Blackburn*

In all the hubbub about political unification of the European Community – which will not happen before 1993 – we should not forget the plight of those who have supplied such a powerful impetus to unification: the peoples of Central and Eastern Europe.

Before the revolutions of 1989 one could say that a key test for the Western European Left was whether it supported the democratic critique of, and opposition to, the authoritarian regimes in the East. At least in recent decades most sections of the Left did clearly reject any 'Soviet model', though sometimes they gave this little priority. Some of the large social-democratic parties favoured doing business with established governments, neglecting dissident movements that were seen as pretty marginal; the independent peace movements – notably END – had a much better record and saved the honour of the radical tradition in the West.

Today we face a new problem. The new test for the Western Left will be whether it is prepared to extend social and economic solidarity to the peoples of Eastern Europe and the Soviet Union as they build a democratic order and tackle the problems of post-Communism in a capitalist world. It could well be that this takes the form of a painful dilemma, since it could be necessary for the Left to support institutional changes likely to give a boost to opponents, the Christian Democratic Right and liberal centre.

In a nutshell, the dilemma is this. Just when the main formations of the Western Left look set to achieve a majority within EC institutions – the Council of Ministers and European Parliament – countries like Hungary and Poland are knocking on the door. If they are accepted, this would immediately swell the ranks of the Right and centre. Take Hungary, for example. The Social Democrats there did not even scrape

together enough votes to reach the threshold required to elect a single
MP. While the former Communists did a little better, they cried foul
when an attempt was made to seat them at the left end of the
parliamentary assembly. While Left parties may hope to win forth-
coming elections in Britain or West Germany, such a prospect is remote
indeed in Poland or Czechoslovakia where Social Democrats will be
lucky to elect more than a handful of representatives.

So on the face of it, expansion of the Community is the last thing that
favours the large West European Left Parties. Indeed, it might seem
more likely to be promoted by the right-wing parties that would reap the
immediate benefits. In practice, the latter are restrained by the severe
digestion problems they anticipate from seeking to admit the post-
Communist societies, with all their problems and expectations. If the
Common Agricultural Policy has been controversial, imagine how much
more so would be its extension to East-Central Europe and the
concomitant elaboration of a common industrial policy.

So the preferred arrangements offered to the Central European
countries take the form of an association which denies them any
representation in Community institutions. The French Socialists seem
willing to fall in with this approach, and other Western social democratic
parties are likely to do so as well. Just as the Lomé Convention regulates
the Community's relations with poorer ex-colonial states, so we may
expect a Lomé-style Convention for East-Central Europe.

This prospect may appear to hold out the promise of a Left-dominated
European Community – but it will be a false one. In fact the Western
labour movement and Left have a powerful self-interest in promoting
economic and social success in Eastern Europe, since the consolidation
of a third-rate capitalism there would make it easier to undermine social
conquests in the West.

When Margaret Thatcher resists the strengthening of Community
institutions, or when the Commission resists the extension of EC
membership, they are really only encouraging a dynamic of economic
integration unrestrained by democratic institutions. The banks and the
multinationals plan to gobble up Eastern Europe whatever the EC does.

The present moves towards European federalism – political union –
should be welcomed so long as they are combined with democratization,
broadening of membership and – as the latter would require – new
institutions of social and economic intervention. Wider membership
would entail a generous programme of socioeconomic and ecological
rehabilitation and democratic transnational institutions to guarantee
economic advance, ecological protection and social justice. Of course
the EC remains an essentially capitalist institution, wedded to *laissez
faire*. But an increasingly united, transcontinental labour movement,

joining with the progressive wing of the green movement and others, could begin to impose another logic.

By sweeping away Stalinism the revolutions of 1989 have removed walls within the Left just as surely as those which divided East from West. Social democrats and Eurocommunists will now find collaboration easier, while many of those in the peace, green and women's movements are finding allies and counterparts in the East. But perhaps many will baulk at accepting the Community as a valid terrain of contest, even though they can hardly deny the need for a continent-wide framework.

While few on the left would now counterpose Comecon or EFTA to the EC, there could still be a refusal to take existing institutions as a starting point. But when it comes to considering which European institution is going to unite the Continent, it is now really a one-horse race. The EC, based on the strongest economies, is clearly decisive. The governments of Hungary, Czechoslovakia and Poland have recognized this fact by requesting membership. Austria has also requested membership, and other EFTA countries, such as Sweden and Norway, will follow suit.

To ignore this real context plays into the hands of those who subscribe to the short-sighted and selfish calculation that, so far as the EC is concerned, 'small is beautiful'. In the medium and longer run it is not. The two- or three-tier Europe proposed by Kohl and Mitterrand would generate a corrupting species of intra-European economic colonialism. If Eastern Europe is successfully relegated to a Central American role, then the West European labour movement is likely to experience accelerated marginalization on the US model, even if the best organized extract some crumbs of privilege. On the other hand, the experience, tradition and institutions of the aspirant members to the EC would boost the eventual maturity and strength of the European Left.

Notwithstanding the political risks, the West European Left should press for measures transitional to full membership of the European Community for all democratic Eastern European countries and the EFTA states which wish to join. Such measures should include a moratorium on debt payments; a social and economic fund of at least one hundred billion pounds; a common industrial policy, eliminating restrictions on East European imports and promoting harmonious and sustainable development; and elaboration of a transcontinental social charter and ecological pact.

If the EC can demand democratic guarantees from the East European states, then it too should be prepared to democratize itself by giving the European Parliament real power and making the Commission directly accountable to it.

Conventional Western thinking will insist that the East European states must undergo a lengthy purgatory of privatization and marketization before they will be acceptable members of the Community – some time in the next millennium. Will it also demand that Austria dismantle its large public sector or Sweden its welfare arrangements, or either their high unionization rates? The Left should, of course, welcome the fact that social provision looms large in the economic pattern of the aspirant new members of the Community and should strongly oppose any attempts to make monetarism or *laissez faire* preconditions of membership.

While pressing for such solutions the Western Left should also work for practical co-operation and solidarity between trade unions and social movements to promote detente and demilitarization, ecological rehabilitation, co-operative economic advance, shorter working hours and better labour conditions, social control of the economy, the strengthening and extension of universal citizens' rights and the improvement of welfare benefits.

Such a programme may seem very ambitious. But it is less utopian than those approaches which imagine the EC can simply be bypassed, and it is more realistic than that purblind egotism which really intends to let the East-Central Europeans fend for themselves.

We should consider the lessons of the East German general election. Whether out of idealism or cynicism, no section of the Left expressed real enthusiasm for German unification. Marx and Engels, those veterans of the German national democratic movement of 1848, must have been spinning in their graves. The result of these attitudes to the Left was to hand victory to the Right on a plate. This was because the Right appeared both more realistic and more generous. More realistic because the East German statelet was scarcely a viable unit, even if it did not have such dismal associations for most of its citizens; more generous because the Christian Democrats seemed willing to share Western wealth. This was, of course, demagogy but it could be exposed only by a Left with its own generous vision. Today the wider challenge of European unity demands precisely such a generous vision.

# 13

# Europe after the Revolutions

## *John Palmer*

The seismic shifts in the shape of Europe's political geography which have taken place in the past year cannot be understood only in terms of developments within Europe, crucial though these have been. The democratic revolutions in Eastern Europe and the preparations of the European Community for economic – and in all probability political – union reflect deep-seated global, economic and political trends, as well as internal factors. The importance of revolution 'from below', of 'people power', in effecting these changes cannot be dismissed, and is rightly a source of great optimism for those in peace and opposition movements throughout Europe. But there is a grave danger that the gains of 1989 will fall prey to forces over which the citizen has little control.

Recent changes mean the end of the bi-polar system, dominated by two superpowers, which has structured our perception of the post-war world. In place of this bi-polar system we now see the disintegration of one superpower and the gradual and uneven emergence of a multipolar system based on a number of regional blocs. Like all other political actors, the peace movements and the Left face the challenge of understanding this newly emerging system, with its new dangers and possibilities. While the dangers of nuclear holocaust may be much reduced, the danger of regional wars – including wars between states armed with nuclear weapons – remains. The global divide between rich and poor, and the various ecological threats to a habitable globe, are also likely to be perpetuated by the West's response to Soviet collapse. Before considering new perspectives in Europe, a brief evocation of the new global configuration is therefore appropriate.

As well as an emerging European bloc – structured around the EC, focused on German economic power but likely to draw in the EFTA (European Free Trade Association) states and many of the countries of Central and Eastern Europe – there is also an embryonic North American bloc and a putative East Asian or Pacific bloc. Together, these would-be regional blocs account for the great majority of the most important advanced industrial capitalist economies, which in turn account for more than three-quarters of the world Gross Domestic Product. The logic of economic competition between these blocs encourages the advanced core states to develop a subordinate periphery, and in each of them centres of economic decision are forming which are remote from democratic control of social accountability.

The basis for a North American bloc has been created by a 'free trade' agreement signed in 1988 by the United States and its economic and political partner, Canada. But efforts are also being made in Washington to secure the integration – on terms that are far from being agreed – of Mexico and a series of other Central American countries which will probably revolve, as minor satellites, around the North American regional economy.[1]

The Pacific Rim region is focused around the economic power of Japan, the so-called Newly Industrialized Countries of East Asia and the Association of South-East Asian Nations (ASEAN). However, many issues remain to be resolved before a credible political relationship of these states to Japan is consolidated.[2] The USA and the EC are locked in conflict over the level of subsidy and support they extend to agriculture.

A key and as yet unresolved question is whether the development of this new system of regional blocs during the 1990s will prove to be merely an interim stage in an evolution towards an integrated global economic and political system, or whether these regional blocs will prove more durable. Moreover, their emergence may be associated – at least initially – with a period of global recession, trade protectionism, and international instability which could set back rather than advance the goal of a new global economic order.

In such a perspective the international economic and trading system might come to resemble the classic intra-imperialist conflicts character-istic of the pre-1914 world. There is now a danger than such conflicts could spill over from the economic into the political, or even military, domain. Nuclear proliferation has already been encouraged by such economic rivalries. International regulatory bodies are certainly quite weak, and cannot be relied on to contain the potential for new conflicts.

Either way, the present international system, which in the West has been based on the hegemony of the United States – as mediated through bodies such as the General Agreement on Tariffs and Trade (GATT) and the International Monetary Fund (IMF) – now seems likely to be eclipsed. GATT itself, which is sponsoring a new round of international trade liberalization, may lose authority as a result of a series of interregional bloc trade deals which retain elements of protectionism.[3]

An international climate of economic expansion, and continuing improvement in East–West relations, would clearly be propitious for the evolution of these new global regions. In these circumstances the regions might play a key role in negotiating a reformed international economic and political order which minimized the dangers of intra-imperialist conflicts and also made less likely the emergence of dominant, imperial superpowers. But even in this relatively benign scenario, global regionalization will tend further to marginalize and deepen the subordination within the international system of Third World countries (particularly of Africa and also of large areas of Latin America). Some groups of states – for example, the Middle East – which might aspire to global regional status will not be able to achieve it. The exceptional relationship between the oil and primary product producing nations in the semi-independent and semi-developed world which occurred briefly in the early 1970s is unlikely to be repeated in the 1990s. These semi-developed states will remain subordinate to the interests of the rich blocs of the advanced capitalist world in Europe, North America and the Pacific Rim. Resistance will encounter economic or military coercion, and access to key raw materials or markets will be disputed by the rival groupings. For example, it is already clear that Europe, Japan and the United States have been contesting control of Middle Eastern oil supplies and backing different sides in conflicts such as the Iran–Iraq war.

The precise frontiers of the emerging global regions are far from settled. Although much – if not all – of Eastern Europe and parts of the Soviet Union will be drawn into the European bloc, a big question mark hangs over the continued unity of the Soviet Union, and hence of the future of the Russian, Baltic, Caucasian and Asian republics. The convulsions of an almost pre-revolutionary character which have gripped the Soviet Union for the past two years have, in effect, already stripped it of its global superpower status. The neo-Stalinist political order, with its related bureaucratic-command-style planning system, is in an advanced state of decay. Mikhail Gorbachev's attempts to control crisis by instituting a process of democratic change and economic reform 'from above' are encountering growing opposition from more conservative layers of the bureaucracy and the nomenklatura as well as from newly politicized and trade-unionized sections of the working class determined to prevent a further erosion of living standards and social rights threatened in the name of perestroika.

That said, the one factor which has more than any other dramatically

changed the international climate for the better has been the commitment of the Soviet government drastically to reduce the size and
firepower of the Soviet military machine. Moreover, the succession of
Soviet disarmament initiatives – some of them unilateral reductions in
force levels – has improved the prospects for far-reaching agreements
involving nuclear, chemical and conventional force reductions in Europe
by both NATO and the Warsaw Pact. These developments are in turn
stimulating a debate about future European security policy. Further-
more, the new security environment has directly led to discussions about
the institutional character of a pan-European association linking the
countries of the European Community, (EFTA), the Council of Mutual
Economic Co-operation (Comecon) and other non-aligned European
states.

## Changes in US Strategy

The deepening crisis of the Soviet system as a whole is meanwhile being
accompanied, albeit in much less dramatic fashion, by the protracted
decline of the United States as an economic and political superpower.
The lineages of that decline and the remarkable transformation of the
USA from the world's largest creditor to the world's biggest debtor can
be traced back at least several decades, but the process has now come to
the point where the United States is being forced to question its
'globalist' political and military pretensions. Already in Washington a
major re-examination is under way of America's capacity to sustain a
worldwide system of military bases and alliances. The haemorrhaging of
US resources – measured in part by its balance of trade and payments
deficits, but also reflected internally by the huge and continuing federal
government budget deficits – suggests that the United States will be
forced to dismantle ever greater elements of its post-war neo-imperialist
role. The growing inadequacy of the domestic American wealth-
producing industrial base to service the international investment,
military and other commitments of the United States means that the
system is now precariously dependent on the inward flow of short-term
financing from outside, most obviously from Japan.
    Although the two Reagan presidencies initially appeared successful in
reversing some aspects of this decline and in reasserting global leadership for the USA, it is now clear that this period disguised an underlying,
even an accelerating, decline. The full political implications of that
decline and the consequent pressure to abandon key aspects of the US
global strategy – such as the maintenance of large overseas military
bases – have now begun to make themselves felt under the Bush

administration. The decline has necessarily underlined the scale of the change in power relations with some of America's major allies – notably Japan and Western Europe. Having at first sought to challenge and contain the shift of power (for instance by seeking to counter the growth of European demands for joint leadership with the USA of the Atlantic Alliance), the Bush administration now appears readier to accept and adapt to the new realities. Nowhere has this foreign policy adjustment been more brusque than in the clear switch from any lingering 'special relationship' with Britain. This has now been replaced by an attempt at a closer and less patronizing relationship with the emerging united Germany, which is expected to play a key role in a strengthened Europe.

Just as the Soviet Union has effectively abandoned any attempt to maintain direct economic and political hegemony in Eastern Europe, so the United States now appears to have begun a process of global disengagement – not least in terms of its military commitments in Europe and the Far East. Under the Bush administration the strategic reorientation of the US military appears to be away from globalist concepts to concepts of regional 'North American' defence. This new regionalist defence doctrine underpins the administration's commitment to the Strategic Defence Initiative, for SDI and the 'magic pebbles' theory of a North American shield against nuclear attack is in the longer run incompatible with a meaningful commitment to America's global alliances – as the European member states of NATO realized with alarm when Reagan unveiled the first versions of SDI in the early 1980s.

It would be quite wrong to suggest that the USA has voluntarily 'given up' its leadership positions in the global agencies of its former economic hegemony such as the IMF, the World Bank, GATT or the Organization for Economic Co-operation and Development. But the signing of the Canadian–US free-trade agreement and the efforts in Washington to restructure a closer relationship with Mexico betoken new priorities associated with a narrower and more limited regionalism in some ways reminiscent of pre-war isolationism.

A further key aspect of this evolution of US strategy has been Washington's attitude to the changing role of NATO. United States opinion-formers are actively debating the extent to which NATO needs to be transformed in the light of the new security prospects in Europe. There is, however, a widespread consensus among governments on both sides of the Atlantic that if NATO is to continue as an active political – let alone military – alliance, it must be primarily under European rather than American leadership. Some argue that this will allow a new 'division of labour' between the United States and its West European allies in the running of a military and political alliance which may be expected to reorientate its 'threat assessment' attentions from the Soviet bloc to the alleged 'security threat' outside NATO's traditional European arena – notably in the Middle East and Africa. Some Western strategists advocate 'a new NATO, to which the USA might be closely linked through an agreement replacing the 1949 Treaty which established the Atlantic Alliance. Such an alliance might retain a diminishing number of US troops in Europe, though it would seek to retain the 'protection' of the still enormous American strategic nuclear arsenal. But its priorities would switch to the non-European arena and it would co-ordinate 'Western' intervention wherever the partners envisage a security threat.

However, there is a reluctance among some NATO strategists to abandon the notion of the Soviet Union – even a rump, post-Communist Russian federation – as a potential security threat. Much emphasis is put on the historic problems which Western Europe has had with Tsarist Russia. An ingenious alternative scenario has a security threat arising not from the strength of the Soviet Union but from the possibility of its disintegration into fractious nationalist mini-states.[4] But such dangers are really more comparable to those which already exist in the Middle East, or on the Indian subcontinent; and it is far from clear that an alliance such as NATO could be seen as the relevant response even in conventional military thinking.

From the standpoint of human interests there are, of course, such easily identifiable 'enemies' as world poverty, the greenhouse effect or a number of other ecological threats to a habitable planet. But the Western military-industrial complex has quite demanding specifications to meet in its new post-perestroika search for a suitable enemy. Preferably such an enemy should be a rival global military formation, requiring long-distance troop movements, possessed of large tank forces and a submarine fleet, with inhospitable terrain and – last but not least – easy to portray as a threat to the Western way of life. As will be seen, neither the drug cartels nor Iraq nor Iran really fit the bill; and to the extent that an enemy with the necessary features is lacking, it will be difficult to justify maintaining military budgets that devote huge resources to specific threats such as a massed tank offensive against Western Europe. There has, of course, been much talk of a 'peace dividend', but many of the proposed 'cuts' in defence turn out, on close inspection, to be cuts in projected increases in military spending.

Getting agreement on the details of how a new Atlantic alliance might work will not be easy. Quite apart from the issue of how the costs of such an alliance would be shared, the facts of conflicting interests in key regions of the Third World cannot be ignored. A case in point is the Middle East, where the traditionally close relationship between the United States and Israel has pointed up the different priorities the USA has followed in the region compared with its Western European partners, who place a higher value on links with the conservative Arab regimes. The serious commercial conflicts between the USA and West European interests in these regions are bound to become increasingly important for foreign and security policy strategists if the early 1990s are years of recession and trade protectionism.[5]

## A New European Community?

The effect of perestroika in Eastern Europe was first to demoralize and then to paralyse the ruling bureaucracies. This allowed the opposition to move from protest to the challenge for state power in breathtakingly short order. There is little doubt that the growing links between the European Community and the *anciens régimes* in Eastern Europe encouraged the population to compare their lives with the greater prosperity in Western Europe. This in turn helped to develop an awareness of allies in the outside world, reducing the sense of isolation which had inhibited opposition in earlier years. However, these factors by themselves do not account for the remarkable revolutionary wave which swept Eastern Europe in the closing months of 1989; this derived from historic sources of civic opposition and, in some cases, dissident socialism.

Whatever the complex – and to some degree conflicting – intentions and goals of the democratic revolutionaries in Eastern Europe, there is little doubt that the basic trajectory of these countries is now back within the international capitalist system. Certainly Western aid and advice push in this direction. All the Eastern European countries are implementing – albeit at varying speeds and with varying qualifications – strategies for the comprehensive marketization of their economies, though the ideological orientation of their leaders seems to be a mixture of free-market radicalism, emphasis on co-operative and democratic forms of economic activity, and a determination to establish a social-democratic-style welfare state. The costs of economic restructuring – and of the opening up of these economies to the international division of labour – are massive and will primarily be borne by those least able to shoulder them. The economic trauma will vary greatly from state to state: Poland, Hungary, Romania and Yugoslavia face a more terrible process of adjustment in terms of inflation, lower living standards and higher unemployment than Bulgaria, the GDR and Czechoslovakia.

One of the cruellest aspects of Western-sponsored economic conversion in Eastern Europe relates to the institutions of civil society which the theorists of Charter 77 and other former opposition groups had hoped to strengthen. Drastic economic measures have meant that theatre groups, publishing houses, research institutes, cultural organizations and the like now find themselves denied all funds. Only those who can find a Western sponsor, or have determined political patronage, can be sure of surviving. The ideal of an autonomous and lively set of intermediary institutions between government and citizen is receding just when it had at last seemed a possibility.

It is true that the European Community is co-ordinating international aid from the twenty-four leading Western capitalist countries, but the scale of this aid and the fact that it is conditional on the implementation of free-market policies will do little to cushion the economic sacrifices which the peoples of Eastern Europe are being asked to make. Measured against the present-day value of the US Marshall Aid programme to Western Europe in the late 1940s, Western aid to Eastern Europe is derisory: as of mid 1990, a mere $15 billion compared with the equivalent of $400 billion made available under the Marshall Plan. Even right-wing free-market economists have warned of the disaster facing the privatization campaign in Poland if it is not accompanied by sweeping 'forgiveness' of Poland's debts to Western governments.

There are also a number of political contradictions evident in the unfolding relationship between the European Community and its new client states in Eastern Europe. For although their incorporation in the European free-market system is designed to be more or less total, the European Community governments are reluctant to offer the East Europeans a clear promise of eventual political membership of the EC.[6] This reluctance is all the more striking since the European Community is embarked on a number of ambitious projects which – if successful – will bring it much closer to becoming a supranational quasi-federal European state. This will involve not only the completion in 1993 of the barrier- and frontier-free internal EC market, but also the parallel realization of a full-scale economic and monetary union. Moreover, the majority of EC states (though with the notable exception of the Thatcher government in Britain) want to go even further and lay the basis for a political union. This will lead to a supranational federal European state which would assume responsibility from national states for a growing range of key political issues, including aspects of foreign policy and defence.

An indication of the seriousness of the drive towards a federal European state was provided by the special EC heads of government meeting in Dublin in April and June 1990. Led by Chancellor Kohl of Western Germany and President Mitterrand of France, the majority of leaders committed themselves to a timetable which would mean the introduction of major changes in the EC decision-making institutions by January 1993. This is the date for the completion not only of the single European market of the twelve, but also of the 'common economic space' to be formed by the EC and EFTA. It is also the date for the final stages of East Germany's incorporation, through a united Germany, into the EC. Thatcher's attempts to block or divert this move were challenged from within the Tory Cabinet in London, leading to tacit British acknowledgement that some form of military union was unstoppable.

The advocates of federalism are bent on the creation of the 'nightmare of a centralist Eurosuperstate', as Mrs Thatcher has alleged. The process envisaged is more complex and would involve not only the retention of national states for a range of functions but also an encouragement to disperse governmental functions 'down' to regional and other bodies with which the EC institutions would have greater direct contact.[7] The federalist case gives major emphasis to the need to extend the role and political authority of the directly elected European Parliament. Under proposals for EC constitutional reform to be discussed under 1991, the European Parliament would subject both the Commission and the Council of Ministers to greater control, and would be given a greater degree of joint legislative powers with the Council. Even the Right acknowledges that there is a 'democratic deficit' in the present functioning of the Community.

The majority of EC governments believe that future Presidents of the Commission – which is the day-to-day EC executive – should be appointed by the European Parliament rather than by national states, and that the President should select the other Commission members in consultation with national governments. More importantly, the majority also believe that, unlike the situation today, no law should be passed by the Council of Ministers (which is the *de facto* legislative power at present) in the face of a majority vote to reject it by members of the Parliament.

The British government argues that in the interests of democratic accountability and national 'sovereignty', control over EC decision-makers should be exercised by national parliaments. But under the treaties of accession which all countries sign on joining the Community, national parliaments lose the right to amend or reject decisions of the Council of Ministers. It is therefore the merest demagogy to claim that Westminster is threatened by the move to give more power to the European Parliament. It is the Council which is truly unaccountable to anyone and now stands most threatened by moves to strengthen the European Parliament.

With this highly delicate process under way, the EC states appear fearful that any enlargement of the Community would risk complicating, or even blocking, the whole process of European Community economic and political union. That is why not only the East European countries, who have latterly adopted parliamentary democracy and market economic systems, but also long-established free-enterprise democracies in Western Europe – including the member states of EFTA – are being actively discouraged from applying for early EC membership.[8]

As far as the ruling interests of the European Community are concerned, it is important that over the next few critical years, when the ideological shape both of the European community and of any wider pan-European confederation is being developed, EC political decision-making should be restricted to the present twelve states. They fear that the existing ideological cohesion of these states – especially regarding the future character of European security arrangements – might be diluted or even undermined by the 'premature' accession of the partly neutralist and social-democratic EFTA states, or by those East European countries whose experiment with Western-style capitalism is at such an early and unpredictable stage of development.

The exclusion of EFTA countries from political membership of the EC – to say nothing of the East Europeans – will not prevent their being increasingly drawn into the all-enveloping dynamic of the EC single European market. But this implies that even the relatively privileged EFTA countries risk becoming politically neutered junior partners of the EC powers, while the struggling East European economies could end up as the *de facto* economic colonies of the European Community.

Not all the twelve EC governments believe that this is the wisest strategy. The Danish government would like to bring its Nordic neighbours Norway and Sweden into the Community as soon as possible, while West Germany and Belgium favour the admission of Austria. West Germany also looks with some sympathy on the idea of at least promising eventual membership to a select number of Central European countries (Czechoslovakia, Hungary, and possibly Poland).

There are also clear indications that some other small non-aligned states in the Mediterranean – Malta and Cyprus – intend to press for EC membership. In Eastern Europe, the Czechoslovak government in particular has made it quite plain that it will not be satisfied with mere economic association with the EC and will want to be guaranteed full membership – albeit after an undetermined period of transition. Several EFTA states may soon follow Austria's lead and make an all-out bid for full EC membership. The Hungarians and the Poles will not want to be left behind by the Czechoslovaks and the East Germans – although the government in Warsaw is under no illusion about the desperate state of its economy and the possible social and political upheavals which may be triggered by its 'Chicago School'-style transition to full market systems. Within Yugoslavia the Slovenes and Croats are already flirting with the idea of direct links with the EC. Austria, Czechoslovakia, Poland, Hungary, Italy and Yugoslavia have formed a 'neo-Habsburgist' trans-Danubian association to push for their interests in the Community.[9]

The odds are, therefore, that by the middle of this decade the pressure for an enlargement of the EC to fifteen, or even twenty or more, member states may become irresistible. The consequences of such a radical shift in economic and political complexion could be significant. It would, for instance, increase the relative weight of social-democratic and left-of-centre governments within the Community's political institutions, and would also involve the integration of avowedly neutral states at a time when the fundamental direction of Europe's future foreign and security policies will be under debate.

For the Left in the European Community, this perspective raises problems and opportunities. While it is not the job of the Left to advocate EC membership to the East Europeans, it *is* its job to defend their right to be members of the Community – whether or not their foreign and security policies conflict with those of the NATO ideologues, and whether or not they are paragons of free-market virtue.

## The Future for European Security

The immediate impact of these developments will be felt by those in Western Europe – notably the British government – who are anxious to preserve as much of the structure and role of NATO as possible. Quite apart from the powerful popular groundswell throughout Western and Eastern Europe for security arrangements which transcend and supersede the organizations set up during the Cold War, many of the Centre Left – and, indeed, Centre Right – governments in Western Europe are now increasingly looking to a future pan-European security order built around the existing Conference on Security and Co-operation in Europe.

This is most clearly the case in West Germany, where not only the opposition Social Democrats but the coalition government of Christian Democrats and Liberals emphasize the need to 'transform the political character' of both NATO and the Warsaw Pact. They are seen as becoming primarily political rather than military agencies which would eventually be subsumed by the CSCE when it is given authority to operate a collective European security order. In the meantime, from the Centre Right leftwards in Germany there is a desire to see the early and rapid reduction in foreign forces and nuclear weapons stationed on

German soil. An increasingly similar line is being taken by the Benelux states, by Denmark and Norway, to a lesser degree by Italy and Spain. Taken together, these developments and the support for giving the CSCE the physical means to assure collective European security is seen by many in NATO as a lethal threat to its very existence. These fears have been encouraged by the pressure on the United States administration to begin examining far-reaching reduction in the 300,000 or more troops it currently stations in Western Europe.

The British and French governments, meanwhile, balance a general political support for the CSCE and a gradual series of disarmament agreements between NATO and the Warsaw Pact with a strategy designed to preserve at least a 'rump' NATO, organized around the key West European states and underpinned by some new alliance with the United States. In the past, London and Paris were keen to use the nine-nation Western European Union for this purpose, but it too reflects a disarray in the face of the rapidly changing situation in Europe which is found in NATO itself.

There are two other contradictions in the Anglo–French hardline alliance which are likely to prevent it from emerging with an agreed strategy. While both sides would like to merge their national nuclear military potential, this is difficult to achieve in practice given the dependency of the British on the United States for its delivery systems – something which the advent of Trident will accentuate. Secondly, there is a major gulf between the British and French governments in their attitude to European Community developments. The Thatcher government wants to restrict the evolution of the EC as far as possible so that it remains merely a more complete and fully decontrolled 'common market' based on an unashamedly liberal economic agenda. This would exclude as far as possible security, social, environmental and other questions from coming within the competency of the EC institutions. This explains in part the British government's hostility to the (mainly rhetorical) European Social Charter of Workers' Rights and moves to toughen EC environment protection legislation.

The French, on the other hand, are essentially EC federalists who give their full support to plans for European economic, monetary, and political union. However, Paris believes that the best way of ensuring a continued West European military alliance would be to transfer some of the responsibilities of the WEU, and eventually of NATO, to the European Community – a process which could entail the 'Europeanization' of France's and Britain's nuclear weapons.

It is unlikely that the British and the French will easily persuade a new united German government to accept their forces remaining – along with those of the Soviet Union – in Germany for anything other than the

short term. A potentially serious clash also looms between London and
Paris on the one hand, and Bonn and its allies on the other, over
retention of nuclear weapons in Central Europe and any attempt to get
Germany to foot the bill for modernizing an Anglo-French nuclear force
loosely dressed up as a new European deterrent.

Superficially, there is more agreement on the importance of CSCE as
the crucial forum for negotiating a pan-European set of arrangements
covering arms control, human rights, political and economic co-operation, protection of the environment and other issues. But Mrs Thatcher
has made it clear that she – unlike most other right-wing leaders – will
oppose any idea of the CSCE being given the military functions belonging
to NATO.

However, there are many other important issues to be agreed in the
construction of what is known as the pan-European architecture on the
1990s. The CSCE involves both the United States and Canada on the one
hand and the Soviet Union on the other, none of which are fully or – in
the case of North Americans – even partially 'European' powers. The
participation of both the USA and the Soviet Union in any future pan-
European Confederation – whether organized around the CSCE or
around the twenty-three-nation intergovernmental Council of Europe –
is seen as crucial for the negotiation of a credible new collective security
order in Europe which will replace the old war alliances. But some West
European governments would prefer the present twenty-three-member
Council of Europe to become the primary organ for pan-European
economic, environmental, social and political co-operation – perhaps
because North American influence would be far less than in the CSCE. It
is possible, however, that the Council of Europe – perhaps together with
the other agencies such as the United Nations Economic Commission
for Europe – might be merged into a pan-European confederal
organism.

Assuming that the North Americans are given only association or
consultation rights within such a body, how should the Soviet Union be
treated? Some commentators have suggested that since the Soviet Union
is moving to a more confederal constitution of its own – and may even
break up into a series of loosely confederated national republics – it
might be appropriate for the pan-European association to embrace the
European Baltic, Russian, Ukrainian and Moldavian republics individually, not the Soviet Union collectively. This would leave an
unanswered question over the future relations with the Soviet Union's
Caucasian and Central Asian republics.

On the West European side it is far from clear how this emerging
pan-European confederation will relate to the European Community as
it moves to economic and monetary union, and then to a federal

political union. However, if – as is quite possible by the mid 1990s – the
EC itself emerges as a federal United States of Europe, will it not
completely dominate or even eventually subsume any wider pan-European confederation?

Quite apart from the concern that an enlarged Community might
imperil the existing strategy of the present EC states for closer economic
and political integration, other political factors are also in play. A
significant section of the Eurocracy – and, more importantly, of EC
national governments – is apprehensive that the accession of countries
such as Sweden, Austria and Norway, with their traditional commitments to a strong welfare state and ambitious environment protection
policies, would push the EC as a whole away from giving free-market
economics priority. These arguments will be easier to resolve if the
international developments in arms control negotiations and East–West
relations generally encourage the emergence of the CSCE as a pan-
European security agency. This would make the accession of 'neutrals'
into the EC less problematic for the main fractions of the European
Community ruling class – particularly since, on most other issues, the
newcomers would be as keen as most of the twelve to move to an
economic and even a supranational political union.

The global trends towards economic and even incipiently political
regionalization are a factor in the thinking of EC political leaders. It is
too soon to say whether the attempt through GATT to negotiate a
worldwide trade liberalization will succeed, but the price of failure
would probably be an accelerated drift towards regional trade protectionism ('Fortress Europe', 'Fortress America'), with all its implications for political and security arrangements.

We are facing the likelihood, then, of a United States of Europe
emerging from the process of European union within the EC and linking
a growing number of other East and West European states. These states
will be economically bound by the 'single' European capitalist market,
but they will also have to surrender to the European 'federal' level a
wide range of powers over politics and defence – powers hitherto the
prerogative of the national state and of alliances such as NATO.

It is a sense of this emerging European state which is lending urgency
to the demands for some greater system of democratic political accountability by the EC institutions. These demands take two forms. In
countries such as Britain they focus on the need for the British state
and/or Parliament to exercise greater surveillance and control over
decision-making in Brussels. The trouble with this is that first the treaties
of accession, under which the EC member states signed the Rome Treaty
as the Community's constitutional doctrine, and subsequently the Single
European Act of 1987, have enormously reduced the scope of national

governments and national parliaments. Only within a perspective of breaking from the EC, and therefore of challenging the economic integration which has driven the Community, does it make sense to seek to restore some role to purely national parliaments. The accountability of individual governments to such assemblies is further undermined by the fact that the Council, collectively, takes more and more decisions on a majority-vote basis.

The only alternative – supported with greater or lesser enthusiasm in most other EC countries – is the case for making the directly elected European Parliament the main legislative body in the Community. This would also involve the existing executives (both the Commission and the Council of Ministers) being fully and directly accountable to the European Parliament.

## The Tasks of the Left and New Social Movements

All this is to confine attention to the processes of building a bourgeois state – with or without bourgeois democracy – first in Western Europe and then in Europe more generally. But to date, working-class and labour-movement bodies have been slow to respond to the new realities of integrated EC economies: transnational companies; the Europeaniza-tion of hours, working conditions, collective bargaining, and increas-ingly of social and labour laws. The new social movements – notably women's movements, the green movement and the peace movement – have been significantly quicker to see what is happening and to begin to respond on a transnational, European basis. Until very recently, however, the political Left has been reluctant to recognize the enormous implications for both theory and strategy of what is happening in Europe – although in a number of countries modest but significant space has begun to open up for independent 'green/Left' socialist movements, as a consequence both of the implosion of Stalinism and of the *de facto* shift to the right by orthodox social-democratic parties.

The construction of a programme (or a series of programmes) for the European green/Left and – more generally – for the labour movement in alliance with the new social movements in both Western and Eastern Europe is an urgent priority. The Western Left, because of as well as despite the bitter years of reaction and defeat, does bring to this task a wealth of initiatives and innovatory ideas which can help to construct a radical European project with real imagination and mass appeal.

The issue of democracy will have to be at its heart: democracy at the level of the regional, national and European state, but also democracy at work and in the community. It should go without saying that the demand for popular control over the process of European integration should encompass – but in no way be restricted by – European Community institutions.[10]

On the other hand, the Left cannot afford to adopt an abstentionist position on the issues raised by the European Parliament's demands for far greater control over the Commission and (even more important) the Council of Ministers. At present the twelve are involved in building a bourgeois state without bourgeois democracy, and many areas of decision-making are deliberately kept secret. Nowhere is this more blatant than in the proliferating intergovernmental bodies – legally not a formal part of the EC institutions or the Rome Treaty – involved in drawing up arrangements for the free movement of peoples within the 1992 single market. Not only is this freedom likely to be restricted in the name of state action against transnational crime and terrorism, but there are grave dangers that the already illiberal rules applying to immigrants and those seeking political asylum from outside the Community will face a *de facto* white, ethnocentric Fortress Europe regime.

Security and defence policy also escape direct democratic scrutiny at present and must be brought within the scope of the European Parliament. But the Commissioners, individually as well as collectively, should be elected by MEPs and not appointed by an indirect and unaccountable process of political office-jobbing. The question of democratic accountability is also posed in relation to any new institutions created out of the CSCE, or the Council of Europe, for the putative pan-European confederation. This is all the more relevant since the Soviet Union, among others, has gone so far as to propose eventually giving such a body some limited supranational decision-making powers – for instance, in setting higher mandatory transnational standards of environment protection.

It is against this background that the Left will also have to review its wider strategy for the labour movement. Quite apart from the issues posed by European unification and integration, the single-market process makes long overdue the development not merely of transnational collective bargaining but also of transnational unions. Significantly, this question has been posed most sharply by those trade unionists – notably in the engineering and metalworking industries – who have had most practical involvement in a co-ordinated European strategy to reduce working hours. Alongside this is the need to develop labour-movement prefigurative policies on transnational democratic planning, new forms of European public ownership, the encouragement of worker co-operatives and innovative applications of human-centred technologies. This must also contain the concept of protected economic zones where less advanced national and regional economies can be safeguarded against distorted developments caused by the unrestricted impact of the international market.

The question is whether, in the radically changed economic and political environment in Europe, there will be space for the re-emergence of a new green/Left movement. There is no point in denying that – however unjustifiably – the entire socialist project has been seriously damaged by an association in the popular mind of even anti-Stalinist and new Left socialist politics with the collapse of authoritarianism in the Soviet Union and Eastern Europe.

It might also be added that confidence in radical politics is inevitably affected also by the failures, omissions and conservatism of mainstream social-democratic politics. Strategies based on national Keynesian and welfare social democracy have suffered substantial setbacks at the hands of both the restructuring of the international economy in the past decade and the aggressive ideological challenge from the right – most notably from Thatcherism in Britain.

A new socialist politics – one which draws its vision from the new social movements and the green movement as well as from the traditional constituencies of organized labour – is going to become relevant as the West European countries face the contradictions of free-market liberalism and in the East as an alternative both to discredited statism and an increasingly predatory capitalism.

During the past decade Left, green and radical democratic strands of thought have enjoyed a certain resonance in the wider political debate. The European Nuclear Disarmament campaign, the environmental movement and initiatives such as Charter 88 in the United Kingdom, which pick up and develop themes of a decentralist democracy, have all affected even the mainstream political debate.

For the first time it becomes possible to develop a dialogue embracing not only the citizens' movements in Eastern Europe but also the emerging green/socialist spectrum in Western Europe. There has been, and still is, a process of learning – both about strategy and in incorporating insights brought by the women's movement and a variety of other 'new socialist forces'.

This is more than a debate between currents which explicitly identify themselves as 'green/socialist' or 'new Left'. It involves also joint reflection and joint action with a broader coalition of radicals in both parts of Europe; working for a democratic, more self-managed society which would give Europe a new, non-militarist, anti-imperialist vocation in a world brought ever closer together by the impending catastrophes of poverty, underdevelopment and ecological crisis.

In some countries these forces even enjoy significant parliamentary representation – as in Denmark, Norway and the Netherlands. Elsewhere the new politics also attracts activists in older political parties of the Left. Much remains to be done. The new politics has yet fully to integrate the realities of European union into its own programmes and modes of working; and this may ultimately require genuinely supranational European organizations and political parties.

The past decade has enabled valuable work to be done on economic strategy drawing on the experience of the trade unions on socially useful production, arms conversion and workers' plans; and the initiatives of progressive local authorities and other bodies. But the new Left is still fatefully weak when it comes to presenting a coherent economic alternative, without which the metamorphosis – in both Eastern and Western Europe – towards mass movements for change must remain problematic.

# Notes

1. *Wall Street Journal*, 5 April 1990.
2. *International Herald Tribune*, 21 July 1989.
3. Some of these issues are examined by Peter Ludlow in 'The Future of the International Trading System', *Washington Quarterly*, March 1990.
4. For example, see article by NATO Secretary-General Manfred Woerner in *NATO Review*, February 1990.
5. The history of these foreign policy conflicts between the United States and the European Community are dealt with in my *European Without America – The Crisis in Atlantic Relations*, Oxford 1988.
6. This was spelled out in a special paper dealing with the European Community's future relations with the countries of Eastern Europe prepared by the European Commission for the special summit meeting of EC heads of government in Dublin on 26 April 1990.
7. The Regional Development Committee of the European Parliament has issued a series of reports suggesting new ways of directly strengthening links between EC institutions and regional and local government bodies.
8. See the declaration of the President of the European Commission, Jacques Delors, at the March plenary session of the European Parliament in Strasbourg.
9. See *The Financial Times*, 10 April 1989.
10. See the *Appeal to the European Left*, issued by the Dialogue Committee of Agenor, Brussels, April 1990. This is leading to discussions between green/socialist and independent Left organizations in more than a dozen West and East European countries about the political basis for co-operation and joint action. See also the April 1990 issue of *Catalyst*, magazine of the Socialist Society, London.

# 14

# The Two Faces of Europe

## *Adam Michnik*

A French friend said to me two years ago that there were two ways for Poland to emerge from its appalling crisis. The first would be through common sense: a miracle would happen and angels would descend to free Poland from Communism. The second would be through a miracle: the Poles – including both the Communists and the opposition – would come to an understanding with one another. This miracle – something that seemed to me utterly impossible – actually occurred in my country. The prisoners and their guards sat down at a table and began to negotiate. The result is that Communism has ceased to exist in Poland today. This was by no means a foregone conclusion – things could have turned out quite differently. The way was smoothed by a specifically Polish feature of the situation: the combination of President Jaruzelski who, as the man who had imposed martial law, could ease Soviet fears; and Prime Minister Mazowiecki, who simultaneously made it clear both to the Poles and to the West that there was a strong will for change.

In the meantime, however, many people in Poland have begun to believe that we are going too slowly, and that it is time to break the agreements that were made with the old ruling power. I contend that we should think twice before disturbing this fragile equilibrium. There are two ways to emerge from dictatorship. The first is the Spanish model. It begins with a pragmatic compromise between reformers from the government and the democratic opposition. This enables the members of the ancien régime to reconcile themselves to the new situation; they have a chance to survive and can hope to find a new place in society; they will even become defenders of democratization because they see that they can gain advantages from it.

The second way was taken in Germany and France: 'denazification', or *expiation* of collaboration. But that way also meant revenge; the settling of accounts; retribution. And when I consider where such an approach can lead, once again I see two variants. First there is the Iranian model: one dictatorship is supplanted by another; the ideology, language, and symbols are new, but a dictatorship is ruling once again. This is the case precisely because democracy is the child of compromise, and violence the child of retribution. Second, there is the situation that gives rise to the 'Kabul syndrome'. In Afghanistan a full year after the withdrawal of Soviet forces the Communists continue to rule. They have no choice because the mujahiddin have not given them a chance to adapt to the new circumstances. The Communists are defending themselves with such bitterness because only one fate awaits them if they lose. In Poland, on the other hand, the Communists can simply give up – an outcome unparalleled in history.

Communism has suffered many defeats in Poland over the years; now, however, it has capitulated. What we are seeing now is the retreat from the centres of power by people who are defending their positions, their money, and their personal security – but who no longer believe in the restoration of Communism. Communism is dead; but what continues to exist is the army and the security apparatus – groups who know that they have lost, who are frustrated and frightened, who feel threatened, and who continue to have weapons at their disposal. This is a very dangerous combination. Military conspiracies such as those of the OAS in France – by small groups that act desperately – can also occur in Poland. This situation compels us to make compromises, and it rules out confrontation.

The greatest threat to democracy today is no longer Communism, either as a political movement or as an ideology. The threat grows instead from a combination of chauvinism, xenophobia, populism, and authoritarianism, all of them connected with the sense of frustration typical of great social upheavals. This is the perspective from which we must view the old conflicts that are now flaring up again in Central and Eastern Europe. The Soviet Union provides an especially vivid illustration of the two types of anti-Communism now locked in struggle with each other. One, as represented by Sakharov, is liberal, pluralistic, and European; the other, advocated by Igor Shafarevich, is xenophobic, authoritarian, turned toward the past and toward restoring the life of the past.* This second type of anti-Communism is distinguished most

---

*Igor Shafarevich is a well-known Soviet mathematician. In the 1970s, he became a prominent ally of Aleksandr Solzhenitsyn and defender of human rights in the USSR. Author of *Russophobia*, a Slavophile history of Russia, Shafarevich has recently written in support of authoritarian, anti-Western, and anti-Semitic policies.

tellingly by its reluctance to do away with the figure of Stalin, because he was the founder of the Great Russian empire. Dictatorship, according to this view, should not be abolished but should rather be continued in a different form. Collective property will also continue to exist, with the collective farms being replaced by more traditional communes – *arteli.* The members of this movement do not see their main enemy in the Communists, but rather in those who aim to create democratic institutions and an open, civil society. What they share with the old Stalinists is the struggle against the influence of Europe, which in their eyes embodies greed, godlessness, and the decline of morals. Russia must be protected against this by the creation of an anti-European bloc within Russian culture.

If Russian history is viewed from this perspective, it is merely the next logical step to reject Communism not because it was a dictatorship, but because it was not Russian. Communism was not invented in Russia; Marx was not born there, nor was the *Communist Manifesto* published there – it was decadent Western civilization that infected Russia with Communism. The Bolshevist Revolution was not the work of Russians, but of foreigners – the Jew Trotsky, the Pole Dzerzhinsky, the Georgian Stalin, Ukrainians, Latvians, and Chinese. The Russians were innocent. This line of thinking can be observed most clearly in Russia. But it is the manifestation of a psychological mechanism that has been set off in all of the countries in which the Communists held power, including Poland. Here as well there are certain people who hold aliens and foreigners – Russians, Germans, Jews, cosmopolites, Freemasons – accountable for bringing Communism to Poland. The most important conflict in Polish culture today is being fought between those who see the future of Poland as part of Europe and those characterized by the Polish sociologist Jerzy Szacki as 'natiocentric' – although the first do not by any means reject national values and traditions, and the latter are not necessarily chauvinist. In any case, these two approaches today divide the Polish intelligentsia; they cut across all political lines and can be found among adherents of the ancien régime as well as within Solidarity and the Catholic Church.

When considering the fate of Eastern and Central Europe, I often ask myself whether chauvinism will once again gain the upper hand. Whether the victors will be those in Berlin and Dresden who screamed *Polen raus,* or wrote those words on walls, in November and December of last year; those in Bulgaria who deny Muslims the right to their own names; those in Transylvania who deny Hungarians the right to their own schools; those in Poland who promote anti-Semitism and a country without Jews. These people could be victorious. They have their chance because we do not know what will flow into the great vacuum left behind by the death of Communism. And also because the democratic idea and Christian thinking are complicated: they do not pretend to give simple answers to the difficult questions of the age. So the chauvinistic approach could win. What we have learned during the past year (the most unusual in the forty-four years of my life) is that there is no determinism in history, that our history depends far more on ourselves, on our will and our decisions, than any of us thought. If we want to stand up to the danger, we have to know where it comes from, and we have to call it by its name. And if there are reasons for assuming that this danger is deeply rooted in certain social attitudes that can only promise new injustice and new oppression, then it is our duty as inheritors of European culture to fight against those attitudes – in the name of all those values of Judeo-Christian culture that were defended for centuries at the cost of great sacrifices.

Just as France showed two faces during the Dreyfus trial, two faces are now being shown in Eastern and Central Europe. Even then, however, the forces of good and evil were not neatly divided along the lines that separated leftist republicans from rightist national conservatives. It is never that simple. For that reason we must always be prepared to understand and acknowledge the values of our opponents, even those we are fighting against. Only then are we truly Europeans.

*Translated by Mariusz Matusiak and Christian Caryl*

# 15

# The Helsinki Citizens' Assembly

## INTRODUCTION

The proposal to found a Helsinki Citizens' Assembly for Peace and Democracy emerged out of the dialogue between Charter 77 and Western peace groups, known as 'detente from below'. The Assembly is supposed to institutionalize that dialogue. Its aims are twofold.

First, it constitutes a permanent pressure for a pan-European security system that would supplant the military blocs and find ways of solving conflicts in Europe without reliance on military force. The Assembly will put forward ideas, suggestions and proposals for disarmament and demilitarization. But it will also tackle problems, injustices, divisions, and so on, in Europe that could lead to violent conflict. Secondly, the Assembly sustains and encourages the creation of a trans-European civil society. Europe has to be integrated from below. The Assembly facilitates networks of autonomous groups, movements or initiatives which can come together to protect each other, to put pressure on governments and to establish a genuine European public opinion.

The term 'Helsinki' refers to the 1975 Helsinki Accords, better known as the Conference on Security and Co-operation in Europe. These Accords were considered to be the high point of detente in the 1970s and first made the link between security and human rights. Under the term 'Helsinki', North American citizens can participate in the Assembly.

The Assembly is a permanent organization with a secretariat in Prague and permanent commissions, working on disarmament and demilitarization; economy and ecology; nationalism and federalism;

women's and human rights. The Assembly will meet regularly and will involve representatives of social movements as well as individual politicians, and individuals from culture and the arts. Individuals will be able to participate in the work of the Assembly even if they cannot participate in the meetings. The idea is to create a kind of pan-European movement.

There are, of course, very different perspectives among the people who are engaged in the work of the Assembly. In particular, a tension arises from the role of the Czechoslovak initiators. When the Assembly was proposed, Charter 77 was a harassed human rights group – its members were constantly under surveillance and periodically imprisoned. The Assembly idea was a brave gesture. Today, the protagonists of the Assembly – Václav Havel, Jiři Dienstbier, Jaroslav Šabata – are prominent members of the Czechoslovak government, and many others, for instance from the Independent Peace Association, are Members of Parliament. On the one hand, this has made it possible for the Assembly to take place. On the other hand, can the Czechoslovak government really be considered part of civil society? This tension expresses a very real contradiction in the conception of civil society; with luck, it could be used constructively to enliven discussions and to develop ideas.

The article by Jiři Dienstbier (now Czechoslovak Foreign Secretary) was written in March 1989, and provides a perspective of the Assembly from before the Czechoslovak revolution. The interview with Jaroslav Šabata was conducted in June 1990, after the Czechoslovak elections. Jane Mayes and Stephen Brown ask Šabata to reflect on the relation between the power-holders and the powerless. Finally, my speech to the closing session of the first Assembly, which was held in Prague in October 1990, expresses my own view on this debate and on what was actually achieved at the Assembly meeting.

## *Jiří Dienstbier:*

## THE HELSINKI PROCESS 'FROM BELOW'

The Prague 88 Seminar in June 1988 was constantly thwarted by the Czechoslovak police, and foreign participants were eventually expelled. Nevertheless a Final Document was drawn up, which included the suggestion that a non-governmental assembly be created – a kind of 'parliament from below' in the Helsinki process. Both the proposal and the circumstances of the seminar are typical of the current situation in Europe – of the dramatic pressure which has arisen due to the penetration of awakening freedom and responsibility into the ossified structures of the Cold War.

Although the post-war division of Europe has not satisfied anyone, until recently only a few dared to dream about overcoming the problem and about practical political work. The idea that military and political blocs might be disbanded and that the safety of nations and states from San Francisco to Vladivostok could be safeguarded not by confrontation between blocs but by peaceful co-operation seemed idealistic – something which would be realized only in the very distant future....

The Helsinki Accords of 1975 did not originally change much of this. Their government protagonists saw them as a strengthening of the status quo rather than as a way of fundamentally changing international politics. The majority of countries, East and West, ignored the Helsinki process. Some considered it to be a capitulation in the face of Brezhnev's power politics. Others saw in it a greater guarantee of safety for the West, obtained through complicity with the inertia in the East. Thus it was with mistrust that they observed independent movements which might cause destabilization in the Eastern half of Europe; for their own peace of mind, they did not try to understand that the source of destabilization is the inertia with which Stalinism, exhausted and on its last legs, strives to delay its departure from the historical scene.

It was in fact these independent movements which uncovered the hidden possibilities in the Helsinki process; also because by its very terms, states accepted international agreements on human rights as a gauge of the behaviour of people and states. In several of the Warsaw Pact countries, committees were formed to monitor their own governments' observance – or rather, violation – of the Accords. From the international agreements on human rights [in 'basket three' of the Accords], ratified by Czechoslovakia in 1976, arose the founders of Charter 77 in Czechoslovakia.

Even in the West some people seized the positive opportunity offered by Helsinki. For example, at the end of the 1970s the US Helsinki Watch was set up. Among politicians the pioneer of discussion in the spirit of those regulations was the Dutch Foreign Minister, Max van den Stoel, who, during an official visit to Prague in 1977, met Jan Patočka, a Charter spokesperson. Some of President Carter's actions resulted in American diplomacy shattering hitherto common clichés about diplomatic relations. Today, meetings between visiting politicians and representatives of independent movements have become a natural part of the protocol.

At the start of the 1980s discussions were also initiated between independent movements, groups and individuals from East and West. The Prague Appeal, sent in 1985 by several dozen Charter 77 signatories to the END Convention in Amsterdam, was an attempt to synthesize these discussions by outlining a strategy for all independent groups. The Appeal proposed that the Helsinki process should be used as a point of departure in preparing the common strategy. The discussion that followed produced a memorandum, *Giving Real Life to the Helsinki Accords*, signed by individuals, groups and organizations from almost all the Helsinki countries. This document was sent to the Vienna follow-up conference just as that conference was getting under way.

European independent activists had agreed, among other things, that issues of peace and security, detente and co-operation, human rights and self-determination were interconnected and could not be treated in isolation. It had also been agreed that concentration on a single issue at the expense of all the others (for instance, the issue of disarmament) was misleading and unproductive. It was necessary to overcome the division of Europe, and it was essential to start at once. The bi-polar superpower manipulation of international politics had to be done away with and substituted by political unity in diversity. It was recognized at the same time that the work of governments was not enough. Independent civil activity was needed if political unity in diversity was to be achieved.

Regardless of all the problems associated with overcoming the rigidified power structures and Cold War thinking, the international situation has become much more hopeful since 1985. There is now increasing opportunity for positive change. The Vienna Final Act, approved in January 1989, is good evidence of this; it amounts to a considerable breakthrough in the field of human rights. At the same time, it offers new opportunities for disarmament talks.

However, even as the Final Act was being signed in Vienna, the Czechoslovak authorities were brutally suppressing independent peaceful demonstrations in Prague. Playwright Václav Havel, peace activists Jan Petrova, Ota Veverka, Hana Marvanova, Tomas Dvořák and others were put on trial. This shows that there is still conflict between the internationally agreed principles and the actual behaviour of certain regimes. As a result, numerous obstacles still stand in the way of full co-operation between independent activists from East and West. (Many East European activists, for example, are unable to travel beyond the borders of their own countries.)

Recently it has been possible to hold joint independent seminars in Warsaw, Budapest, Cracow and Moscow. Independent activists from Hungary and Poland (and sometimes from other East European countries) have been able to attend meetings in the West. However, if we wish actively to contribute to a major breakthrough in international relations, we must adopt higher forms of co-ordination. Governments alone are unable to overcome the existing situation. They are too closely tied to the management of the current political status quo. They are captives of the existing internal and international structures. In pursuit of popular support, they often have to act in accordance with what they see as the momentary demands of the voting public, and with other demands. The electorate's demands are often misunderstood by politicians. Independent activists and movements are free to formulate the social tasks that lie ahead much more openly and realistically, because they do not need to take heed of power politics.

It is desirable that the Helsinki process at government level be complemented by an independent international assembly that would consistently strive for the peaceful and democratic reunification of Europe. This assembly should work towards the creation of a free, economically strong, ecologically orientated and socially just society in Europe, North America and the Soviet Union.

The Helsinki process would thus take place at government level and at the same time be pursued by individual citizens. Activities on both levels should be parallel. There should be co-operation between both levels of the Helsinki process. Constructive criticism should be voiced. The independent Citizens' Assembly would be a continuous source of initiative. It would generate new proposals. It would be free to examine critically the ongoing Helsinki process from an independent standpoint and would create grassroots pressure. Apart from tabling their own proposals, it would be the role of government structures to codify the results achieved by altering international law in the Legal Codes of the countries concerned. The independent peace assembly would thus function as a kind of international 'round table'.

Representing differing political groupings and movements which are independent of governments, the Assembly would express a plurality of views. The minimal programme of these groups would be the implementation of the agreements reached through the Helsinki process. These groups would aim to express and further extend the individual articles of these agreements in concrete terms. The ultimate aim would be a European unification on a new footing. The new unified Europe would do away with the current practice of disregarding the individual human being and his/her dignity, and it would pay special attention to environmental issues.

If Europe were reunified in line with these principles, the impact would be major and worldwide. If Cold War structures and thinking were done away with in Europe, North America and the USSR – an area which has a decisive potential for the further development of our civilization as a whole – and if people and nations in this area came to coexist in pluralist and democratic societies, it would have a strongly beneficial effect on the situation in the Third World.

Anyone who accepts that relations between individuals and states should be based on democratic principles could become a member of the Assembly. Respect for human rights would therefore become the commonly accepted point of departure and mode of behaviour in our civilization. Supporters or advocates of terrorism would not be tolerated. If open political dialogue is to be the Assembly's basic principle, its members must be duty-bound collectively and openly to condemn acts of terrorism aimed at independent activists and their work, even in their own countries.

The list of issues that should be put on the Assembly's agenda is just as endless as the list of problems which still plague us. They include: abolition of military and political blocs; gradual nuclear and conventional disarmament; withdrawal of troops from other countries; implementation of consistently defensive military strategies; protection of the environment; and a transition towards an ecologically conscious economy.

But there are also a number of seemingly less important problems the solution of which would be of exceptional psychological value. For instance, people should be free to travel abroad; conditions should be created for young people to visit other countries on an exchange basis; people should be able to attend language courses in the countries where the languages are spoken. By devoting attention to these problems and by its other work, the Assembly would contribute to demilitarizing the international community as well as individual societies. It would help people to overcome outmoded prejudices and misunderstandings and would work towards the creation of a friendly and peaceful climate in the area of the Helsinki process.

It has been proposed that the seat of the assembly should be Prague. Numerous significant events in European history are associated with this city. In the twentieth century alone, it has witnessed several such major events. Czechoslovakia came into being in 1918 as a result of the victory of the democratic powers in the Great War. Munich 1938 not only heralded the destruction of the democratic Czechoslovak republic, but paved the way for Hitler's attempt to conquer the world. February 1948 [when Communists took power in Czechoslovakia] confirmed the division of Europe and led to the creation of the two power blocs. The Prague Spring of 1968 constituted a hope, soon destroyed by the Warsaw Pact invasion.

Now, twenty years on, this hope seems to have returned. Prague is at the geographical centre of Europe. Of all the capitals of the countries in Europe's eastern half, Prague is situated nearest the borderline between the two blocs. The January 1989 massacre at Wenceslas Square in Prague, when riot police attacked peaceful demonstrators at the very time the Vienna Final Act was being signed, and the political trials and other persecution that followed, also underline the psychological importance of choosing Prague as the symbolic seat of the new Assembly – even if it proves impossible for the Assembly to convene there. The struggle for Prague is a struggle for the disposal of the debris of the rusty Iron Curtain.

The debate about the setting up of the Helsinki 'grass-roots parliament' has now reached the stage when concrete proposals regarding organizational structure are being discussed. If the 'parliament' is to become a politically productive forum, it will have to have governing bodies, a secretariat, and permanent working committees, as well as *ad hoc* committees to deal with specific questions as they arise. It will be necessary to provide technological back-up and to set up a press and documentation centre. Financial resources will have to be found which are not tied to political conditions.

It is therefore clear that the setting up of a Helsinki Citizens' Assembly will be a long-term task. It is impossible to say in advance when this task might be completed. It will depend on the ability of the individual working committees to gain authority and recognition through the concrete results of their work. These committees can start tackling some of the simpler and more burning issues even before the whole Assembly can be set up as the Supreme Body of the Movement. However, the Assembly's international preparatory committee should strive from the outset for the recognition of the Assembly as an independent institution working within the framework of the Helsinki process.

Six years ago, I wrote to the second END Convention, in Berlin (which I was unable to attend because I had been denied a passport):

I agree that we must act as though a free Europe, united in creative plurality, already existed.... There is no other way of testing the real will of governments except by confronting their promises and statements with the free will of citizens in any particular country and in the international community as a whole. If we find that governments represent the mere specific interests of the power-wielders within a given country or a given bloc, we should attempt to create a European movement of people who strive for common, universal human values. The tradition of European civilization and culture places us under an obligation to do so. At the same time, this tradition is the source of our optimism.

I am glad that these days, we are much nearer to this goal than could have been expected when I wrote those words.

*Translated by Emma Davies and Pavel Stránský*

# AN INTERVIEW WITH JAROSLAV ŠABATA

**Q:** For a number of years, before the events of last autumn, there was a dialogue between representatives of peace organizations in the West and social movements such as Charter 77, Solidarity, and independent peace and human rights groups. Do you think that this dialogue has played a role in the development of Czechoslovak foreign policy today?

**A:** Of course. The official Czechoslovak policy, as formulated by the government and the President, is not a policy which is bound to the status quo. It has a wider perspective. Take, for example, Havel's speech to the Council of Europe. The perspective is basically the original perspective of Charter 77 as it developed through contact with peace groups. The basic declaration from 1985, known as the Prague Appeal, was written at the height of an argument within Charter 77, epitomized by the names Raček and Thompson. Some of the Charter people rejected co-operation with the 'peaceniks'. The letter from Václav Benda in spring 1984 supported this view. It was a rejection of END, of CND, of co-operation. Even President Reagan quoted this letter as proof that Charter 77 did not agree with the peace movements. The crisis within Charter 77 that thereby arose led to the development of an all-European – including an all-German – perspective. We should be grateful to the peace movements for causing this crisis, which compelled us to work out a strategic position that could be shared by all democratic positions within Charter 77: left and right, or centre-left and centre-right. One can say that the communication with the peace movement led us to this policy. It was not shared by the right-wing forces, the ultra-conservatives, but basically it became the consensus position. This consensus was maintained later in the Manifesto 'Democracy for All', from autumn 1988. Most Charter people united behind this manifesto, this programmatic declaration; and this in turn became part of the policy of Civic Forum. This was the development which today is official Czechoslovak policy.

**Q:** But how do you see the opportunities to implement these perspectives politically? You are no longer talking simply about these perspectives in unofficial groups, but about a situation where this policy has become state policy. Can the perspective of the Prague Appeal be realized in Europe today? The Prague Appeal was developed by people who had no official role in politics. Now they are co-responsible for state policy. Can these perspectives be realized politically?

**A:** Of course, of course. the basic idea was to overcome the blocs.

This was the idea of the first half of the 1980s – your idea as well – and this idea, which today is linked to the idea of a new security system, is completely realistic politics. That can be seen in many ways. And alongside the official policy there is also, so to say, a civic, a citizens', dimension, which is found in what we call the Helsinki Citizens' Assembly. So we are following the policy of 'Helsinki from Below' from above, but also continuing from below. These are complementary parts of one whole policy. I am both Chair of the Czech Preparatory Committee of the HCA and Chair of the Parliamentary Foreign Affairs Committee. It will develop further. It is a question of the idea of a radical democratic integration of Europe, which should lead to the total overcoming of the division of Europe. In the last six months it has really been possible to see that we are following this policy officially. Perhaps you know that many diplomats – American, but British as well – call Havel and Dienstbier 'peaceniks'. You know, of course, that they do not hold the classic pacifist position, but the aim is the same.

**Q:**    You spoke of the concrete opportunities to implement these aims. What are they?

**A:**    The Warsaw Pact has already agreed that within a short time it should be only a political alliance, and that it should actively participate in disarmament activities. Those are practical steps. We are going further. We are working with a medium-term perspective of founding an Organization of European States. Today it is still not clear how this will develop, but the principle that the European process, the Helsinki process, should be institutionalized has wide support and a large measure of consensus. The Soviets, who had been less keen on this idea, have now developed a similar proposal. Also the German Question, which now has a totally new dimension, has to be seen from this perspective.

**Q:**    The Prague Appeal supported the right of the Germans, as of other nations, to self-determination. Now there is a political situation that makes German unity possible. But in NATO it is said that the territory of the GDR must be integrated into NATO, and a united Germany must be part of NATO. What would be the implications of this for countries in Central and Western Europe, such as Czechoslovakia?

**A:**    We often hear from the West that the unification of Germany is not a positive factor for European unity but rather a negative one. We do not agree. We think that Germany, the unification of Germany, can and must contribute to the unification of Europe. The question is whether the European states, both in the West and in the East, clearly comprehend this new challenge and energetically make progress towards the integration of the two parts of Europe. It is not important for us whether Germany remains part of NATO or not. Perhaps it is for Soviet policy, but not for us. For us it is important that NATO changes its strategy and its whole concept in that it contributes to the abolition of the military blocs. I do not want to discuss all the implications of that now. You will know that there have already been some steps in this direction. That must happen 'from above' in official forums, in the two-plus-four talks, but we must also develop a bridge 'from below' that will lead to the phasing out of the military blocs. That is also the task of the Helsinki Citizens' Assembly: to formulate very concrete steps in this direction.

**Q:** How do you see the possibilities of the HCA developing such a political strategy?

**A:** I am an optimist. At the beginning of this new phase of Czecho-slovak policy, we were not completely agreed on the weight to be given to this citizens' (civic) dimension, now there is a large measure of agreement between officially orientated people and less officially orientated people. You know that Havel, in Strasbourg, mentioned the Helsinki Citizens' Assembly. In Eastern Europe, or in the Eastern part of a divided Europe, there has been progress since the spring. In Moscow we spoke with rather important people, both official and unofficial, about the Helsinki Citizens' Assembly. We have spoken to representatives from the Baltic states. (A Lithuanian may work in the HCA office and at the same time serve as an unofficial Lithuanian ambassador to Czecho-slovakia, since we do not have official relations with Lithuania.) We have spoken with Poland and Hungary and further steps will be taken to unite all forces who wish to promote the radical democratic integration of Europe.

**Q:** There was some debate in the eighties about the relation between stabilizing and destabilizing strategies; between democratization and demilitarization. Where is the HCA within this debate?

**A:** The question of so-called nationalism – a problem in Central Europe, the Soviet Union and the Balkans – will be very much to the fore. The HCA should contribute to the important political forces uniting to overcome these destabilizing tendencies. As far as Central Europe is concerned we are in favour of regional co-operation, the core of which should be Czechoslovakia, Poland and Hungary; that is state policy today, but we also want support from below. A declaration based on the Bratislava decisions has been published which speaks of comprehensive co-operation by these three states, so that they can become an important force in European politics. This formation should have links both to the south and to the north. You know of the regional group of Czechoslovakia, Hungary, Yugoslavia, Austria and Italy. A similar group around the Baltic Sea will be developed step by step. This group in turn will have good relations with the Council of Baltic States, an important aim of which is to play an autonomous, independent role in the Helsinki process, not only within the framework of the Soviet Union but also directly. These are all aspects of the dynamic of the policy which we represent both in official institutions and in regional groupings.

**Q:** But you speak of the links between state policy and citizens' policy on the other side. Is there not a danger that this citizens' level could be instrumentalized in the service of state policy?

**A:** Of course. There is such a danger, a great danger. But we can overcome this danger if we reflect critically on developments as a whole; if we don't move only in the orbit of official policy. Look at the question of Lithuania. Should Czechoslovakia recognize Lithuania as an independent state or not? That is a very concrete question. The government does not dare to do that yet – not yet. It would like to, but there are barriers – you can imagine what I mean. We do not think we should destroy the Warsaw Pact; we must transform it. One has to find ways which will lead to the recognition of Lithuania. That should be the business of all democratic forces in Europe, and in this sense the citizens' level should be ahead of the government, and do what the government cannot do, so that the changes which are necessary in the Soviet Union and in the whole of the East can be made sooner. But it is also the case that the demand for recognition is not supported by some pacifist or left-orientated forces in Western Europe. It might be. Then the question is whether these forces are not more conservative than some forces in government circles in Eastern Europe. That is an area for dialogue.

**Q:** But are you now a bit too optimistic about the citizens' movements? Some say, at least in the West, that citizens' movements have become increasingly institutionalized so that the Citizens' Assembly is not really an assembly of movements, but rather of institutionalized organizations, with fixed structures, their own organizational interests which are more important than the political subject matter itself.

**A:** Yes, but then we see the institutionalized civic initiatives in the same way as we see the official policy. That is a bit too speculative. One must analyse where institutionalization has taken place. For example, we know END, where this institutionalization has led in the course of time to bureaucratization; where we have lost a feeling for the important challenges of the time; where we – so to say – are thinking about whether we stay or go. That is also a question of a dialogue between us.

**Q:** On what does participation in the HCA depend? How should organizations be represented? How can this Citizens' Assembly really be representative?

**A:** That is the main question, a question which can be solved only in practice and is not solved yet. We have the feeling that in the West the invitation policy has still not been sorted out. In the East it is much easier. The dynamic is so strong that it is straightforward to involve the forces from below and from above. Look at Landsbergis, the President of the Lithuanian Parliament – is he above or below? Where is he, in contrast to Gorbachev? I discussed with him pushing forward the transformation of the Soviet Union in the name of European transformation. Was I a person from below or from above? What I mean is that in the East, genuine representatives of the important forces in the Assembly can and will come: people like Grigoryants, from the Glasnost group; the Social Democrats; the Inter-Regional Group in the Soviet Parliament; and even Gorbachev's people. That is to say: if we look at Russia, we need to consider all these things. The contacts are developing very dynamically. In the West, there is a great danger that the basis, the sociopolitical basis, will be very narrow. We have drawn the attention of our friends from the pacifist movements to this danger a number of times.

**Q:** But this question of whether the invitation policy is too narrow or not is linked perhaps to another question: what the political direction of the Assembly is intended to be: an assembly of the Centre such as Charter 77, or one with a centre-left or a centre-right orientation?

**A:** If possible, a centre with both sides. If there is only one side, it will not be correct. That is our opinion. In the West, the HCA has had a centre-left orientation until now, in a way we want to bring people from the Left and from the Right together at the same table. Both sides don't have to have the same weight, but step by step we want to go in this direction. The most important thing is to focus on the new situation, rather than getting stuck in the Left–Right antagonism. We don't see the perspective of a democratic united Europe from the old left-wing position, but neither do we see it from a right-wing position. We are looking for a new order that will transcend the status quo in all its aspects.

**Q:**   Until now, the Citizens' Assembly has been mainly organized from Czechoslovakia; the first meeting takes place in Prague. Do you think that the preparatory work will be taken over by other groups in other countries, or will it stay in Prague?

**A:**   Not at all. I'm aware of the accusation. We don't want it to become the project of just a small group in Prague. In the tradition of Charter 77, we want as wide a spectrum of participants as possible. We have no Pragocentrist thoughts. For us it is vital that it should not be narrowly pacifist or left dominated. I say that quite openly.

**Q:**   Do you see any chance that this will not be both the first and the last Assembly, but rather an assembly as part of a process?

**A:**   If it is not an assembly that is part of a process, it has no point at all. We see the Assembly as just one step in a direction that will continue to develop.

*Translated by Stephen Brown*

## *Mary Kaldor:*

# SPEECH TO THE CLOSING SESSION OF THE HELSINKI CITIZENS' ASSEMBLY

The Helsinki Citizens' Assembly has been founded!

It was chaotic. There were too many boring panels. There were not enough women speakers. There was a lot of misunderstanding, difficulty in communicating. It was exhausting. It was overcrowded. There was not enough time. People couldn't find their beds. They couldn't find their working groups. They had the wrong colour stripe on their pink tickets for meals. They didn't have time for the cultural events.

But despite everything, it happened! If you think where we were ten years ago, this was an extraordinary achievement. Just the fact that Azerbaijanis, Scots, Welsh, Canadians, Swiss, Hungarians, not to mention Germans and Russians, actually met and talked together, this was a great event. It was also an extraordinary organizational achievement. It is still very difficult to organize meetings in Eastern Europe. We have a tiny secretariat, very little money, only one telephone, and only recently a fax and computers.

It was a happening. But it was also more than that. What I found, at any rate in my working group, despite all the difficulties, was energy, enthusiasm and commitment. People sat through all the frustrating meetings and stayed to the end. Listening to all the proposals and ideas, you can see that there is a real readiness to work together.

So who are we? We represent democratic and human rights groups; peace movements; green movements; national groups; popular fronts; women's groups; gay groups; groups for minority rights – especially immigrants; community groups. We include politicians from a wide range of political parties. We include people from universities, churches, trades unions, cooperatives, enterprises, and even banks, newspapers and magazines.

We came together because of a common commitment to the democratic integration of Europe. What I felt was a sense of relief, the satisfaction of a real need, at finding each other. During the past year, after the euphoria of the revolutions, events have moved at a furious pace. Many of us have experienced a kind of helplessness. Once again, we seem to be swamped by imposed models of society. Many people here from the West (and also, I found, quite a few from the East) are really concerned about the new ideology of free markets that seems to be sweeping the East, aided and abetted by Western governments and institutions. Don't get me wrong. I am not against markets. But I am against the ideology of markets. I am against the notion that the market should be the dominant regulative principle of society; that profits, prices and costs are more important than concern about unemployment, environmental degradation, or the situation of women. I am against the privatization of the individual; the transformation of citizens into consumers; the way in which videos, home computers, cable TV, replace civic and social life.

On the other hand, even *more* frightening, is the growth of new fundamentalisms which have been nurtured by forty (or seventy) years of totalitarianism; exclusivist nationalism – nationalism which is not just about self-determination, but is directed against an other; xenophobia, racism, anti-semitism, homophobia, religious fundamentalism. The space for democratic alternatives, for choice about lives, for participation in decisions about our society, seems to be squeezed out, on the one hand, by consumerist culture, and, on the other hand, by the wave of fundamentalism.

There is a real parallel with the Cold War period. There are two models of society which appear to be fundamentally opposed. But, in fact, they complement and reinforce each other. Consumerism, the unchecked market, needs ever more resources. It breeds on economic inequalities. An exclusivist culture, it creates outside the charmed consumerist circle the conditions in which fundamentalism can flourish. Markets are both creative and destructive. They provide an entrée both to the consumerist West *and* to the crisis-ridden South. What is more, consumerism needs a horrible alternative to legitimize itself. The joys of private consumption may not satisfy those who have a social conscience. Now we have lost totalitarianism, fundamentalism has come to the rescue, to explain why all is well in our society.

The new cold war between fundamentalism and consumerism is being played out now in the Gulf crisis. It is symbolized in a military confrontation which squeezes out the space for democratic and peaceful alternatives. The dictatorships that the West created through its greed for oil and the sale of arms now stand counterposed to the West as its opposite, not its creation.

If we are to find a democratic alternative, we really need each other. We in the West, who are concerned about the erosion of democracy and of civic responsibility under the impact of consumer culture, really need East and Central Europe to help us build a peaceful democratic Europe; not an isolated, rich, fortress Western Europe. And I think that people in the East need a responsive concerned West that really wants to solve the problems of poverty and the environment. What I have felt during these last few days was how much we needed each other.

We are here to expand the space for democratic approaches in both

East and West, to ensure that a united Europe is a democratic Europe and not a consumerist and/or fundamentalist Europe.

So what kind of an organization are we? Are we a lobbying organization for the Helsinki process from above? Are we a citizens' network? Are we an embryo parliament? Do we represent civil society? Well, we are some of those things. We are definitely a citizens' network. There are a lot of proposals for networking, for mutual information, for joint activities, meetings, seminars, and so on. We are definitely a lobbying organization. There are a lot of proposals to be addressed to governments, especially the governments engaged in the Helsinki process. But we are not an embryo parliament and I do not think that we represent civil society.

We are a citizens' assembly not a parliament. We are concerned about democracy not in the sense of electing representatives and delegating responsibility. That is important. It has to happen; there have to be parliaments. But we are concerned about democracy in the sense of participating in public debates, offering opinions and discussing alternatives in a context that is not influenced by electoral gain, in the sense of having to take responsibility ourselves for our societies.

We are not representative of civil society; we are a part of civil society. If we were representative of civil society, we would be no different from a parliament. We would include people committed to consumerism and people committed to fundamentalism. Of course, those people can come to the Assembly; we are ready to discuss with anyone. But we certainly don't represent them. In fact, we don't represent anyone but the movements and institutions in which we are involved. In many cases, we represent no one but ourselves. And our power rests not on whom we represent but in what we do – in what we say, in our ideas, in our quest for truth, in the projects we undertake. It rests on our energy and commitment.

So where do we go from here? I want to stress that where we go depends on us. The Helsinki Citizens' Assembly is us. Whether or not we can establish a permanent and significant organization to strengthen democracy in Europe depends on what each of us does now. There is no one else to do it but us. So it is up to us to establish functioning national committees, to participate in commissions and working groups, to turn all these wonderful ideas into reality. If only a fraction of what was proposed here today happens, the Helsinki Citizens' Assembly will be very successful.

*21 October 1990*

# Postscript

## ADDRESS TO THE OPENING SESSION
## OF THE HELSINKI CITIZENS' ASSEMBLY

### *Václav Havel*

Dear friends,

It seems to me that it is first and foremost my pleasant duty as Head of State to welcome you to Czechoslovakia and to express my joy that this meeting is taking place here.

I will use the opportunity of having been given the floor for a moment to consider one issue in particular. At the time of dissent and opposition, of the so-called dissidents; at a time when we 'fought for human rights', struck up our first friendships, our first contacts, and began our first cooperation with various independent and peace-orientated and democratic organizations in Western Europe, we were pariahs in our own society. We lived on the fringes of society. We were persecuted, we were imprisoned. We were, if it can be put like that, the lowest of the low. Now, some strange and miraculous quirk of history has elevated us to the highest office. Literally on returning from boiler rooms and police interrogation rooms, we found ourselves in the top positions of government.

At the time when we were the so-called dissidents, we did not like that expression very much. We emphasized many times that the struggle we had taken on had little in common with what is traditionally understood by the expression 'politics'. We discussed such concepts as non-political politics, and stressed that we were interested in certain values and principles and not in power and position. We emphasized the importance of the spirit, the importance of truth, and we said that even spirit and truth embody a certain kind of power. I remember very well Western journalists visiting me for years and telling me: You are just a small group of lunatics who write some papers or other and circulate them among yourselves, but you don't have any real physical power at your disposal. You face a gigantic police force, a gigantic state bureaucracy of the totalitarian system, and the army. Who is on your side? Certainly not the workers. The workers are apathetic. They are not interested in your struggle. They are barely aware of it. You are totally quixotic. Why do you do what you do?

We were asked such questions extremely frequently and we replied over and over again that under the conditions of a totalitarian system (though not only under such conditions) social impact and importance is not measured by numbers of votes or by the number of open supporters or by the size of the organization. True social impact resides in the strength of the word of truth, in a person's courage to call things by their true names, regardless of consequences. But the journalists told us, in a nutshell, that the spirit cannot prevail over brute force, that we were utopians and totally naïve.

Yet a strange thing happened. The spirit did prevail over brute force. The truth did prevail over the lie. It did not need any instruments of coercion; it did not need weapons; it did not even need the breaking of a single shop window. And this strange turn of events – which was very surprising even to us – vindicated our views. We always used to say that we did what we did for the sake of the principle; that we did not rely on any outcome; that we were simply forced to wage the struggle by our consciences. And suddenly, the struggle did have an outcome. The circumstances did change. The totalitarian system did crumble. And more than that. Another very strange thing happened: we were elevated to the highest positions of state.

From that time onwards the same people who used to doubt whether there was any point in our struggle have naturally started to ask us other pointed questions: Are your ideals of non-political politics still valid? Do you still believe that truth outweighs the number of your supporters? Are you still not interested in positions of power? Is it still true that you are unwilling to use tactics and manoeuvres and that you do not want to pursue that brand of politics which relies on the technology of power and the technology of the power struggle? Aren't you forced to give up your earlier views, concepts and ideals now that you have assumed top positions? Aren't you forced to drop all these ideals as the naïve notions of dissidents? Aren't you actually doing in your posts exactly what your predecessors, those 'technologists of power', used to do, with whom you either clashed directly or whom you at least criticized.

I think that in certain regards these questions are fully justified. Because what has come about in this country is truly a great change. We daily realize that although we have acquired a degree of dexterity in demolishing the old system – we really had learned to do that rather well over the years – we were not properly prepared or sufficiently equipped for the building of a new system. Now that the old system has collapsed, we face the task of building a new, different, truly democratic system. It turns out that, no matter how difficult it is to bring down a totalitarian system, it is even more difficult to build a new and better system from its ruins. Since we entered the world of high politics, we have realized that in this world one does have to take account of various conflicting interests, of various ambitions, of the balance of power represented by different groupings; one also has to take into account the various illusions which persist in one's society, or which tend to rise anew. Simply, a person in the world of high politics is forced to manoeuvre, to behave diplomatically. Simply, we are now in a different arena. That is true and in this sense all these questions are understandable.

In short, it is undeniable that we are now moving in a totally different environment and have a totally different kind of responsibility from when we were in opposition. But in my view and in my experience, this fact cannot change the essence of our efforts and ideals, although the forms and the ways in which these ideals are being implemented may have been modified. I think it is possible to remain true to our original ideas. Czechoslovakia is trying to do so. Czechoslovakia has emphasized over and over again in its various international initiatives that the new government does not follow any ideology, any doctrine, and that the only idea on which our new policies are based is the idea of human rights and freedom. We want a democratic, prosperous and socially just state. We want Europe and the whole world to live in peace and friendship. We want Europe to become a democratic community of democratic states and free nations. These are not merely empty phrases. We are trying to incorporate these ideas into various specific international initiatives, into our concrete everyday work, both in Czechoslovakia's internal policy and in its foreign policy. All this is extremely difficult. It is more difficult than we could ever have imagined when we took over those posts at the time of the revolutionary euphoria. It is extremely difficult, yet it is possible. It is possible to pursue what we perhaps imprecisely called 'non-political politics' – i.e. a policy which is based on the dictates of conscience. It is possible to do this even when you hold power. This I firmly believe and stand behind.

I could now tell you in concrete terms the particular ways in which we are trying to use these ideas, formed in our dissident years, in our political practice, both at home and, especially, in our international foreign policy. I am sure that, as delegates from a number of foreign countries, you would be especially interested in our foreign policy initiatives. But I don't think it would be a good idea to delay your deliberations with too long a speech. I won't go into any detail; just a few sentences.

Firstly, in Western Europe, as well as in Eastern Europe, there exist various structures and organizations: the Atlantic Pact, the European Community, the Council of Europe, the Warsaw Pact, the CMEA. It seems to me that the new situation which has arisen in Europe, as a result of the emancipation of the countries of the former Communist bloc, places all these institutions in a totally new position. They have to consider their future. It seems to me that these organizations can be divided roughly into two categories. Some of these organizations do have a future. They are meaningful. They have proved viable. They should now quickly try to open themselves up to the newly emancipated countries. They should look for ways of getting closer to them, of making contact with them. These organizations probably now face the task of self-transformation. They will have to adapt to the new times.

Then there are institutions which will obviously sooner or later come to the end of their natural lives: organizations which are now obsolete, which played their role at the time of the Cold War and have now lost their raison d'être. For instance, some of these organizations were the material expression of Stalinist expansionism. These are the structures which will go to the wall.

But over and above these existing structures, it is naturally important to create totally new structures and associations which grow directly from the spirit of the here and now, from our totally new situation. Many people in Europe, from politicians to ordinary people, are giving this intense thought. You will undoubtedly have heard of the idea of a European confederation, which President Mitterrand explained in more or less concrete terms during his recent visit to Czechoslovakia. Margaret Thatcher on her visit to Prague talked about her idea of a European Magna Carta of human rights, which could be a point of departure for a new Europe of integration. Naturally, your gathering – as a meeting of grassroots initiatives; purely civic, social initiatives – is also a totally new development. It shows that on various levels and in various corners of Europe people are considering the same task: the task of building a totally, thoroughly new Europe; a Europe undivided into blocs; an integrated Europe; Europe as a continent which would not emanate rays of war into the world at large, but rays of peace. Two world wars were started in Europe; Europe became the largest arsenal of weaponry; it was through Europe that the main line of confrontation between two great power blocs ran. This unfortunate role of Europe in modern world history sets a challenge to our continent. Europe must now seize this unique historical chance to transform itself into a truly peaceful continent, into what President Gorbachev calls a Common European Home. It is Europe's historical duty and responsibility to embark upon this path and to react to the challenge of its unpropitious past history. These are issues which we in Czechoslovakia contemplate daily and which we are trying to implement, in practice, in various international initiatives.

To conclude, I should perhaps say that during all our deliberations on the future of Europe, we ascribe great importance to the Helsinki process, which is in the background of this gathering. This process played a very important role in the emancipation of Central and East European countries because all our opposition movements relied on the fundamental commitment to human rights established in the Helsinki documents. We believe that the Helsinki process is far from outdated and that the time has come when it can become active once again. The Helsinki process can be given new content, it can become something much more than it has been to date. For instance, the existing system of pacts and treaties, which only had the power of recommendation to governments, could now be transformed into an assembly of truly binding treaties. The process could be institutionalized in some way or another. The Helsinki process could form a broad security background for an integrated Europe. We consider this to be very important, which is why we have started certain specific Czechoslovak initiatives within the Helsinki process.

Finally, it seems to us that the most important thing, an essential point of departure for the future, is the notion of citizenship. This idea recurs again and again in all the alternative deliberations and parallel initiatives. It seems that a future united Europe should be based on the principle of an open civic society. It is quite natural that after the many years during which national identity and national independence was suppressed in Central and Eastern Europe we are now entering times when individual nations are fast seeking their identities and demanding they be acknowledged, be made visible. They want to present themselves as nations on the European scene. Naturally, this process, which is historically inevitable and logical, contains a danger of nationalism, of national rivalries and conflicts of various kinds. This is why I think it is very important to emphasize the idea of citizenship. We must stress that first and foremost we are citizens enjoying certain freedoms, certain rights and certain duties. Borders between states should gradually lose importance. We should eventually create a varied and intricate network of horizontal and vertical ties as a true guarantee of freedom, democracy and peace. These ties will contribute to the establishment of civic freedom over the whole of Europe, while at the same time guaranteeing this freedom.

I believe that your Assembly is also moving in this direction. Its work is based on the awareness of all the above. I therefore wish you success. Thank you.

*Translated by Lesley and Jan Čulfk*

# The Contributors

NEAL ASCHERSON is a columnist for the *Independent on Sunday*, and author of *Games with Shadows* (1989).

ANTHONY BARNETT is a writer and co-ordinator of Charter 88.

ROBIN BLACKBURN is Editor of *New Left Review*.

JIŘI DIENSTBIER is Czechoslovak Foreign Minister. He was a founder member of VONS (the Committee for the Defence of the Unjustly Persecuted) and a signatory of Charter 77.

BARBARA EINHORN is East European Co-ordinator of END. She is a research fellow at the School of European Studies, Sussex University, working on a comparative study of women in East-Central Europe.

MIENT JAN FABER is General Secretary of the Inter-Church Peace Council (IKV) of the Netherlands, and co-Chairman of the Helsinki Citizens' Assembly for Peace and Democracy.

J.K. GALBRAITH is Emeritus Professor of Economics at Harvard University, and a former US ambassador to India. His many publications include *The Affluent Society* and *The New Industrial State*.

TIMOTHY GARTON ASH is a fellow of St Anthony's College, Oxford University, and author of *We the People: the Revolutions of '89* (1990).

LYNNE JONES is a psychiatrist, and former chair of END. Her latest book is *States of Mind* (1990).

MARY KALDOR is a researcher at Sussex University, and a senior fellow of the World Institute of Development Economics Research (WIDER), United Nations University, Helsinki. She was a founder member of END and Editor of the *END Journal*. Her latest book is *The Imaginary War: Understanding the East–West Conflict* (1990).

GEORGE KONRAD is a novelist, and President of PEN International. He was a leading member of the Hungarian Democratic Opposition; his extensive writings about domestic and international politics include *Politics and Anti-Politics*.

ADAM MICHNIK is editor-in-chief of the Solidarity newspaper *Gazeta Wyborcza* and a member of the Polish parliament. He was a founder member of KOR, the workers' defence committee, and some of his important political writings of the 1980s are contained in *Letters from Prison and Other Essays*.

JOHN PALMER is European editor of *The Guardian*.

JAROSLAV ŠABATA is Minister without Portfolio in the Czechoslovak government. He was General Secretary of the Brno Communist Party in 1968 and urged resistance to Soviet military pressure. He was a signatory of Charter 77, and is now co-chair of the Helsinki Citizens' Assembly for Peace and Democracy.

MILAN ŠIMEČKA, a political philosopher and writer, died in September 1990. He was a signatory of Charter 77; his books include *The Restoration of Order*.

DAN SMITH is Associate Director of the Transnational Institute in Amsterdam. His latest book is *How America Runs NATO* (1989).

AAFKE STEENHUIS is a writer living in Amsterdam.

TAIR TAIROV is a founder member and chair of Civic Peace in the Soviet Union, and is on the board of the Foundation for Social Initiatives. He was formerly Soviet representative of the World Peace Council in Helsinki, and head of department at the Institute for World Economics and International Relations (IMEMO) in Moscow.

E.P. THOMPSON is a historian and writer. He was a founder member of END and originator of the END Appeal of 1980. His books include *The Making of the English Working Class* and *The Poverty of Theory*.

CHRISTA WOLF is an East German novelist. Her books include *Cassandra, A Model Childhood, Accident* and *The Fourth Dimension,* a book of interviews.